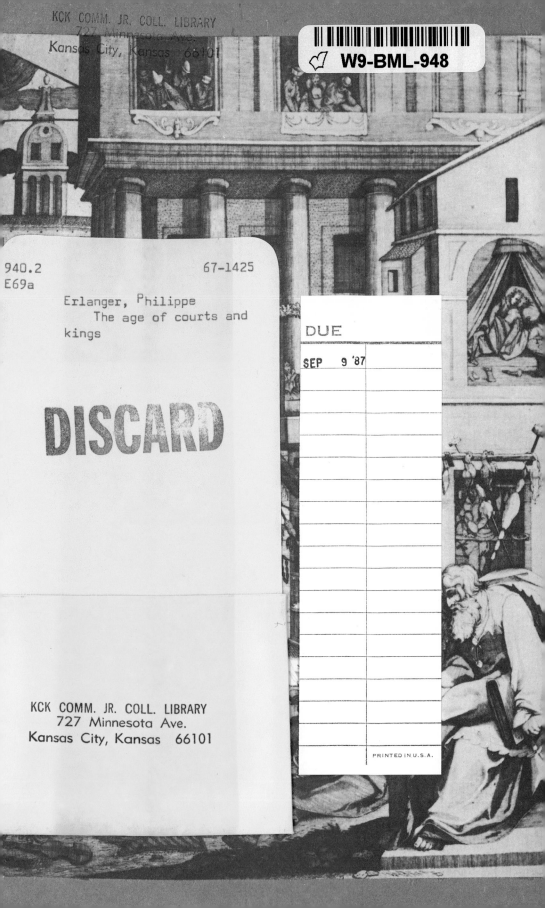

DUE

SEP   9 '87

PRINTED IN U.S.A.

The Age of Courts and Kings

Manners and Morals
Editor: Richard Friedenthal

The Age of Courts and Kings

Manners and Morals 1558–1715

Philippe Erlanger

HARPER & ROW, PUBLISHERS
NEW YORK AND EVANSTON

Contents

Illustrations

Figure des Brisilians; C'est la deduction du sumptueux ordre plaisant spectacle et magnifiques theatres, 1551. London, E.P. Goldschmidt

Joris Hoefnagel, *The Marriage Feast at Bermondsey*. Hatfield House (by courtesy of the Marquess of Salisbury)

Hans Bock I, *The Baths at Leuk*, 1597. Basel, Oeffentliche Kunstsammlung

Title-page of Melchior Borchgreuinck, *Giardino Nouo Bellissimo di Varii Fiori Musicali Sceltissimi*, 1605. British Museum

Tennis, from Dikinger's engravings of Tübingen University, 1589. Oxford, Ashmolean Museum

Title-page of Turberville, *The Noble Art of Venery or Hunting*, 1611 (1575). British Museum

Exercises in the gymnasium, from Dikinger's engravings of Tübingen University, 1589. Oxford, Ashmolean Museum

German hunting-piece (detail), *c.*1600–10. Victoria and Albert Museum (Crown Copyright)

Cazza del Toro, engraving from Giacomo Franco, *Habiti d'huomeni et donne venetiane*, 1597. Oxford, Bodleian Library

TRAVEL AND TRADE   73

The Merchant, engraving from De Bry, *Emblemata*, 1593. British Museum

Adam Willaerts, *Departure of an East Indiaman*. Greenwich, National Maritime Museum

The Exchange at Antwerp, illustration from Guicciardini, *Descrittione dei Paeggi Bassi*, 1588. British Museum

Sailor using a cross-staff. Greenwich, National Maritime Museum

Thomas Morgan, *Santa Sophia in Constantinople*. British Museum, Sloane Ms. 5234 (by courtesy of the Trustees)

Christoph Amberger, *Christoph Fugger*, 1541. Munich, Bayerische Staatsgemälde-sammlungen

Silver dish made in Augsburg, late sixteenth century. Florence, Palazzo Pitti, Gabinetto degli Argenti (*Alinari*)

Golden Hall in Schloss Bückeburg, *c.*1605, by Ebert and Jonas Wolf (*Dr Wiedemann, Hildesheim – Deutsche Kunstverlag*)

Tunny-fishing off Cadiz, engraving, *c.*1580, after Hoefnagel. Greenwich, National Maritime Museum

P. Brueghel I, *Battle of Carnival and Lent* (detail), 1559. Vienna, Kunsthistorisches Museum

Sign of the St Gall (Switzerland) Butchers' Guild, 1564. Zürich, Schweizerisches Landesmuseum

Annibale Carracci, *The Butcher's Shop*. Oxford, Christ Church Library (*University Press – Kindlers Malerei Lexikon*)

F. Villamena, *Mendicant*, 1595. Rome, Pecci-Blunt Collection (*Josephine Powell*)

RELIGIOUS TROUBLES   97

Fructus Noui Euangelii, engraving from *Theatrum crudelitatum Hereticarum*, 1587. British Museum

Jean Perrissin I, *Execution of Amboise*, 1560. Vienna, Nationalbibliothek (*Bildarchiv der öst. Nationalbibliothek*)

Jean Perrissin I, *Atrocities of the People of Tours*, July 1562. British Museum

French School, *Procession of the League*, 1590. Paris, Musée Carnavalet (*Bulloz*)

Le Diable est déchainé (detail), 1590. Vienna, Nationalbibliothek (*Bildarchiv der öst. Nationalbibliothek*)

Scenes from the Massacre of St Bartholemew. Paris, Bibliothèque Nationale

Spanish soldiers entering Antwerp and Oudewater, illustrations from Eytzinger, *De Leone Belgico*, 1585. British Museum

P.Brueghel I, *Massacre of the Innocents* (detail), *c.*1565. Vienna, Kunsthistorisches Museum

Adam Elsheimer, *Narcissus*. Berlin, Stiftung Preussischer Kulturbesitz, Staatliche Museen – Kupferstichkabinett

Annibale and Agostino Carracci, *Wandering Peasants*. Oxford, Ashmolean Museum

Georges De La Tour, *Woman with a Flea*. Nancy, Musée Historique Lorrain (*Royal Academy of Arts*)

Louis xiv receives ambassadors from Siam. Oxford, Ashmolean Museum

Birth of the Dauphin, 1674 (*Bildarchiv der öst. Nationalbibliothek*)

Apotheosis of Leopold i, engraving after Burnacini of scene from *Il Pomo d'Oro* (*Prestel Verlag*)

Equestrian ballet at Viennese court, engraving from *Parte delle Figure del Balletto, Festa a Cavallo*, 1668. British Museum

Fountain in the gardens at Versailles, illustration from Le Clerc, *Labyrinte de Versailles*, 1677. British Museum

Scene from *Plaisirs de l'Ile Enchantée* by Israel Silvestre, 1664. Paris, Bibliothèque Nationale

Scenes from Molière's *Le Malade Imaginaire* (detail) and Lulli's *Alceste*, illustrations from Félibien, *Relation de la feste de Versailles*, 1679. British Museum

Frontispiece to Caspar von Lohenstein, *Cleopatra*, 1680. British Museum

Décor by Torelli for *Andromède* by Corneille, 1650. Paris, Bibliothèque Nationale

Design for a *Gloire* and the machinery used to produce it, made for the theatre of San Salvatore, Venice, 1675. Paris, Musée de l'Opéra (*Pic*)

Lely, *Nell Gwynn*. Denys E. Bower Collection (*Royal Academy of Arts*)

W. Hollar, *St Paul's on Fire*, 1666. British Museum

Scenes of the Plague of 1665 in London. Cambridge, Magdalene College, Pepysian Library

John Halys, *Samuel Pepys*, 1666. London, National Portrait Gallery

Pepys's Diary. Cambridge, Magdalene College, Pepysian Library (*John Marmaras*)

Lely, *Idyll* (*Lely and his Family*). London, Courtauld Institute of Art

The Countess of Shrewsbury. London, National Portrait Gallery

J. G. Eccardt, after Lely, *Elizabeth Hamilton*. London, National Portrait Gallery

Mignard, *Hortense Mancini*. Earl of Sandwich Collection (*Port of London Authority*)

Lely, *Nell Gwynn*, London, National Portrait Gallery

Thomas Johnson I, *King's and Queen's Bath at Bath*, 1672. British Museum

Van Tilborgh, *The Tichborne Dole* (detail), 1670. Sir A. Doughty-Tichborne Collection (*Royal Academy of Arts*)

Endpapers: Italian Carnival Scene. Oxford, Bodleian Library

Layout of illustrations by Shashi Rawal

ACKNOWLEDGMENT

The author and publishers wish to thank the museums and collectors mentioned above for kind permission to reproduce works in their possession.

They also wish to thank Mrs Gabriele Tergit for additional text material supplied for chapters on Germany and the Low Countries.

Part One

1558–1610

1 Spain

The Spaniard of 1560 not only boasted that he held dominion over a vast empire; felt himself stronger, more awe-inspiring, more civilized, more chivalrous and nearer to God than any man who belonged to a foreign nation: he *was* the cynosure of every eye, he *was* the glass of fashion. Even satire proved his prestige: in his *Emblems Of The Deeds, Perfections And Customs Of The Spanish Señor*, Simon Molard declared him 'a devil in his house, a wolf at table, a pig in his room, a peacock in the street, a fox with women'. For Spain, whilst scorning the rest of the world, forbidding her subjects in the Low Countries to study outside her frontiers, and withdrawing her student doctors from Montpellier, was copied by the whole of the West, including France, the foremost of her rivals.

In Paris, an agency flourished for translating from the the Castilian, the wits decked out their speeches with Castilian phrases, the women wore Spanish powder, rouge and scents. Civilized people everywhere would have gloves only if they came from Spain, leather if it came from Cordova, steel if it came from Toledo. The Spanish (silver) pistole was an international currency.

Philip II was determined to erect a Kingdom which was impervious to the Protestant revolution. Hence the autocracy became inflexible, enforcing doctrines more rigidly than the Popes themselves, ratifying the monarchy in the assumption of boundless power. The Society of Jesus was its inspiration, the Inquisition its shield.

Under the influence of the Jesuits militant evangelism superseded the ideal of pious withdrawal. The thirty Jesuit colleges opened in Spain during the generalship of Francesco Borgia initiated what we now call secondary education, and, although often regarded as intolerant and sectarian, offered the middle class laity access to a culture which was formerly the exclusive preserve of the clerics. The King himself was greatly influenced by Jesuit teaching, and resisted only their most blatant casuistry.

Philip likewise shared the bitter intransigence of the Dominicans and supported the Inquisition. This terrible machine had been set up in the thirteenth century by Innocent III and St Dominic to exterminate the Albigensians, and, since 1478, had become integral to the Spanish State. Valdés, the Archbishop of Seville, had established the ultimate code of its operation.

Henceforth the moral life of the nation was submitted to the Dominicans: on the strength of a mere innuendo a Grandee or a beggar could be arrested, questioned and tortured. Even the Infant Don Carlos, heir to the throne, had to appear before the tribunal when it was examining the future saints (John and Theresa of Avila, John of the Cross, Francesco Borgia) and prosecuting the King's confessor, Cavanza. The report of the trial filled eighty thousand pages.

The Inquisition hunted out the Moriscos, the Marranos, the Jews, the sorcerers, the visionaries, the sodomites – in fact all the non-conformists. The smallest difference of opinion or ambiguity of expression was enough to lead the perpetrator to the pyres, which would continue to burn until the days of Napoleon. Spain was a land of contrasts: her Golden Age was also the age of her Black Legend.

Faith filled the monasteries at the expense of the secular development of the kingdom. In 1570 a quarter of the adult population had taken the vow: there were 400,000 monks, 312,000 priests and 200,000 people belonging to the minor orders. This fanatical and militant faith ranged from the mysticism of St Theresa to the mortifications of the Flagellants; every extremity was a commonplace.

Inferior only to God himself was the King: a monarch untouched by the power of facts, convinced of the infallibility of his principles, and blind to whatever did not accord with his inner view of the world. And so jealous that he lost the fruits of victory both at St Quentin and Lepanto rather than accord to his generals the glory they had won.

Philip II was sedentary, parsimonious and secretive; a procrastinator and ever the prey of his conscience. When not making an appearance, he led the life of an official tied to his desk and submerged in his papers. As Cardinal de Granvella put it, his proverbially slow government bogged public life 'in a flow of slimy mud'. It was an autocracy tempered by fear, where (apart from the Duke of Alba) the administrators were not noblemen, but theologians, lawyers, police-agents and secretaries.

Personally, the son of Charles V had simple tastes, as his recreations proved. He enjoyed walking, fishing, hunting as a spectator, and most rural pleasures. On 20 May 1576, at the request of Queen Anne, some thirty shepherds sheared in the presence of the two sovereigns; the bewildered folk sang songs and drank themselves to distraction.

Philip II preferred painting and music to bullfights. His art collection bore witness to his eclectic and original taste: the works of Hieronymus

Bosch appearing side by side with paintings by Titian and El Greco. Such were the diversions which the austere and parsimonious monarch allowed himself. His existence otherwise was absorbed by his work or by the mysteries of ceremonial.

The ceremonial had been created by Philip the Good, Duke of Burgundy, and revived by Charles v. Since 1548 it had become an institution the like of which was not found in any country until the France of Louis XIV. It was the transposition of a religious cult to the secular plane, a cult devoted to a monarch set up as an idol. The monarch had thus to be guarded from hostile influences, and his subjects appraised of his super-natural power; for these two reasons he was set apart from the ordinary commerce of living.

Philip II, enamoured of his solitude, suspicious and dissembling in the extreme, made these barriers well nigh insurmountable. His service became a mystery celebrated according to sacred rites. His every act or whim assumed the importance of an affair of State and demanded the creation of a post at court. In consequence, his individual freedom was strictly cur-tailed.[1]

The King's apartment was a sanctuary. At the doors of the first two rooms, the *sala* and the *saleta*, ushers stood on guard from eight o'clock in the morning until seven at night to deny access to all unworthy of reception.

In the *antecamera* and the *antecamarilla*, 'physiognomists' among the guards kept watch over the visitors and made sure that they bowed before the royal canopy. Officers and functionaries, priests, scholars and artists did not penetrate beyond the *antecamera*. Grandees of Spain, bishops, ambassadors, Councillors of State, knights of the Orders of the Golden Fleece, Santiago, Alcantara and Calatrava, penetrated as far as the *antecamarilla*.

After the *antecamarilla*, His Majesty's study. The only people allowed to enter were the Nuncio, the cardinals, the President of the Grand Council of Castile and the viceroys. Beyond the study were the bedroom, the dressing-room, a closet and the privies.

A multitude of dignitaries ensured that the cult was observed. The Grand Majordomo, at their head, ranked immediately after the President of the Grand Council of Castile. Seventeen people worked under him, from the eight majordomos and the Captain of the Guards to the First Upholsterer to the King. The ordinary majordomos, generally sons of Grandees of Spain, commanded the other officers of the household. They surrounded the King when he appeared in public, received ambassadors or performed his religious ceremonies.

[1] Cf. Ludwig Pfandl: *Philip II*.

The Grand Chamberlain had the duty of waking the sovereign and supervising the table service. He wore a gold key on his hip, like the other chamberlains specifically entrusted with dressing His Majesty. The Grand Almoner had the title of Patriarch of the Indies, the First Chaplain said mass, the Confessor (sometimes Franciscan, sometimes Augustinian, occasionally Jesuit) was in fact the principal personage at Court. The Master of Apartments led the King to the Queen at night. The bakery, the fruitery, the cellar, the sauces, the kitchen itself were each supervised by a Grand Master. So also were the stables.

The King dined alone in the presence of bareheaded and unarmed courtiers. He did not eat with the Queen except on feast days.

As a precautionary measure, there were no less than three Guards: the Dutch, the Spanish and the German. The Queen had a somewhat similar household, but less grandiose.

The conduct of affairs at the Council of State illustrates the rhythm of the court. The councillor who was to speak rose to his feet, doffed his cap, knelt, and made his case. If the King agreed, he said: 'So be it', and the councillors raised their caps. If he wanted further information, he said: 'You will report to me again'; the assembly rose and then sank to its knees. When the King withdrew, everyone doffed his cap and knelt on one knee.

Philip II considered it imperative to respect every detail of the cere-monial; and, in doing so, he met the aspirations of his people. The con-sequence was the exacerbation of national pride, and the hardening of the Spanish character into a rigid and arrogant mould. This was to reveal itself in the mania for titles (hundreds of people usurped the 'Don'), in extravagant dress, in the epistolary style. You prostrated yourself when you wrote to the King, you lavished compliments on your equals. Both writing and typography were subject to arbitrary and changing fashions. St Theresa complained about it in her autobiography: sometimes the margin should be on the right, sometimes on the left; one day you should put the conventional civilities at the beginning, next day you had to put them at the end of the letter.

It was characteristic of Philip that he should build his final retreat, the Escurial, on a site remote from all profane influence. The Escurial, com-pleted in 1584, was a monastery and palace combined. It was planned in the form of a gridiron in memory of the torture of St Lawrence, and centred on the chapel. The King himself supervised the work and personally selected the artists.

At Christmas and at Pentecost, during Holy Week and on All Saints' Day, Philip II was at the Escurial. During the last fifteen years of his life, he spent a considerable part of his time in the little *Capella Mayor*, from which he could follow all the gestures of the priest during the services.

So it was that he strove to deserve the supreme reward received by his father (Charles V) when he was greeted in Heaven by the Holy Trinity. A picture by El Greco illustrated the event and Philip II was convinced of its veracity. When he lay dying after a terrible illness, stoically borne, he was to feel himself assured of the same honour, and to repent only that he had failed to exterminate sufficient Jews, heretics and infidels.

Thanks to the sale of Court situations, the extortions of the Inquisition, and the confiscations made among the Moriscos, the nobility grew rich. On the other hand the members of the *caballeria* (knighthood) and the *hidalguia* (provincial nobility) grew poorer, even destitute. They all alike led haughty, idle lives, which resulted in the stagnation of industry, agriculture and commerce. Some held commands in the armies, which were chiefly composed of mercenaries. Combats and tournaments remained their favourite diversions.

Centuries of warfare had inspired a taste for tales of chivalry, and these were in great vogue, even in the convents: St Theresa herself wrote one. The influence of these tales varied according to the reader: some were incited to adultery, revenge and luxury, to scorn of the social order; others, on the contrary, to an enhanced code of honour, valour and nobility of manner, courtesy and sublime passion.

This code of behaviour, to which the Spanish señor owed so much of his prestige, had been particularly admired during the reign of Charles V. In 1528 the Venetian, Baldassare Castiglione, Bishop of Avila and favourite of the Emperor, had published *The Courtier*, a guide to civility and polite manners. It was addressed to the young and translated into several languages. Whilst the subjects of Philip II still respected his commands, they were less interested in the art of living than in personal advancement. A hundred years after *The Courtier*, appeared *The Courtier's Manual* by Baltazar Gracián, a dry and skilful work designed for the ambitious, which by the end of the sixteenth century had superseded the earlier work.

Likewise, the extravagancies of the chivalric tale were finally discredited in 1605 by the publication of Cervantes' satire *Don Quixote*. Cervantes was a veteran of Lepanto, a former quartermaster who had helped to victual the Armada; a prisoner in Algiers before being imprisoned in his own country, when at the age of fifty-eight he produced his masterpiece.

While the nobility grew rigid in its conceit, the middle class came discreetly into being and began to expand; and the peasants, who despised country life, struggled to become townsmen. Knowledge of the tilt-yards was no help in agriculture, and the vast estates were badly cultivated. 'The Spanish desert' was immense, but the cities flourished. In 1600, Madrid had 200,000 inhabitants. Seville, the port where the gold was unloaded from the New World, grew even more. Ostentation replaced ancestral austerity, and the Church was powerless against the corruption of these cities, which were the great cross-roads of international trade.

At Seville, the home of vagrants and rogues of every kind, St Theresa observed that the climate was fit for an ante-room in Hell. When she was there, she felt so 'faint-hearted and enervated' that she could barely recognize herself any more. Justice, administration, and even the agents of the Inquisition, could all be bought. The monopolists enjoyed them-selves to the full. The women spent huge sums on clothes. The men showed themselves no less frivolous: 'They are effeminate dolls without virtue, or the nature of a man,' wrote Brother Juan de Los Angeles. 'They paint and titivate themselves, are carried round in chairs, and preen themselves in front of the mirror. They will soon . . . be wearing distaffs on their belts, since they are evidently tired of swords.'

This Spain, partitioned into castes as rigid as those of India, contained a great many 'undesirables'. There remained nearly 50,000 Jews, a remark-able élite including many doctors, scholars, and merchants, all of whom were ruthlessly persecuted.

The Moriscos were even more numerous (nearly 400,000). They were descended from those Moors who, since 1492, had been forcibly converted to Catholicism. They practised the *mudéjar* cult, in which Arabic replaced Latin (the rite is still celebrated today in a chapel in Seville Cathedral). In fact, it was often no more than a façade, and in Andalusia and Valencia whole villages practised both religions. The Moriscos played an important part in the economic life of the country, a fact which did not, however, prevent them being subject to persecution. They revolted more than once, and for a time held the King himself in check. Don Juan of Austria was to find it hard to master them. In 1609 Philip III banished them from the kingdom, thereby ensuring its ruin.

There were other pariahs: the *gitanos*, the slaves taken from the Infidels, and, finally, the beggars, who grew in numbers as agriculture declined. Foreign travellers were astonished to see them. Here were the richest states in the world, those of the Church and the Catholic King, and the wretched creatures were allowed to multiply.

It is often supposed that religious tyranny stifles artistic and intellectual development, but in Spain this proved not to be the case. There were some thirty Spanish universities: the one at Salamanca had no less than seventy professors and 7,800 pupils; at Alcala 2,000 students were studying medicine. In the scientific field results were remarkable. In medicine, mineralogy, metallurgy, mining, astronomy and ophthalmology, Spain found herself in the van of progress. Rogete was constructing telescopes, Deza de Valdés was greatly improving spectacles.

Likewise in theology, in the brilliance of Benito Arias Montano, Juan Baptista Perez, Molina and Francisco Suarez. The historian Ambrosio de Morales was the first to support his narratives with proofs and documents. It was perhaps under his influence that Philip II created the Archives at Simanca and made this noble pronouncement: 'Chroniclers and historians are ill-informed of affairs of State. It is therefore desirable to assemble all the materials that might help them.' The Archives at Simanca still exist, but unfortunately they are not often consulted: the Spanish government has all too frequently decided that, after all, it is undesirable for historians to be too well informed.

Law, political sciences, literature, including Cervantes and the authors of the picaresque novels, were also at their zenith. Artists were reacting against the tendencies of semi-pagan Italy, which admired Antiquity and beauty of form. Spain proscribed mythology, nudity, and the exaltation of the flesh, and developed a Christian aesthetic in which line was less important than colour. Spanish painters received strength and inspiration from the Church, although this sometimes led to monotony.

El Greco, although he was born in Crete, was the one who best translated this mixture of realism, pride and spirituality, characteristic of the Spanish soul. No one could more eloquently dramatize the atmosphere of the country which El Greco discovered at the age of forty. The Inquisition was to reproach him for contravening canon law by the way he painted angels' wings. El Greco pleaded his cause with ardour and had the rare good fortune to convince his judges.

Many famous portrait painters have transmitted the court style to us: a style which was gradually adopted in Paris and London, Vienna and Florence. The model is always standing, with his hand resting on a table, on the back of a chair, or even on the head of a dwarf.

At the beginning of the century, the costume followed the contours of the body, but as it evolved it became a sort of pillory, a symbol of intransigent pride. The doublet took on the appearance of a cuirass. Whalebone and squares of cardboard were inserted between the material and the lining, to give it stiffness. After 1570 it was stuffed with horsehair. The *cappa*, the Spanish cloak, was typically short, with a high collar, but greatly enlarged to cover ceremonial dress. Over the knitted hose, were worn puffed-out pantaloons, very short, padded, and almost spherical, with the lining visible through the slashings. Caps were tall and voluminous and sword-hilts were shaped like baskets.

Women wore a straight bodice, stiffened with whalebone and wire, which allowed no suggestion of a curve. The skirt was supported by cane hoops. The strip of cane was called a *verdugo*. Hence the French *vertugadin*, the English *verdingale* (or farthingale), the Dutch *fardegaljin*. The dress reached the ground.

'The Queen of Spain has no legs', so the *Camarera Mayor* informed the young Elizabeth of Valois, third wife of Philip II; she was terrified, and supposed the Queen was in danger of an amputation. The ladies of the Court glided noiselessly as they moved from place to place, a feat only Russian folk-dancers can perform today. One wonders by what miracle thirty of them managed to serve the Queen *on their knees* when Her Majesty was at table.

Cloaks were very long, with a pleat at the back, those of the bourgeois completely enveloping. The ruff, which was worn by people of both sexes, was made of tulle with lace edging. It grew larger and larger until 1600. Hair was brushed down flat in front, and piled up and constellated with precious stones. Black was the favourite colour for both men and women.

Such were the Spanish fashions which conquered the West, except for Venice, for generations to come. And even when the English and the French grew out of them, they were regarded still as the epitome of good style. The marriage of Louis XIV and the Infanta Maria Theresa, which confirmed the end of Spain's supremacy, saw the last victory of Spanish fashion. The Catholic King and the Grandees, in black velvet, wearing the Orders of the Golden Fleece, crushed with scorn the upstart *nouveaux riches* who had conquered them, the absurd French popinjays, laden with jewels, lace, feathers and finery.

2 France

'A court without women is a springtime without roses.' 'I can create a nobleman, only God can create a great artist.' From this double tribute to beauty paid by François I, was born the court of the Valois, 'a true paradise, the ornament of France'. It had no equal.

If we wish to imagine the setting, which was hardly to change for half a century, we must imagine the rooms painted entirely in bright colours picked out with gold, from the wainscoting and the piers to the ceilings, which were coffered or supported by cross-beams with prominent joists; the walls were all hung with Cordova leather in vivid colours, decorated with flowers, foliage and arabesques on reddish-brown grounds with a tinge of red or bronzed green like old copper. The parquet floors were strewn with Oriental carpets which Queen Catherine des Médicis had ordered from Venice. The furniture also was painted in bright colours picked out with gold.

Men and women wore sumptuous clothes of silks, brocades, cut velvets and lace; precious stones and gold nets on their hair. Materials streamed with silver and were always vivid in colour. Warm, flesh-tinted cosmetics were applied freely. Servants, pages, lackeys and ushers were also clad gaudily, half red and half yellow, or half green and half white. The young noblemen had slashed sleeves, and puffed-out breeches with scarlet or vivid yellow silk linings which showed through to heighten the effect. 'The world,' cried Brantôme, 'has never seen anything like it'.

Catherine des Médicis, despite her widow's weeds, was an incomparable mistress of the house; she never tired of entertaining even in the worst moments of the religious wars. Ronsard sometimes organized the cavalcades and balls, the tournaments and spectacles which the Queen-Mother considered to be an aid to government. She believed that the habit of pleasure and the need for extravagance would keep the King's potential enemies in his service.

Round her were grouped a number of young ladies chosen for their wisdom and high birth who were, however, expected to display an aptitude for seduction rather than virtue. These ravishing ladies formed the famous *Flying Squadron*. They never submitted to their worshippers without the Queen's permission, and, like new Delilahs, they could at times deliver a factious Samson into her hands. Sometimes their charms served to reward the loyal servants of the monarchy, sometimes to surprise the secrets of the rebels.

During the last years of the reign of Charles IX, this Court 'of silk and blood', which condoned the Massacre of St Bartholomew, became the focal point of passions and intrigues which tore France apart. Love-affairs, plots and crimes were all inextricably mixed.

The accession of Henri III did nothing to appease the tumults in the palace, but gave it an aspect which no one had foreseen. At the age of eighteen, the new king had been a victorious general, and won the throne of Poland. He had spent little time in Cracow, but before returning to France, he had sojourned for a time in Venice. This Venetian visit had had a decisive influence on his character. It brought to flower a personality which had been trammelled by education, religious precepts and accepted customs. Henri had been warlike, a womanizer, an enthusiast of violent exercise, because those about him had valued these tastes above all others. In Venice, he found a different world, and there discovered his contradictory nature: mystic and frivolous, ardent and versatile, sensual and sensitive, gentle and cruel, avid to undertake some great enterprise and imbued with his responsibility to the future. The French were stupefied when he came home: a strange person covered with rouge and precious stones, surrounded by parrots and little dogs.

The French court, so hard to rule, for long refused to accept that their sovereign was preparing to draw up the first code of laws, that he was presiding over an academy (the precursor of Richelieu's), that his Edict of Poitiers (later copied by Henri IV as the Edict of Nantes) could have ended the civil wars. Harassed by calumnies and insults, Henri replied with defiance – particularly during the remarkable fête at Chenonceaux.

Under the trees of this admirable park the King presided over the banquet, dressed as a woman. He wore a gown of pink damask, embroidered with pearls. His enormous sleeves were tied with gold and silver threads held in place by trefoils of pearls and emeralds. Emerald, pearl and diamond pendants distended the lobes of his ears, and diamonds shone in his hair which, like his beard, was dyed with violet powder.

For His Majesty and his principal gentlemen readily appeared in feminine disguise at the great Court pageants. 'So much so,' wrote Agrippa d'Aubigné, 'that the people who saw him found it hard to tell if they were looking at a woman-King or a man-Queen.'

That particular evening the young ladies of the *Flying Squadron* waited

Monarchs and Courtiers

The Virgin Queen. Elizabeth as the symbol of monarchy, after the defeat of the Spanish Armada.

The ceremonies of the Order of the Golden Fleece carried on the elaborate traditions of the court of fifteenth-century Burgundy, and were the model for Hapsburg court ceremonial in Spain and in Germany. Here Emperor Rudolph II is received into the Order.

Above. Sir Walter Ralegh, traveller, writer, and courtier *par excellence*.

Right. El Greco, *The Dream of Philip* (detail). The artist expressed the sombre dignity of the court of Spain under Philip II in his portrait of the king, dressed entirely in black.

A TOVS ACCORDS

Left. The Hermaphrodites, a satire on Henri III and his *mignons*. 'No need to choose between being a man or a woman: better to be both together and have double the pleasure.'

Below. Henri IV, whose court was perpetually on the move, making a triumphal entry into Rouen in 1599.

Below. Gabrielle D'Estrées, the mistress of Henri IV, with her sister in the bath.

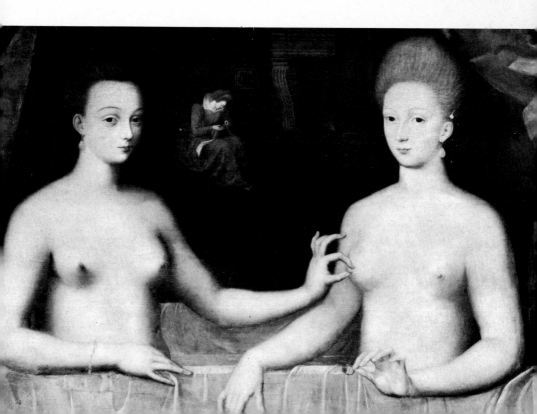

A portrait of Princess Isabella of Savoy, which shows the richness and ostentation of French fashion: the fantastic ruff, the rich brocade and the jewelled aigrettes and pendants.

Hierbey da hanget der Schminden Krug
Vnd. So du werst Nicht Schön genug
dar zu so bleich alß wie der thot
damit kan Ich dich wol machen rot

So Ich zu ihnen thriw Hebt bey
So werden auß dicken zweien vier drey

A German print satirizing
the French fashions of
1590: ruffs, painted faces
and finery are all inventions
of the devil.

A scene from *Don Quixote*,
Cervantes's novel, which
ridiculed the pretensions of
the Spanish court and
society.

Medieval 'chivalric' pastimes still survived at the European courts. In 1559 Henri II of France had died of a wound received at a tournament; here a less perilous version of the joust is practised.

Ball at the court of Henri III to celebrate the marriage of the Duc de Joyeuse, one of the king's most intimate *mignons*, in 1582.

The European courts vied with one another for the services of distinguished musicians. Roland de Lassus, one of the greatest composers of the age, was in the service of the Duke of Bavaria, and is here seen directing the choir in the court chapel.

A vivid allegory of the vanity of courtly life.

at table; under their dresses, which left their legs and breasts and shoulders free, they were completely naked. After the supper, a saturnalia worthy of ancient Rome continued for a long time in the shadowy groves.

Public indignation, cleverly orchestrated, was aimed in particular at the King's favourites: Saint-Mégrin, Quélus, Gramont, Livarot, Sagonne, d'O, Maugiron, Epernon, Saint-Luc. These brilliant youths, who were endlessly discredited, were none the less handsome, valiant, clever, and passionately devoted to their prince. Their ridiculous costume excited satire. Philippe Desportes wrote:

> This curly-headed Minion serves as woman or as man
> To you, in your lighthearted mood, still taken by surprise.
> He is your Adonis, you are Venus in his eyes,
> You are his sweetheart, and he is your life, your soul, your own. . . .

And yet these Minions (or Mignons, as they were called) were terrible duellists, prodigal of their blood, fighting with a laugh or a leer of contempt. Nearly all of them gave their lives for the King before they were thirty, and their heroic end should have spared them the ignominious meaning which history attached to the once common title of His Majesty's Minions.[1]

We know exactly how the last of the Valois spent his time. Since the King always went to bed very late at night, at about nine o'clock in the morning the princes of the blood, the high dignitaries, the gentlemen-in-waiting entered the audience room next to the royal bedroom, in company with the jesters and the musicians; the ministers, with a few courtiers among them, remained in the State Room. The officers and *maîtres-d'hôtel*, the equerries and gentlemen of low degree crowded the ante-room.

The King was woken, and clapped his hands. The privileged people in the audience room went in to him at once, giving place to the guests in the State Room. Behind the gentleman bearing the towel on a salver, came the first *maître-d'hôtel*, leading several servants armed with covered dishes. This procession solemnly invaded the sanctuary, and the first *valet de chambre* drew the curtains. The sun burst into the splendid room, and cast a glow on the cabinets of rock crystal, the Florentine enamels, the brocade cushions, and the tapestries with representations of Classical myths. In the midst of these treasures the bed rose up, like an altar, with its bed-posts of solid gold, its counterpane in green figured velvet, its double canopy in gold and silver cloth on which legendary scenes were embroidered in multicoloured silks. A mosaic censer cast an exotic aroma round the room.

Henri III was reclining in an ocean of cushions. He wiped his hands and face, drank a cup of soup, ate a few sugared cakes. A nobleman presented

[1] The word meant 'servant'. In the fifteenth century, 'the King's Minions' was a phrase in current use.

him with his shirt. The long and delicate process of dressing had begun: barbers, perfumers, hosiers, tailors, masseurs, valets of every degree applied themselves to this august person entrusted to their care.

The intimate attentions over, Henri put on a closely fitted costume, generally black or dark brown, and pinned a cap with a jewelled aigrette on his hair. He chose three rings from his casket, which was presented by a gentleman, hung a gold chain, with a medallion full of musk, round his neck. Other dignitaries presented him with a handkerchief, a sword, a comfit-box, two pairs of gloves, the first being fine and close-fitting like a sheath, the second with big cuffs, fastened with silk cords.

Thus apparelled, the King went to the council, and thence to mass.

Next came dinner time. The King ate alone, to the sound of music, divided by a barrier from the Court. Conversation was restricted to topics of learning or of virtue. Carrying his sybaritic habits to extremes, Henri disdained to eat with his fingers; into the sauces he plunged a curious tool which had been devised for him, a two-pronged fork.

When he grew tired of riding on horseback, he had a glazed litter built for himself, large enough to contain not only five or six friends, but also jesters, dogs, a table and a desk. This gigantic machine moved slowly. Henri beguiled the tedium of the journey by cutting out splendid pictures which had been printed specially for him. The pictures and the litter, like the pekinese, caught the fancy of song-writers. The legendary cup-and-ball was to appear only two years before the end of his reign.

On certain days, the King was seized by a superstitious fever that he did not live like a true Christian, and then he revolted against his own weaknesses. A nostalgia for purity, a desire for humiliation threw him into a fit, and an astonished populace saw the Minions file past in the coarse robes of flagellants.

When he returned from such expeditions, the King went back to work: councils, dictation, signatures, audiences. He supped with the Queen in his mother's apartment. At midnight he went back to his own room. All day long, it had remained open to the public, and those who filed through it had to bow before the bed.

Now, a thick carpet of roses, violets, carnations and lilies hid the floor, incense burned in the perfuming-pans. A skilful barber covered the royal face with rose cream, and put on a linen mask to preserve the make-up. His hands were washed with almond pastes before they disappeared in enormous waterproof gloves. And lying on his idol's couch, which had been warmed with coriander, benjamin and cinnamon, the King listened to a chapter of Machiavelli.

The assassination of Henri III, and the anarchy which followed, ended all Court life for a long time. Henri IV, who returned in triumph to Paris, seemed ill-equipped to resume the tradition. He was often to be seen wearing a torn habit, his face and arms bathed in sweat, his beard and hair covered in thick dust. Unkempt hair and Rabelaisian talk delighted him as antitheses to the refinements of the Minions.

The Spanish Ambassador was speechless to find the King of France carrying his children pick-a-back. And they were not even legitimate children! Until 1598, people had to accustom themselves to the unheard-of spectacle of the Most Christian King living with his concubine, Gabrielle d'Estrées, and the children of this double adultery.

When Henri married Marie des Médicis, the scandal, far from disappearing, assumed new proportions. The ladies' man had an Arab conception of marriage. He obliged his wife and his mistresses, his legitimate children and his bastards, to live all together. Nearly every year saw an increase in the little 'flock'. Of course, in this domain as in others, the King set an example. The licence and excesses of the great noblemen exceeded even those of the Valois period. The Grand Duke of Tuscany's envoy wrote: 'In truth, I have never seen anything more like a brothel than this court.'

A court? It was really more a camp, or indeed a kirmess, which would have come to mind at the sight of the royal ante-room, filled by a truculent, begging, quarrelsome crowd, with foul language and a preposterous smell. You went into the room 'as into the mill'. An embroidered habit and hired lackeys were sufficient passport. Every one shouted in order to make a stir. Men and women rivalled each other in the brilliance of their dress. The King briskly made his way through the crowd in which a Marshal of France brushed shoulders with a needy younger son from the provinces, and a Jesuit father talked to a contractor. He called everyone by their names and passed on, saying: 'Your servant, so-and-so, your servant'!

The Code of Etiquette, promulgated under Henri III in 1585, was still technically in force, but le Béarnais ignored it. He detested constraint, pomp and ceremony. The only servitude to which he readily submitted was the one which seems to us most intolerable: from morn to night, from birth to death, the monarch and his family lived in public. These were tribal fetishes, and, throughout the day, their performance was a sort of religious mystery which their subjects were at liberty to witness. Whether the King consummated his marriage or sat on his commode, whether the Queen gave birth to a child or attended to her dress, nothing was without witnesses.

Henri IV had three passions: women, hunting and gambling. And so the Louvre looked unpleasantly like a gambling house. The gains and losses there were enormous: at least twenty thousand pistoles a day. A dubious Portuguese, Pimentel, won 200,000 écus from His Majesty: a third of the dowry of Marie des Médicis!

Hunting expeditions and travels were the order of the day, although the King's health was affected by them. He was a man who could not keep still. He could never assemble his council round a table: affairs of state were transacted as he walked through his gardens. The seat of monarchy was mobile, too, nothing being further from the Capetian tradition than the idea of power based on a city or a palace. The government was found wherever the sovereign and his people happened to be. A whim was sufficient to set the whole apparatus of the State on the road: the King would say, as he rose, 'Gentlemen, we shall be leaving soon'; and, that afternoon, everyone would be astride his horse (there were very few carriages, the fashion for litters was over). Noblemen, soldiers, pages and servants travelled on horseback; ladies on ambling nags; priests and secretaries on mules. The luggage, including the bed and table equipment, was carried in enormous carts. The royal apartment would be erected on arrival.

Enveloped in a cloud of dust, the prodigious caravan crossed the countryside like a swarm of locusts. Wayward routes were chosen, for otherwise the regions visited would be impoverished. The rural folk watched in wonderment.

The King had become, as a former rebel said to him, 'the great sun which gave life, light and strength'. A continuous movement bore all aspiring men towards him: all those who, deep in the provinces, in cities, towns and austere châteaux, in forgotten dioceses and ruined manors, nourished an ambition or desired to taste of the richness of life. Only by approaching him could they hope for a public office, a regiment, the blessed pension, thanks to which they could repair the breaches in their inheritance. Everything came from the King and so everything was concentrated round him.

However, the survivors of the old reign found it hard to accustom themselves to the violence and vulgarity which had replaced the former refinements. There was no trace, nowadays, of courtesy and politeness. Feasts degenerated into orgies, banquets into drunken brawls, masquerades gave rise to fixed battles, and even Court ballets were full of ribaldry.

A number of great ladies decided to protest, and began a crusade against 'barbarity'. The year 1606 was decisive. The Marquise de Rambouillet escaped the odious crowd which gravitated round their Majesties, and settled in the rue Saint Thomas du Louvre in a *hôtel* which was thenceforward consecrated to immortality. Her blue room, so frequently described, was still not open to men of letters. Only great noblemen and great ladies, chosen from the most 'amiable', diverted the Marquise and founded the reputation of her house. This was the return to sophisticated manners.

L'Astrée, by Honoré d'Urfé, published three years later, furnished a code. This book, which was to delight and influence three generations, was also a manual of love and a work of diverting knowledge. It described a code of ethics which was to echo through the rest of the century: 'If reason conceives . . . the beauty of goodness, if the will is firmly resolved to attain this ideal, what obstacle could prevent it from doing so? It is perseverance in the face of obstacles which proves that we are rational and not sensual beings.'

Honoré d'Urfé was already a long way from the Minions and the Ladies' Man.

From the death of Louis XI to the death of Henri II, the monarchy and the nobility lived in peace. It was the moment when this class, which was solidly attached to the land, eager to fight, and loyal, but not yet domesticated, found its balance. Unhappily for the nobility, as for the whole of France, the wars of religion reawakened base instincts. Heads of great families once again treated the sovereign as an equal, the Guises nearly siezed his crown. As in the Middle Ages, the lesser noblemen followed their suzerains. Masters of their towns, fortresses and regiments, they indulged in the worst of excesses in the name of the Lord. For more than thirty years battles and brigandage devastated the country, after which the most important among them returned to the fold, selling their allegiance to Henri IV.

The time of the troubles increased the power and fortune of the great: princes and dukes, peers and governors, the principal officers of the Crown, courtiers and ministers transformed by royal favour. These last survivors of the feudal system owned immense estates, raised troops, and lived surrounded by vassals, clients and servants. Some of them, who reigned over independent principalities, were even ready to declare war on the King.

The great nobleman of this period still enjoyed an almost religious prestige. His birth set him far above the rest of humanity and above the laws which were destined for the common man; neither he nor anyone else felt the slightest doubt on this point. He was usually a man devoid of culture, a man of boundless pride and physical courage; haughty, arrogant, ostentatious, truculent, brutal, greedy and prodigal, generous to his own people and pitiless to the rest, profoundly devoted to his house, touchy on points of honour. He had dissolute habits and boasted publicly of his successes with women. His wife, no less haughty, no less violent, no less wanton, was equally gay and given to adultery – and all was well, provided only she avoided a scandal.

In spite of the fighting, death reduced the number of women faster than the men. Many of the nobility had two or three wives in succession.

Sparing of affection towards their children, they worked furiously to build up their fortune. Civil wars might be fomented simply to 'establish' a younger son, to arrange for him a splendid marriage.

The nobility behaved amongst themselves with savage hostility or savage loyalty, or at best with an uneasy mistrust. Their glory was proclaimed in their dress. The Comtesse de Soissons and the Princesse de Conti wore so many jewels that the material of their bodices was invisible. A man's attire might be worth the value of several farms, and new clothes were often needed. Henri IV tried to restrain this extravagance by sumptuary edicts; the only result was to incur the wrath of the noblemen and the merchants alike.

The minor nobility, also, enjoyed fine weapons, noble steeds, gambling and women. As long as people were fighting, paying ransoms, raping and looting, the minor noble led the life of his dreams. Alas, all good things must come to an end! Peace arrived, the value of land decreased, and so did the revenues it brought; gold depreciated, the old incomes fell to derisory rates, and prices rose dizzily.

A gentleman could not do anything except fight, hunt and train a horse. So he had to choose between the château, where (if he was the eldest son) he was free to lead a wild, austere, rural life, and the Louvre, that palace of mirages, in which everyone stood a chance of receiving a few drops from the golden river. 'But,' wrote the Venetian Ambassador, 'when they arrived at Court, the French gentlemen spent more in a week than they had saved at home in a year. They gambled even their clothes away. I have seen more than one of them go off in the rain and snow without a shirt or breeches.'

Recognizing these ruined gentlemen as a source of unrest, the King would occasionally secure their allegiance by granting them a pension. All the idle in the kingdom depended on the hand which distributed the annuities. This system, contrived by the cunning of Henri IV, remained until 1789 one of the essential props of the régime.

Above all, the nobility of this period was characterized by a passion for duelling: the hunger for power, the love of adventure and the free reign of passion, could be satisfied only by mortal combat. Valour was the one indispensable virtue. Between 1583 and 1603, 7,000 duellists who had killed their adversaries received letters of pardon. The English Ambassador wrote: 'There is scarcely a Frenchman worth consideration who has not killed his man.'

Money did not enjoy in France the prestige it had won abroad. Governments founded on fiscal strength like those of Venice, Genoa and Florence were inconceivable here. The great banking houses and their dynasties, their loans, credits and bills of exchange had originated elsewhere. The Capetians were ignorant of the vexations of sovereigns across the Channel, forced to capitulate to the demands of financiers.

The economic revolution which occurred from the end of the fifteenth to the beginning of the sixteenth century did, however, have profound repercussions. It was then that personal fortunes appeared, as piety declined. The two phenomena might appear foreign to each other, but they were to engender a new species: the commoner, who could equal and surpass in wealth the noble, the cleric, the heirs of landed property; the Christian whose supreme God was money.

The middle class did not covet the magnificence which was in any case forbidden it. It did not make war, and it avoided pleasure. Its only happiness lay in increasing its wealth. The civil wars had established its prosperity. They had:

... accelerated the movement which impelled it to acquire noblemen's estates and to invade public service. Noble families, often disabled by the loss of their head or his heir presumptive ... were obliged to sell or mortgage their fiefs to commoners, or to borrow on security at a rate of interest which might be as high as thirty per cent. While the middle class was installing itself in the decaying châteaux of the nobility, it was also taking possession of posts in the magistracy, and of ecclesiastical livings which had once been largely reserved for the younger sons of aristocrats.[1]

The new class ranged from the common people to the *noblesse de robe*. At the summit of the class stood the members of parliament, the dispensers of royal justice.

Under the First President, who was appointed by the King, 200 chief justices and judges convinced themselves that they were 'the image and the summary of all the orders in the kingdom'. In their wake thronged a veritable army of lawyers including 20,000 judges and King's sergeants, besides barristers, solicitors, clerks of the courts and 'other illustrious persons' who, if we are to believe Noël du Fail, numbered no less than 300,000!

These people bought their offices from the Crown. François I had founded this fatal method of reimbursing his treasury and of levying a tithe on the wealthy who paid all too readily. Henri III alone had the courage and foresight to curtail this abuse, but far from following his example, Henri IV perfected the old system. On the advice of Judge Paulet, he made the offices of the magistracy hereditary, on condition that the incumbent paid annually one-sixtieth of the value of his office to the State. This office then became wholly the property of the purchaser, who could bequeath it, sell it, or trade it as he pleased. Public service thus became the monopoly of a few families. The 'Paulette' dated from 1604. It was to rouse constant indignation, but was not abrogated until 1789.

The office of a counsellor in parliament was then worth some 100,000 livres in Paris, 60,000 in the provinces; that of treasurer general represented

[1] Fagniez: *L'Economie sociale de la France sous Henri IV*.

30,000 livres, that of counsellor at the Cour des Aides 25,000. Buying it brought dispensation from paying tallage and aids, from serving in the *arrière-ban* of the army, from lodging the King's soldiers. And so the lawyers proudly ranked themselves among the privileged.

However, the magistrate earned very poor wages. How could he redeem the invested capital, pay his debt to the Crown and live 'honestly'? How, above all, could he amass those vast fortunes which would enable his family to dislodge the ruined nobles? In 1560, François Grimaudet gave the answer in his speech to the State-General:

The ministry of judges, their jurisdiction and distribution of justice, is only a shop in which they sell retail what they have bought wholesale. The nobleman and the priest, the commoner and the pilgrim, the widow and the orphan, the cripple and the beggar will have no sentence, either interlocutory or final, which has not been taxed and valued and bought before it has been passed.

This scandalous state of affairs raised at best a few satires. Universally accepted, it did not even shake the prestige of the Law. The judge who sold his sentence did not feel any scruples of conscience: just as the nobleman had his prerogatives, so he possessed the right to venality. So much so that people who were otherwise morally irreproachable, did not hesitate to conform to this practice.

On the other hand, the *bourgeoisie de robe* did not know the depravities, the prodigality, the follies of the nobility. The golden écus piling up in the depths of coffers were hardly ever visible to the outsider. The illustrious Président de Thou went to mass on a mule, his wife behind him. Parliamentary gravity, the antithesis of aristocratic extravagances had its own emblems: dark woollen stuffs, judge's ermines, square caps, 'plain linen and smooth watered silk'. Grave were the interminable beards, grave were the looks, grave were the speeches, the gestures and the bearing.

The wives, in their straight dresses, white linen, and severe coifs, the bunch of keys at the waist, had something puritan about them, too. Youth learnt early to restrain the impulses of its years, not without a secret envy of the fine, exuberant gentlemen clothed in silk.

The merchants, whom the lawyers had left so far behind, having set out from beneath them, watched them now with jealousy and anger. For their profession was devoid of glory. In Italy, Germany and England commerce was highly honoured: it bordered on the patriciate, it gave power. There was nothing like it for the French, whose only renown and virtue were in their arms. They scoffed all the time at the 'petit bourgeois', money-grubbing, shabby, obsequious, nervous, huddled in his shop like an animal in its pen.

And so the merchants kept together and rarely left their particular neighbourhood. There they were, in a dress to be deplored by the characters of Molière, wearing 'the fine doublet, very long and properly done up', the plain black or brown trunk-hose, the woollen stockings with thick garters, the huge hat beloved of painters, the shoes 'that did not torture the feet'. The greater part of their existence was spent in dark and airless chambers on the ground-floor in the shelter of an arcade.

Commercial habits resembled those of the oriental bazaar. People haggled, and indulged in long verbal duels before settling on a price. The shopkeeper, man or woman, was hard and mistrustful. The moment the evening came, he locked himself in, 'having cheated people all day', and counted the takings. He piled up and arranged his écus, his pistoles and his livres, and this, apart from religious festivities and a very occasional country outing was the merchant's only distraction and reward.

When the piles were sufficient, the couple could retire from business. Those who were more ambitious might buy a post for their son. Thus, provided they had amassed enough, the draper could cherish a hope that his great-grandsons would be gentlemen and courtiers.

Commerce grew to include no less than 150 corporations. First came the woollen-drapers, the goldsmiths, the mercers, the furriers and hat-makers (who were considered worthy of municipal functions because they did not work with their hands). After them followed the doctors, surgeons and pharmacists, who could be recognized at a distance by their famous dress. Then came the crowd of miscellaneous trades, whose fraternities quarrelled fiercely with each other and indulged in frequent lawsuits.

We have now reached the bottom of the hierarchy, the level of the 'vile persons', in other words the industrial class. In this superstitious century one prophecy at least would have met with total disbelief: the prophecy that this class was to preponderate 300 years later. To do 'mechanical work', to work oneself, invited a sort of opprobrium. The frontiers of the middle class could therefore be considered as crossed when one came to men incapable of buying a position, and so of rising above their social class.

For we have to come back to this: that in a society where rank was fixed by birth, advancement was possible only by the sale of offices. So what family that was in a position to do this failed to seize such an opportunity? If one of the sons entered the royal service, their destiny could be transformed.

This dream of the French middle class was so continuous, so obsessive that it survived revolutions and crises and upheavals of every kind. Even today it is thanks to this dream that the State easily recruits its functionaries among the élite and gives them derisory salaries with impunity.

In the large towns there were not rich quarters and poor quarters, aristocratic and plebeian quarters. Social distances were too vast, too visible, too well recognized for there to be any need to mark them geographically.

On the Pont-Neuf, in the Marais, in the Rue Saint-Honoré, in front of Notre-Dame, plumes and cassocks mingled with sober doublets, satin or fustian dresses, liveries and rags.

The lowest class, whose hovels nestled beneath the Louvre, and who were immortalized in the engravings of Callot, were an indescribable company of beggars, cripples, ruffians and hired assassins waiting for the chance of a thrust.

In the depths of their dens bands of criminals drank and gambled, ready to use their daggers on behalf of a jealous man or for someone too cowardly to settle his quarrel himself, perhaps an impatient heir. It was in vain that the pillory was set up near les Halles, that the bankrupts, the forgers, the blasphemers, the prostitutes, the pimps were put in it pell-mell. Neither the insults of the delirious crowds nor the executioner's whip intimidated these delinquents, who included in their number students and lackeys.

As for the lackeys, these tough determined men did not have the servile position which later they would have with their master. They really belonged to the nobleman's house, and they reflected his haughtiness, his insolence, his brutality. If they were treated roughly, and often beaten, they also knew that they were assured of unconditional protection. To touch a livery was to touch a coat-of-arms. Those who wore it therefore gave free rein to their bad instincts. The Comte d'Auvergne, the natural son of Charles IX, did not pay his valets: he sent them out to plunder passers-by.

These potential gallows-birds kept a permanent tumult going throughout the town; through it one might discern the pious rumour of processions and the cries of street vendors. A thousand voices announced: 'Cherries, sweet cherries', 'come buy muffs, and ruffles and bands', 'come buy cakes and hot cheesecakes', 'kill rats and mice', 'roasted chestnuts', 'brandy to rejoice the heart'. At night the wafer merchant, holding his lantern in one hand, and shaking his clappers with the other, would sing out: 'Wafers, wafers, where are they?'

The corporation, a distant ancestor of our own trade unions, had formerly rendered great services; it had assured its patrons a minimum of security, and given the workers protection against the employers' demands, a ruling on hours of work and on salaries. Then the abuse had begun, and under Henri III the corporation gradually assumed the aspect of an oligarchy; the richest patrons had hedged in its freedoms and assumed the privileges of an élite. And so, side by side with these organized trades, a number of free trades had arisen.

Through the institution of the sale of 'freedoms' the worker was more than ever tied to his corporation. For mutual assistance, charity, religious practices and, above all, for pleasure, he had his fraternity. The subscriptions which he paid did not only serve to help the needy; they also helped to subsidize merry-makings, banquets fit for Pantagruel, with interludes of song and dance where the wine might rouse people's spirits and even make them conceive ideas of sedition. The fraternities were more than once prohibited by the kings, but they were always re-formed.

The workers led a hard life. Nature and politics regularly afflicted them with the worst scourges, epidemics, famines, floods, civil wars; they suffered these with an impassive stoicism which came from several sources – religion, fatalism, the ancestral habit of misfortune. The worker enjoyed no consideration; neither philosopher, nor writer sang his praise.

On the other hand, he was far from lost in an anonymous mass. He could make his own worth appreciated, he could aim at a 'masterpiece' and, which was invaluable, he could keep his character. Taxation did not worry him and military service was foreign to him. All of this helped him to bear his wrongs in patience and, meanwhile, neither to impair his spirit, his courage, his passion for certain national or religious problems: nor to extinguish a little flame of revolution which burned within him from generation to generation.

What can be said of the peasants – that multitude of men dragging out their existence in endless toil from which they themselves were not to benefit? What can be said of these victims who were given over to the rigours of tax-collectors, the extortions of functionaries, the avarice of usurers, the ravages of campaigning troops, the abuses of noblemen and prelates: these nameless men who, by their misery, their tenacity and their sweat, were to make the restoration of the kingdom possible?

As for these indispensable beings, charged not only with feeding the privileged, but with assuring their magnificence; these people could hope for neither gratitude nor honour. Far from that, they were mocked and scorned. They were considered stupid, underhand, wicked and filthy; they were compared with animals. Vincent de Paul, who had come from their midst, called them 'savage tribes'.

An astronomical distance divided the Court, the gentlemen with dazzling plumage, and the rich, cultivated, refined bourgeois from these grey masses: these peasants who worked the land of France until excessive persecution forced them to seek refuge deep in the forests. Among the pious souls whose mystic disquietude was to echo throughout the centuries, amongst all those who were anxious about their salvation, there was no visible scruple of conscience about the condition in which the rural population was kept. That the whole burden of the State should be imposed on its shoulders seemed perfectly natural.

And yet, however pitiful he might appear, the common man had already made considerable progress towards that ownership of the land which was his daily thought, his obsessive concern. Despite the vastness of the Church estates, and despite the servitude, the small property existed. The impoverishment of the nobility, obliged to sell part of its fiefs, had rapidly increased it. The villein, the serf of former years, had often bought the fields and mills which some fine spark had changed for velvet and gilt. He owned the property he had bought, he would hand it down to his eldest son or share it like La Fontaine's labourer. In no other country in Europe could he enjoy such liberty. The change was not yet remarkable. But what a way he had travelled since the end of the Middle Ages!

The struggle to cheat consuming taxation, to escape the plunderer, never ended. At night, between one raid and another, the common man would go mysteriously to work. If necessary, he would harness his wife and his children (from the age of ten!) to the plough, he would harness himself to it, 'all dressed in canvas like a windmill'. He suffered and toiled and often fled like game. An old countryman could hardly distinguish him from the wolf or the wild dog. But if, suddenly, the rainbow shone, if destiny, the state or war allowed him a moment's respite, he rose again, and found his good humour intact; and out of his rotten mattress he brought the écus which would make him a landholder despite his persecutors.

It was a kind of miracle, in the year 1598, when Sully extolled tillage and pasturage as the breasts of France: when the King, realizing the need to re-create something taxable to clear his liabilities, decided to let the country populations 'get their breath back'.

It is not very easy for us to form a clear idea of these 'men liable to tallage and statute labour': these men who, in succeeding reigns, extolled the first decade of the seventeenth century as the equivalent of a golden age. Every imagination hesitates before these millions of beings isolated by their ignorance, the scorn in which they were held, their almost complete inability to circulate, their fear of a hostile society. What ideas did they have of their country, of politics, of the wars they suffered from, of the castes they fed, or the religion, sometimes mingled with pagan superstitions, which inspired them with the 'charcoal-burner's faith'?

Their body was no better cared for than their spirit. Old wives' cures and simples, the recipes of bone-setters and spells, were their only weapons against the illnesses and epidemics which were so frequent. They died in hundreds, often in their prime. Their work, their appalling lack of hygiene made them deformed and repulsive. But the stock was strong and it assured France a population which was considerable in relation to that of other countries.

The peasants lived in hovels, sometimes devoid of windows, made of cob and thatch, and dried mud, sometimes capable of lasting for centuries. Heating and lighting had hardly changed for a thousand years. The dirt was shocking, even in this century of stenches. Many families lived together with their animals. Besides, if ruthless saving allowed a little comfort, the fear of attracting the tax officials would prevent their yielding to any temptation.

Rye bread, cooked for three weeks, formed the basis of the diet. The potato was yet to be discovered. As for meat, only pork was eaten, and that on solemn occasions: marriages and baptisms. The inventories of possessions, made out for inheritors, are shorter in certain regions than in others. Sometimes one includes furniture, a big bed made soft with poultry feathers, linen, clothes and crockery. Sometimes there is a pathetic absence even of essentials.

Such is the setting of a peasant life, completely regulated by the length of the day, submitted both to the tyranny of nature and to the head of the family.

3 Italy

ROME

At the end of the sixteenth century, Italy existed as a mosaic of states as different from each other as could be. The form of government, social progress, the development of commerce and the arts, the rôle of the clergy, the nobility and the bourgeoisie, the burden of foreign occupation utterly different in each region. There was a crowd of principalities whose capitals remained important centres, although the intensity of the life there had been exhausted in the course of the wars. Between the principal towns stretched vast tracts of land, thinly populated by peasants, who were generally unconscious of the changes brought about by the centuries.

Rome, the heart of Christianity, kept its primacy and its radiance. For the rest, it was undergoing profound transformations. The year 1559 saw the end of a thirty-nine years' war and the accession of Pius IV, and so marked the beginning of a new era. Pirates and bandits remained a cause of alarm, but otherwise Rome ceased to be submitted to threats from outside and enjoyed a veritable restoration. The cause of her prosperity and peace was paradoxical for a continental city, little given to commerce, for a city which professed to scorn the riches of this world and looked in principle towards the spiritual guidance of nations. It was the influx of American gold. For, with a few exceptions, the conquerors of the New World had embarked from the Catholic countries.

Even when war and domestic troubles consumed part of the manna which had been harvested beyond the seas, the clergy was powerful and skilful enough to gather in the principal; either by exploiting popular credulity, or by selling its indulgences and sometimes its political compliance; or by partaking of the imported gold. And where did it go to, this gold which had been collected in humble churches, drawn from the royal coffers? It went to Rome, whose wealth was therefore unequalled.

These almost limitless resources allowed the Holy See to pursue a policy of magnificence and to restore the war ruins which had accumulated in

46

Rome. The sacking of 1527, in particular, had caused terrible damage to the brick houses, which were huddled together in narrow alleys, most of them squalid.

At the end of the century, the city was transformed. It swelled with life, and became a gigantic workyard. Its population increased; architects, painters, sculptors, everyone whose profession was to drink the waters of the Pactolus, the golden river, hastened thither. While St Peter's was being finished, the church of Gesù was built under the direction of Giacomo Vignola. It was the first Jesuit church. It was to be a model to all Christendom for at least two centuries. Every religious order wanted to build its own monuments and to display its splendour, regardless of cost. As Stendhal noted, 'it was the countries which had not had to tremble for their authority which produced the greatest works in painting, architecture and sculpture of modern times.'

Jesuits, Carmelites, Dominicans, Franciscans, rivalled with one another not only to embellish the city but also to propagate its new architectural fashions abroad. While they all contributed to this proliferation, the heirs of St Ignatius proceeded with particular fervour. That is why the term 'Jesuit style' seems fairer and more meaningful in the circumstances than the term 'Baroque'.

The movement of mystic renovation accompanied and emphasized the movement towards architectural restoration. That was one of the more surprising 'revolutions from above': a considered, conscious, calculated revolution. The civilization which brought it about was militant. Art was used, not as an end in itself, but as a means to glorify the Church. Guido Reni, Domenichino, Caravaggio, were all employed with this end in view. The fame of their paintings spread throughout Europe, and contributed by their imaginative appeal, to the cause of the Catholic Church in its struggle against the Protestant reform. The medieval Mystery Plays were likewise revived and exploited by the Jesuits for this purpose.

While she was putting on her new and magnificent apparel, Rome saw the birth of her bureaucracy. The popes continued to be assisted by a Secretary of State or a Cardinal-nephew, but the congregations kept much of their power. During and after the reign of Sixtus v, who created most of them, there were more than fifteen congregations, which ranged from the Holy Inquisitions, and the Index, to the congregation 'for revictualling' or 'for the building of new churches'. The power of the congregations corresponded to the executive power of the tribunals: the Penitentiary, the Signature of Justice, the Signature of Grace, and above all the terrible Rota, which was feared almost as much as the Inquisition.

The 'great services' included the Chancelry, the Datery, which conceded livings, the Apostolic Chamber which supervised finances and

47

was presided over by the cardinal-camerlingo: there were the Prefect of Administration, the governor of the city, the governor of the Castel Sant' Angelo, the six legates of state; and so many cardinals, services, offices, secretaries, employees and servants that the old feudal Rome underwent a complete metamorphosis.

There was more unearned wealth in Rome than anywhere else. Splendour was displayed without shame, sanctified by the holy services of those who enjoyed it and by the accepted conviction that this luxury served the glory of God. In 1595, the Venetian Ambassador, Faruta, wrote:

Spending has increased in a quite excessive fashion, and this splendid way of life, which was once the privilege of a few cardinals and barons, has now been adopted by an astounding number of people.

The Duke of Urbino's envoy added: 'Merchants dress their wives like noblewomen, and allow themselves every pleasure, whatever the cost.' The servants grew rich so fast that it became difficult to maintain the household that befitted a cardinal or a great nobleman (every palace had from one to three hundred people to feed). Luckily the gaps could be filled by buying Turkish slaves.

The love of pleasure naturally went with the taste for ostentation. Hunting, which had been much in fashion early in the century (the Caraffa had kept more than 1,300 dogs at the time), became less fashionable, but banquets remained Gargantuan. At a banquet given in honour of the Venetian ambassadors, there was a procession of seventy-four dishes of *poulet à la Catalane*, served to the sound of harps and cymbals and violins, followed by eight dishes of roast meats and by eighteen dishes each composed of two pheasants and a peacock, followed in turn by eighteen dishes each composed of eight pigeons.

Keeping a carriage was the ultimate proof of wealth and fashion. Only the courtesans were forbidden them. 'You need two things to succeed in Rome,' said St Charles Borromeo: 'to love God and to own a carriage.' Hence there was a traffic problem in the narrow streets.

It might be supposed that the Church, with her vast wealth, would have encouraged the birth of new industries. She did not do so. Despite the increase in the population, Rome was to remain, until 1870, almost exactly as she was in 1600. Montaigne wrote: 'This city has hardly any unskilled labourers . . .'; in other words it was difficult to find recruits for humble jobs. In fact the money which they earned so rapidly in the workyards gave most workmen the ambition to become employers and middle-class citizens as fast as possible. The increase in the number of guilds clearly shows the evolution of the classes of labour: there were eighteen of them at the end of the fourteenth century, thirty-two at the end of the fifteenth. Twenty-three more were created in the course of the sixteenth century.

Recreation

Festivities at a competition for cross-bowmen in Germany.

'The beautiful dance of Zan Trippu at his wedding with Madama Franceschina.'
A group of Italian comedians in the typical characters of the *Commedia dell' Arte*.

Brueghel's painting of a group of travelling actors. Several well-known companies
of 'English Comedians' toured extensively in Germany and the Low Countries.

Above and below. Two designs by
Inigo Jones for court masques. Many
architects combined the design of
buildings and the planning of
theatrical spectacles for the courts.

Ceremonial battles were the gladiatorial sports of
the sixteenth century. Here a naval battle is
enacted on the Seine in honour of Henri IV.

Left. The Brazilian forest recreated in Rouen on an island in the Seine, complete with savages, for a visit of Henri II to the city. This human zoo was shortlived, owing to the untropical weather of Normandy.

Opposite. Hans Bock the elder, *The Baths at Leuk*. Thermal baths were enjoyed as much for the company as for the cure.

Below. Procession of dancers and revellers at a wedding in Bermondsey.

A group of musicians from *The New Most Beautiful Garden of the Choicest Musical Flowers*, a song-book of 1605. Social music has probably never enjoyed as much popularity as it did around 1600.

Below and opposite. Tennis, played in an indoor version, and every sort of contest of strength and skill were popular pastimes throughout the period.

THE NOBLE ART OF VENERIE OR HVNTING.

Wherein is handled and set out the Vertues, Nature, and Properties of fifteene sundry Chaces, together with the order and manner how to Hunt and kill euery one of them.

Translated & collected for the pleasure of all Noblemen and Gentlemen, out of the best approoued Authors, which haue written any thing concerning the same : And reduced into such order and proper termes as are vsed here in this noble Realme of Great Britaine.

AT LONDON,
Printed by *Thomas Purfoot*.
An. Dom. 1611.

Title-page of the most famous Elizabethan hunting book: Turberville's *The Noble Art of Venery.*

Detail from a German hunting-piece. As in the Middle Ages, hunting was an important courtly pursuit, and a new dimension had been added by the development of firearms.

The Venetian bull-fight, held in the streets of the city.

Within the guilds, which were divided according to streets or districts, the rules restricted personal initiative but offered the resources for a genuine social security: medical care in case of illness, assistance for widows.

It was not only building which caused money to circulate. Innkeepers and tavernkeepers grew rich thanks to the enormous influx of travellers, pilgrims and merchants. So did the tailors, embroiderers, jewellers, and all the tradesmen connected with clothes, church linen and finery. The yardage of material sold every year was considerable, but the Romans contented themselves with selling and tailoring it; the textile industry was hazardous and undeveloped.

It is a sign of wealth to take meticulous care of one's health; it is also the celibate's mania. There were therefore an impressive number of surgeons and doctors in the service of the prelates, and among them were a good many Jews.

And so, whether it was a matter of buildings, dress, food, or medical science, most of the money which circulated during this fortunate period was used to promote prestige. This capital was bequeathed to posterity, but it produced no income.

Side by side with excess there existed poverty. With the increase in wealth went a corresponding increase in the number of beggars, cripples and thieves. Rome was an international capital for poverty and for opulence, for believers and for profiteers. Sixtus V wrote in 1587: 'These vagabonds swarm over all the streets and squares in the city in search of bread; they fill public places and private houses, and even the churches, with their groans and cries . . . They wander round like animals, and their one concern is the search for food.'

In 1595, the pontifical police concluded from the interrogation of a young boy that there were nineteen companies of beggars in the city, each with a different occupation. In 1601, C. Fanucci wrote: 'In Rome you see nothing but beggars, and there are so many of them that it is impossible to walk in the streets without having them around you.' The only solution seemed to be to assemble the genuine poor, the pilgrims, the sick and the foundlings, and to group them together in workhouses. At the beginning of the sixteenth century, there were already seven such establishments in Rome. Nine others were built in the course of the century. They were not enough. An appeal was made to private charity, but it was no use. From every region of Italy, the poor converged on Rome, the country was depopulated, and the working-class districts grew full of the unemployed.

On 27 February 1581, it was decided to take a census of them. They were conducted – a strange procession preceded by standards and prelates – to the ancient Dominican monastery of San Sisto. They numbered 850. Sixtus V wanted to build a workhouse to hold them all; this building cost 18,000 crowns and received an annual grant of 15,000 crowns, both considerable sums. But in 1591 there were 1,034 unemployed. All solutions proved to have been provisional. In 1613 the lame, the halt and the blind were authorized to form themselves into a corporation. It was at least a recognition of their social existence.

There was one trade which could not be formed into a corporation, but remained of prime importance because of the number of those who lived by it and by the money it earned. This was the trade of the courtesan. In the city of the popes, in spite of the increase in places of prayer, the influx of pilgrims and the great quantity of priests, this profession grew to a disturbing degree and became proverbial throughout Europe. Every traveller talked of the venal beauties of Rome.

Montaigne wrote:

The courtesans show themselves at their windows with such deceiving art that I have often wondered how they attracted our attention; and frequently, having leapt from my horse, and obtained immediate entrance, I have marvelled at this: how much more beautiful they appeared than in fact they were.

Du Bellay wrote:

Their outward show is splendid, there is naught so fine or brave,
But the inside bears a likeness to the inside of a grave.
Oh, what greediness there is, and oh, what poverty!
Oh, what a horror just to witness their impurity!

There were two categories of courtesan, which should not be confused; on one hand there were the 'honest' courtesans, rich and cultivated, and equipped with palaces and protectors, asking up to twelve crowns a night: on the other hand there were the prostitutes who were known as 'candle tarts' because they often operated in a candle-merchant's back shop. These hardly ever charged more than a crown, and they risked harsh treatment from the police.

Pontifical authority found it hard to tolerate them. Sixtus V tried to impose a ruling and to canton them in a single district; but the tide was difficult to stem: 800 prostitutes in a population of 35,000 women, according to an official census of 1599. Another census gives the figure of 484 'honest courtesans', that is to say courtesans who were suitably maintained; this figure allows us to imagine a much more considerable number of poor prostitutes.

Some of those who had enriched themselves knew how to present themselves as great ladies. Pietro Fortini, from Siena, described the interior of one of their houses:

A broad, spacious staircase, a room hung with gilded leather and decorated with very fine paintings. On a splendid chair there sat a beautiful, ravishing young girl, eighteen years old, sumptuously dressed, with an infinite number of golden, pearl-headed pins. The room was all hung with silken hangings, and the bed had magnificent curtains, a royal counterpane . . .

The Spanish Ambassador, paying a visit to Imperia, preferred to spit in a servant's face rather than spit on the ground, for he was afraid to dirty the carpet. Imperia was obliged to him for this courtesy . . .

These ladies had strange rivals to contend with. In 1580 Montaigne wrote in his account of his Italian journey:

In this church [St John Lateran], some years ago, a number of Portuguese entered into a curious brotherhood. They married each other, man and man, with the ceremonies we use at our own marriages; they received their sacrament at Easter together, read the same nuptial mass, and then slept and lived together. The Roman wits said that because only marriage legitimized the conjunction of male and female, it had seemed to these subtle people that this other conjunction would be legitimate, too, if it were authorized by the ceremonies and mysteries of the church . . .

It may seem surprising to call such behaviour Portuguese when it had its followers in every country, and it was called Italian when it spread through France.

The popes fought hard against depravity. They created a monastery for the ill-married and a monastery for the repentant. They gave dowries to poor young girls. Montaigne described the ceremony of 'giving alms to virgins'. Thirty-five crowns a head! Alas, it was not enough to convince the girls that they could remain honest women.

They would have been remarkably noble had they done so, considering the morals which were prevalent even at the summit of the Church. The first pope of the Counter-Reformation, Paul III (the brother of a mistress of Pope Alexander VI), had children whose scandalous behaviour was a byword. One of them took a fancy to the young Bishop of Fano, and engineered his death in conditions which defy description. Pope Gregory XIII also had a son whom he was bold enough to legitimize: he became in fact the Governor of the Papal States. Cardinal Farnese prided himself on his daughter, Clelia, who was, he said, the most beautiful object he had made apart from his palace and the Jesuit church.

With such encouragement as this, it was not surprising that the lay nobility set out to indulge their passions with a frenzy which often led to crime.

The Cenci family contrived to surpass all others. Painting and literature have often recalled how the beautiful Beatrice Cenci, raped by her father, Francesco, took revenge, in agreement with her brother and sister-in-law, by having him murdered. The woman whom Shelley would identify as 'the Angel of Parricide' was executed together with her brother on the order of Clement VIII. But the flame of the Renaissance which still burnt in human beings could also push them to the opposite extreme. The ascetic life was as extreme as the life of depravity; saints like Charles Borromeo and Philip Neri, the founder of the Oratory, were found side by side with prelates whose immorality was infamous.

Charles Borromeo, who had been made Inspector of the Sacred College, one day reproached Cardinal Farnese with spending a fortune on his villa at Caprarola instead of helping the poor. 'I am doing something much better', replied the stately cardinal, who had the mentality of a modern man, 'I am giving them work'.

Another singular event is recorded in 1585, when a former swineherd, who had become a strict theologian, succeeded to the Papal throne. Cardinal Peretti was elected because his apparent infirmities promised that his reign would be brief. The very moment he became Sixtus v, however, he cast aside his crutches.

For a brief period he restored to the Church the authority which it had practically foresworn for the benefit of the King of Spain. While he was inflaming the wars of religion in France and urging Philip II to attack England, he completed the cupola of St Peter's in Rome, restored many monuments, and brought in the waters of Aqua Martia through a wonderful aqueduct. At the same time he reformed the religious orders and prepared for a crusade.

Rome was haloed for a moment with its ancient glory. After him, once again, it became that strange metropolis, full of gold and poverty, of masterpieces and monstrosities, lost to vice but determined to exalt the glory of God.

FLORENCE

The evolution of manners in Florence at the end of the sixteenth century was the correlative of its political history, or at least depended upon its political history.

The Grand Duke of Tuscany, Cosimo I, was accused of accelerating the decline of industry and commerce, the former sources of national prosperity. In fact, signs of exhaustion were already visible in the final years of the Republic. Florence suffered at the expense of the immense prosperity which religion brought to Rome, and maritime trade to Venice.

Cosimo de Medici, whose ancestors were merchants, did not forget the origins of his ancestral wealth. He took an interest in the commercial affairs of all Europe – of which he was one of the principal bankers – including trade in the Near East. But if this activity filled the treasure-chests of the rulers and of certain great families, it did nothing to help the middle or lower classes who remained in poverty.

Despotism was the symptom rather than the cause of the economic decline of Florence; and although the Medicis claimed new resources from the land and undertook a long-term agrarian policy, they needed time, and for nearly a century Florence was considered the poor relation in Italy.

Cosimo I, who was treated as a parvenu by his fellow sovereigns, resorted to the artists in order to enhance his splendour. At his instigation, Cellini cast the bronze Perseus, Vasari built the Uffizi, rebuilt the bridge of Santa Trinità, joined the Pitti Palace (which had become the grand-ducal residence) to the Palace of the Signoria. To him also is due the completion of the Laurentian Library, opened to the public in 1571, the creation of a botanic garden and the foundation or transformation of several academies, including the Academy of Drawing. Thus Florence underwent a renaissance which was further enhanced by the Mannerist school of painters: the school which sought to conciliate paganism and religion, corresponding to the work and thought of St Philip Neri. The founder of the Oratory appealed to the heart rather than the head, and he extended to Florence the work which the popes of the Counter-Reformation had commissioned in Rome; he propagated faith through the love of beauty.

The reign of Francesco, Cosimo's successor, was a period of political humiliation, social corruption and police terror. The Grand Duke was less interested in affairs of State than in festivities, orgies, and in scientific experiments. He had a notorious love affair with the beautiful Bianca Cappello, whose husband was murdered at his instigation. Bianca and Francesco died within a day of one another, possibly by poisoning.

Montaigne showed small indulgence to 'Florence, a city smaller than Ferrara, situated in a plain surrounded by a thousand highly cultivated little mountains.' He complained that he had never seen a nation with fewer beautiful women than Italy. He found the lodgings less comfortable than those in France and Germany, and he complained about the food: '. . . meat is not in such abundance as in Germany, nor so well prepared; it is served without larding in both countries, but in Germany it is much better seasoned . . .' Florence seemed to him to be 'the most expensive city in Italy'.

> . . . I do not know [he continued], why this city should have the privilege of being called beautiful; it is beautiful, but it in no way surpasses Bologna and it is little better than Ferrara, and it is without comparison beneath Venice . . . Yet, to tell the truth, it is fine to look down from the Duomo on the infinite multitude of houses which cover the hills for two or three leagues around . . .

Ferdinand I, the brother of Francesco, was a cardinal before he became Grand Duke, a matter which did not prevent him from taking a wife in order to ensure his lineage. The festivities which were organized for his marriage to Christina of Lorraine were marked by an important artistic event: the birth of the opera. The Florentine *Camerata*, an association of poets and musicians under the leadership of Count Giovanni Bardi di Vernio, had already made several attempts to devise an opera. Vincenzo Galilei, the astronomer's father, had helped to introduce the recitative into musical works. But on the occasion of Ferdinand's marriage came the first attempt at a dramatic performance with a musical accompaniment. In 1595, the poet Ottavio Rinuccini wrote *Dafne*, which was set to music by Jacopo Peri. In 1600, for the marriage of Marie des Médicis and Henri IV, the same artists presented their *Euridice*. Finally, in 1608, for the marriage of the Grand Duke Cosimo II with Maria Maddalena of Austria, Rinuccini wrote his *Arianna*, the music for which was composed by Monteverdi.

Ferdinand patronized not only the arts, but also literature, which had long been neglected; and at his instigation the Accademia della Crusca compiled the first dictionary of the Tuscan language, which was published in 1612. The humanist passion was not extinct and numerous Classical authors were at this time translated into the vernacular: Apuleius, Ovid, Livy and Plutarch.

Florence, although in decline in Italy, shone with unforeseen radiance in France, thanks to the reigns of Catherine and Marie des Médicis. These princesses perpetuated the traditions of their city in politics and manners and, which was more important, in patronage. Under the last Valois and during the minority of Louis XIII, the court of France became known as 'a little Florence'.

VENICE

The patriciate of Venice did not – understandably – originate with land-holders. It was an oligarchy of merchants, bankers and administrators, whose manners show the influence of the trade with the Near East. The great Venetian names, which were not taken from estates as they were elsewhere, already dated back six centuries. It was lineage, rather than the possession of domains or even wealth, which attested to nobility.

The chief families were descended from the twelve tribunes who had elected the first Doge. People called them the Houses of the Twelve Apostles. Then came those of the so-called Four Evangelists. These were the signatories to the charter of foundation of the abbey of San Giorgio Maggiore, in the year 800: the Giustiniani, who claimed descent from the Emperors of Constantinople, the Cornari, rendered illustrious by Catherine Cornaro, Queen of Cyprus, the Bragadini and the Bembi. Eight other houses belonged to the first class by virtue of their antiquity. These twenty-four families governed the Republic and administered the affairs of State.

About the year 1200, at the time of the creation of the Grand Council, all the families then settled in Venice were declared to be noble (eighty of them still existed in the seventeenth century). Seventeen others were ennobled in 1380 in reward for services rendered to the Republic during the war against the Genoese. Together they constituted the second class. Finally there came those who had more recently solicited and obtained the favour of being called citizens of Venice. This was a kind of 'naturalization of honour': it was granted to the younger sons of some of the great houses of Italy, to the nephews of popes, and to Henri III of France when he visited Venice. In return Henri granted letters of nobility to certain merchants and glass-makers of Murano; as a result of which the glass-makers and all the merchants claimed themselves noblemen.

The Venetian nobility, as all nobility, had its pride of caste and its prejudices. Family prestige was a matter of birth, rather than of the largeness of the estate, military prowess or chilvalric honour. In this sense it resembled a republican nobility.

Citizens of Venice had to be Venetian by birth and origin. Doctors, lawyers, merchants, and glass-makers from Murano had the right to this title. They were eligible for the offices of secretaries of the senate or the tribunals, even the title of Grand Chancellor of the Republic; they were also, of course, eligible for all the secondary posts too.

The government – the most stable of all governments, since it was to last without any perceptible change for a thousand years – approximated to that of a police state. Espionage and informing were veritable institutions, and this with the co-operation of the citizens themselves. We read in the account of Saint-Didier's travels:[1]

The places where informers cast their notes of denunciation are like trunks set in the thickness of the walls: the open mouth of a gargoyle swallows up the information and passes it through a hole one cannot see. The whole of the Palazzo San Marco and every place in the city where magistrates preside over tribunals have a quantity of dangerous mouths like these. If the denunciator declares himself, he receives a reward; otherwise, he sends a stranger with the other half of the paper on which he has written the denunciation and they pay him in cash. The Republic is not content to maintain a great number of spies quite publicly, it also has secret spies in private houses and, in particular, it slips them into the embassies. And so it is informed of the slightest word that affects its interests. Of all the spies, none are better treated than those who are connected with state inquisitions; and though this profession is considered the lowest of the low, and the greatest insult is *spia d'inquisitori*, there are spies in every class, artisans, citizens, officers, even noblemen . . .

Tyrannical in the political field, the Republic showed great tolerance in matters of religion. The Greeks, the Armenians and the few Protestants practised their religions unimpeded. The domain of the Inquisition

[1] Chapter 35: *Of Secret Denunciations and of Spies.*

was strictly limited to heresy. The 2,500 Jews, who were recognized by their red caps lined with black taffeta, were better treated than Shakespeare would have us believe in *The Merchant of Venice*. The richest of them associated with merchants and could, on occasions, bring considerable sums to the State. One can still see the tall houses of the ghetto shut by double doors.

The same liberalism was often practised in individual families. The foreign chroniclers of the time observed with surprise and disapproval the excessive independence given to children, especially the children of the nobility.

Fathers and mothers so idolize their children that they never restrain them . . . They soon grow accustomed to being treated like princes. That is why foreigners do not usually find honest people among these gentlemen unless they are those who have learned to live abroad, and, among these, the ones who have been to France are happily distinguishable from the rest. However carefully one tries to educate these young people, they only study as much as they feel inclined, whether it be at college or at home.

Gambling was the favourite passion of the Venetians. Many young noblemen chose this way of squandering the money so laboriously earned by their father's employees, and they were never reproached for it.

Wives and daughters, however, were strictly guarded against temptations. Rarely were they permitted to leave their houses unless it was to attend a religious service. Most of them remained at home and saw no one but their family. And yet their dresses were renowned for their originality, their extravagance and their fantasy, whilst in every other city in Italy women had adopted the Spanish uniform.

Moryson in his *Itinerary* of 1605, thus describes the Venetian fashion:

The women wear gownes, leaving all the neck and the brest bare, and they are closed before with a lace, so open, as a man may see the linnen which they lap about their bodies, to make them seeme fat, the Italians most loving fat women. They shew their naked necks and breasts, and likewise their dugges, bound up and swelling with linnen, and all made white by art. They wear large falling bands [ruffs], and their haire is commonly yellow, made so by the sunne and art, and they raise up their haire on the forehead in two knotted hornes and deck their heads & uncovered haire with flowers of silke, and with pearle, in great part counterfeit. And they cast a black vaile from the head to the shoulders, and necks, and breasts, may easily be seene.

Another text informs us: 'They seem a foot taller than the men because they walk on high leather-covered blocks of wood. They have their breasts bare, the old women as well as the young ones.'

And, finally, Montaigne, always valuable for his original views, wrote:

I did not find that precious beauty which people attribute to the ladies of Venice, and I saw the finest of those who traffic in it. But it seems to me quite as admirable to see so many of them, a hundred and fifty or so, spending like princesses on their furniture and clothes, with no other means of maintenance than this practice. And several of the nobility even had courtesans in their service, in the sight and to the knowledge of everyone . . . I hired a gondola for day and night for two livres, but without spending anything on the gondolier. Living is dear as it is in Paris, but of all the cities in the world that is where one lives the cheapest, inasmuch as one needs no suite of valets, everyone goes there alone, and only spends on his own clothes; and then one does not need to have a horse . . .

This was the time when Venice belatedly attained in the arts the glory of Rome and of Florence. She displayed the magnificence which bursts forth from the canvases of Titian, Tintoretto and Veronese; the magnificence of the bronze well-heads in the Ducal Palace (an unheard-of splendour for the time), the magnificence which marked the unforgettable visit of Henri III, on his return from Poland. During those days in July 1574 banquets were held for 3,000 people, which included displays of fireworks, and a ball during which the ladies and daughters of the nobility filed past the King of France. They all wore white dresses with jewelled collars and great golden belts studded with diamonds. Twists of pearls held back their hair, pearl necklaces encircled their necks, enormous chains of pearls held up their diamond crucifixes. Their beauty barely withstood the weight of this overwhelming luxury.

Likewise Venice itself; founded on gold, offered a distracted world the enviable image of a civilization at its zenith.

NAPLES

The kingdom of Naples was less a kingdom than a province, less a province than a Spanish colony. The Viceroy who governed it in the name of the Catholic King exercised absolute power. 'I send you as a second self to my kingdom of Naples,' wrote Philip II to one of these noblemen. 'I grant you complete jurisdiction, complete domination, and the power of the sword; I confer on you the right to order punishments, to legitimize natural sons, to create knights, to grant fiefs and bishoprics, and even to do what, by right, would demand the presence of the King.'

The Neapolitans were vowed to submission, because of the threat which the Turks and Berbers held over them, a threat from which the Spaniard alone could protect them. And not only against foreign pirates, but also against the brigands in their midst, they needed the 'sword' of Madrid.

The clergy might have fostered a spirit of independence had they not been bound, through the office of the Holy See, to the regulations of the Inquisition. So tyrannical was the Inquisition that on one occasion the nobility and the bourgeoisie combined forces to oppose it – but they won few concessions from the Viceroy before the revolt was crushed.

65

D

Most of the nobility fled from their estates in order to live under the aegis of the Viceroy; but it was a life potent of extravagance and recklessness and made them easy prey to the ambitions of their Spanish masters. The people themselves were poverty-stricken, primitive in their customs, ignorant of the world. The revenues of the kingdom rose from 1,770,000 ducats in 1558 to more than 5,000,000 in 1620, without any rise whatever in its standard of living. This is the best proof of what the wretched kingdom suffered as an occupied country. The latter part of the sixteenth century was a period mainly of passive suffering for the Neapolitans.

SAVOY-PIEDMONT

A rural, mountainous country, hardly touched by change or progress, or by artistic inspiration, Piedmont would have had only a trivial history if its geographical situation had not made it important to its powerful neighbours, a vital pawn on the diplomatic chessboard. Annexed by France, then given to the Duke of Savoy by the treaty of Cateau-Cambrésis, it had difficulty in maintaining its independence.

Every country wished to secure a marriage alliance with Duke Charles Emmanuel, and Philip II of Spain did not hesitate to outbid them all. He promised to assist the Duke to conquer Saluces, Montferrat and Geneva, and dangled before him the royal title of the Island of Cyprus. Finally he offered his daughter, the Infanta Catarina Micaela, with a dowry of half a million ducats, subject to eight per cent interest until it was all paid. How could such an offer be resisted?

The contract was signed at Chambéry on 23 August 1584, and the young Duke left for Saragossa in January 1585. Philip II, very simply dressed as always in contrast to the sumptuous turn-out of the Spanish Grandees, came to meet his daughter's fiancé in person. Charles Emmanuel had ruined himself with equipages and finery, but what did it matter? The splendid dowry would cover his expenses. Philip II granted him the title of Highness, and made him ride at his right hand. Charles Emmanuel soon showed his wit: as his horse was rearing, he exclaimed gallantly: 'Sire, this animal understands that neither it nor its rider is in place.'

The marriage was celebrated with great pomp on 10 March, and the Spanish visit continued for three months. Philip II overwhelmed his son-in-law with attentions and honours and even went so far as to give him the sword that François I had surrendered at the Battle of Pavia. But not even the first instalment was paid on the dowry, no precise engagement was entered into on the subject of Montferrat and the rest. Charles Emmanuel had run into debt for the honour of seeing himself the son-in-law and the vassal of Philip II; Piedmont, in its turn, became a satellite of Spain.

No one was surprised in those days that a nuptial benediction should decide the fate of a nation.

4 England

Early in the sixteenth century an Italian traveller remarked of the English at that time:

> The English are great lovers of themselves, and of everything belonging to them; they think that there are no other men than themselves; and whenever they see a handsome foreigner, they say 'he looks like an Englishman', and that 'it is a great pity that he should not be an Englishman'; and when they partake of any delicacy with a foreigner, they ask him 'whether such a thing is made in their country?'

This insularity of the people was not easily to be modified, though in coming generations there were to be many influences flowing in from outside. The sixteenth century saw England drawn into the general trends that were forming national states, with centralized governments overcoming many of the old forms of feudal anarchy. But the English state had its own distinctive character with a comparatively wide basis of support – from the larger landowners and the gentry, to the yeomanry and the prospering town-classes. It was strong enough to put down any section which might protest or rebel. Not that the first Tudor years were lacking in upheavals, revolts, and disturbing swings between the Papal and the Protestant systems. But despite the many points of strain the state weathered the storms; and when Elizabeth came to the throne, her own wish for a settlement coincided with the mood of a large part of her people.

By creating a national Church with no allegiances outside the country, and by expropriating the monasteries, the state had gained control of the main sources for disseminating social and religious ideas, and at the same time had at its disposal huge landed estates with which to enrich its supporters and consolidate its position. A new body of administrators was needed however. At first the Crown used the medieval system of appointing prominent churchmen, but later it also recruited foreign scholars who, as men imbued with the thought of the Renaissance, had a secular approach to politics, their minds orientated towards the Greeks and Romans rather than the Christian Fathers. At root the Tudor policy was to conserve as much as possible of the medieval content within the new forms, but there were continual intrusions of radical change. 'England was never merry since the new learning came in,' said the Duke of Norfolk, meaning that the new forms had upset the way of life in which he felt at ease. The Crown kept on trying to face both ways at once, to build new systems of administration with the new men who alone could make them work, and yet to resist any thorough-going changes. Men like the Duke of Norfolk wanted to dress up the new forms in old guises, and so tended to romanticize the past; the new men, aware of their lack of roots, wanted also to perpetuate old dignities. Hence the mania for collecting imaginary portraits and fabricating ancestral effigies; and the length of time before the provincial master-mason using late-Gothic forms, was supplanted by the book-learned amateur with his subordinate surveyor, and subsequently by the artist-architect.

The Tudors set out to transform the great feudal magnates into courtiers and office-holders, and the lesser gentry into Justices of the Peace controlling the countryside at the lower level of administration. Many of the monastic lands had been granted to the king's officers or sold to merchants and lawyers; wool was in demand, so that the arable fields were liable to be enclosed and turned into sheep-runs. The government was anxious about the unsettling effect of an increasing number of landless beggars, but left the task of checking the enclosures to the Justices of the Peace who were themselves the local landlords responsible for the enclosures. The Crown's desire for stability was continually upset by the changing economy. England was caught up in a general inflatory crisis which had been caused in part by the huge influx of precious metals from the New World. Elizabeth's calling-in of debased coins in 1560 helped to steady the market, but could not cure the crisis. The price-level seems to have risen at least threefold during the century. Wheat which had been selling at four shillings a quarter, brought in four times that sum in 1549. Food prices continued to rise fairly fast until about 1620. Thus prices rose quicker than wages, which were kept down by law; and the poorer classes were the hardest hit.

But the Crown, whose customary revenues were rather inelastic, also suffered. Hence Elizabeth's drive to economize, which was often regarded as parsimonious. She disliked creating new peerages: though, of the sixty-two peers in 1560, thirty-seven held titles conferred since her father's accession. The great lords, who took for granted that they had the right to high office, were dissatisfied with her methods, and their revolts in 1569–72 against the power wielded by William Cecil discredited them in her eyes, so that she largely excluded them. The Duke of Norfolk, executed in 1572 (as had been his father, the poet Earl of Surrey before him), wrote in his farewell letter to his children, 'Beware of the Court' (except, he added diplomatically, to do the monarch service) 'for that place hath no certainty, and either throweth a man down headlong, or he liveth there unsatisfied.' They could live, he said, 'a great deal richer and quieter in your low degree, wherein I wish you to continue.' In time the discontent of the nobles, together with that of considerable sections of the gentry, led to the rebellion of Essex.

The Court, however, remained the centre of much ceremony and splendour and attracted those of the nobility who could not resist the itch to make a show. Here is a glimpse of it near the end of Elizabeth's reign, set down by the traveller Paulus Hentzner. The occasion is a Sunday visit to the Chapel at Hampton Court:

First went the gentlemen, barons, earls, knights of the garter, all richly dressed and bare-headed; next came the chancellor, bearing the seals in a red silk purse, between two, one of which carried a royal sceptre, the other the sword of state, in a red scabbard, studded with golden fleur-de-lis, the point upwards. Next came the queen, in the sixty-fifth year of her age, as we were told, very majestic; her face oblong, fair but wrinkled; her eyes small, yet black and pleasant, her nose a little hooked; her lips narrow and her teeth black: (a defect the English seem subject to, from their too great use of sugar). She had in her ears two pearls, with very rich drops; she wore false hair, and that red; upon her head she had a small crown, reported to be made of some of the gold of the celebrated Luneborg table; her bosom was uncovered, as all the English ladies have it, till they marry; she had on a necklace of exceeding fine jewels. Her hands were small, her fingers long, and her stature neither tall nor low; her air was stately, her manner of speaking mild and obliging. That day she was dressed in white silk bordered with pearls of the size of beans and over it a mantle of black silk, shot with silver thread. Her train was very long, the end of it borne by marchionesses. Instead of a chain, she had an oblong collar, of gold and jewels.

As she went along in all this state and magnificence, she spoke very gracious, first to one, then to another, whether foreign ministers or those who attended for different reasons, in English, French, and Italian: for besides being well skilled in Greek, Latin, and the languages I have mentioned, she is mistress of Spanish, Scotch and Dutch. Whoever speaks to her, it is kneeling; now and then she raises some by her hand. While we were there, W.Slawata, a Bohemian baron, had letters to present to her; and she, after pulling off her glove, gave him her right hand to kiss, sparkling with rings and jewels – a mark of particular favour. Wherever she turned her face as she was going along, everybody fell down on their knees. The ladies of the court followed next to her, very handsome and well shaped, and for the most part dressed in white. She was guarded on each side by the gentlemen pensioners, fifty in number, with gilt battle-axes. In the antechapel next to the hall where we were, petitions were presented to her, and she received them most graciously, which occasioned the acclamation of, Long live Queen Elizabeth! She answered it with, I thank you, my good People.

The big landlords could often recoup themselves, in the midst of the price-rise, by putting rents up despite the check of long leases; but many were hard hit, especially those who wanted to cut a fine figure at court, like the Earl of Oxford. Some tried to move with the times. Harrison in 1577 noted, 'Men of great port and countenance are so far from suffering their farmers to have any gain at all, that they themselves become graziers, butchers, tanners, sheepmasters, woodmen, *et denique non*.' Some of the gentry were able to introduce improved methods of farming; but large numbers went downhill. In 1617 Fynes Moryson could still declare, 'The gentlemen disdain traffic, thinking it to debase gentry'. The yeomanry on the other hand were doing well, as they did not need to make the same display as the nobles or the gentry; they could sell their surplus at rising prices, get food and clothing from their own farms, and be troubled with few expenses beyond their rent. They could thus save money and move up the social scale.

Sir Thomas Smith in *De Republica Anglorum* (written 1551, published 1583) divided English society into nobles, knights and squires, gentlemen, those 'who can live idly and without manual labour, and will bear the port, charge and countenance of a gentleman'; citizens and burgesses, 'of some substance to bear the charge' of town-offices; yeomen; and finally 'day labourers, poor husbandmen, yea merchants and retailers which have no free land, copyholders, and all artificers who have no voice nor authority in our commonwealth, and no account is made of them but only to be ruled.' We see what prestige attached to the ownership of land.

But, though in theory there was a sharp division between the estates, in fact the changing situation kept on breaking down boundaries, even if they quickly re-formed. Even Smith goes on to jeer at the upstart who manages to 'be taken for a gentleman' by obtaining a coat-of-arms from the heralds 'for money'. By 1593 Nash wrote of an increasing nicety in class-distinctions, at least in London:

In London, the rich disdain the poor. The courtier the citizen. The citizen the country man. One occupation disdaineth another. The merchant the re-tailer. The retailer the craftsman. The better sort of craftsman the baser. The shoemaker the cobbler. The cobbler the carman. One nice dame disdains her next door neighbour should have that furniture to her house, or dainty dish or device, which she wants. She will not go to church, because she disdains to mix herself with base company, and cannot have her close pew by herself.

The gentry who tried consistently to show the port of a gentleman, to dispense medieval hospitality or keep up a court-show, were more than liable to fall into debt and other troubles – unless they could get a court-post. Moryson, after noting the gentleman's scorn of trade, says that they 'daily sell their patrimonies, and the buyers (excepting lawyers) are for the most part citizens and vulgar men. As to the causes, he is unsure 'whether it be the prodigality of the gentry (greater than in any other nation or age), or their too charitable regard to the inferior sort, or rashness, or slothfulness.' He was writing after the process had gathered pace, but it had begun under Elizabeth. The more reactionary gentry struggled along with fewer disasters:

A Country Gentleman is a thing, out of whose corruption the generation of a justice of peace is produced. He speaks statutes and husbandry well enough to make his neighbours think him a wise man; he is well skilled in arithmetic or rates; and hath eloquence enough to save his twopence. His conversation among his tenants is desperate; but among his equals full of doubt. His travel is seldom farther than the next market town, and his inquisition is about the price of corn: when he travelleth, he will go ten miles out of the way to a cousin's house of his to save charges; and rewards the servants by taking them by the hand when he departs. Nothing under a subpoena can draw him to London: and when he is there, he sticks fast upon every object, casts his eyes away upon gazing, and becomes the prey of every cutpurse. When he comes home, those wonders serve him for his holiday talk. (Overbury)

Below him, but not far below, was the solid farmer or yeoman:

He hath religion enough to say, God bless his Majesty; God send peace, and fair weather: so that one may glean harvest out of him to be his time of happiness: but the tithe-sheaf goes against his conscience; for he had rather spend the value upon his reapers and ploughmen than bestow any thing to the maintenance of a parson. He is sufficiently book-read, nay a profound doctor, if he can search into the diseases of cattle: and to foretell rain by tokens makes him a miraculous astronomer. To speak good English is more than he much regards; and for him not to condemn all arts and languages, were to condemn his own education. The pride of his house-keeping is a mess of cream, a pig, or a green goose; and if his servants can uncontrolled find the highway to the cupboard, it wins the name of a bountiful yeoman. Doubtless he would murmur against the Tribune's law, by which none might occupy more than 500 acres, for he murmurs against himself, because he cannot purchase more. To purchase arms (if he emulates gentry) sets upon him like an ague: it breaks his sleep, takes away his stomach, and he can never be quiet till the herald hath given him the harrows, the cuckoo, or some ridiculous emblem for his armoury. (John Stephens, 1615)

Harrison, about 1577, says, 'the gentility commonly provide sufficiently of wheat for their own tables, whilst their household and poor neighbours in some shires are forced to content themselves with rye or barley, yea and in times of dearth many with bread made out of beans, peason or oats and some acorns among.'

The Tudors lacked a standing army or civil service, but by the end of Elizabeth's reign a professional governing class had appeared and consolidated itself at the centre. In the countryside we still find the medieval system of local administration. In manor, parish, town, hundred or shire, there were offices and juries to be filled, returns to be made, taxes collected, the peace to be kept. More and more duties and powers were handed over to Justices of the Peace, and in time they came to censor or control almost every other local official or institution, from sheriff to village constable. They were the channel through which the Crown's will was carried to the populace and numbers of treatises and handbooks witness to their growing importance. But this deputing of authority was linked with measures that modified medieval forms of government to make the new centralization effective. The country was ruled in effect, under the Crown, by twenty or thirty men in Council or Star Chamber and by some 600 or 700 Justices of the Peace in quarter and petty sessions. The number of boroughs with representation in the Commons grew; by the end of the century there were half as many again as at the start. The Commons was thus in the hands of the landed gentry who had captured the boroughs, disregarding the law that required a Member of Parliament to reside in his constituency. The boroughs did not want to pay members the parliamentary wages, and they wanted some important gentleman to represent them and act as patron. The Speaker in the Commons was the Crown's official for controlling the House, and Elizabeth held firmly that Parliament existed only to vote such taxes as she needed, to legislate on the topics she submitted, and to give advice when she asked for it.

The Crown's need of money, as well as the lack of experience in building up and running a large bureaucratic machine, ensured that as many as possible of the controls or exactions were farmed out. Elizabeth paid out as little as she could for the Navy, although Sir John Hawkins, employed as Navy Treasurer from 1573 to 1595, at a salary of £66 13s. 4d., did much to save the situation, curbing the extreme corruption and himself designing great warships. (It was Hawkins who also had been bidden Godspeed by Elizabeth when he sailed from Plymouth on the first official expedition financed to capture Negro slaves.) But at least some of the navy's inadequacies were made up by the privateering gentry who, by licenses to plunder, sought to recoup their fortunes. As Sir John Oglander later remarked, 'Get a ship and judiciously manage her.' Thus it was the excluded or declining gentry, such as those backing Essex, who wanted war; the court-party of office, that of Cecil, wanted peace.

In the attempt to exercise complete control over trade and manufacture, Elizabeth fell back more and more on handing out monopolies to unpaid or underpaid officials and courtiers. In her last decade there was hardly an article in common use – coal, salt, soap, starch, iron, leather, wine,

Travel and Trade

The merchant. The vast development of trade created new social hierarchies in England, Holland, Germany and Italy.

Departure of an East Indiaman. The trade with the Indies was mainly responsible
for the commercial successes – and rivalry – of England and the Low Countries.

The Exchange at Antwerp, which led the way in developing more sophisticated
techniques of trade and finance.

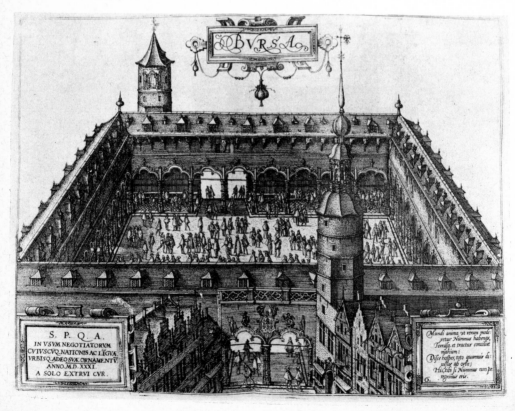

Sailor using the cross-staff, one of his aids to navigation.

Santa Sophia in Constantinople, drawn by Thomas Morgan, mariner, who had
been fifteen years 'bond & thrall in the Turke gallies'. His drawing is patriotically
inscribed: *Vivat Elizabeth Regina Semper Eadem.*

Opposite top. Christoph Fugger (d. 1615), member of the most influential banking and trading family in Europe.

Opposite bottom. Silver dish made in Augsburg, the home town of the Fuggers and the commercial centre of southern Germany. The design shows the labours of the month of December.

Below. The Golden Hall at Schloss Bückeburg, near Hildesheim, an example of the ostentatious decoration of the *nouveaux riches* in Germany.

Left. Tunny-fishing off Cadiz.

Bottom. A fish-seller's stall – detail from Brueghel's *Battle of Carnival and Lent*.

Opposite top. Sign of the St Gall (Switzerland) Butchers' Guild, 1564.

Opposite bottom. Annibale Carracci, *The Butcher's Shop*.

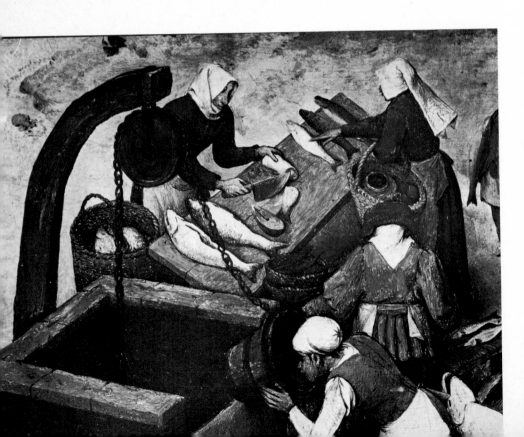

A mendicant in Rome in 1595. He feigned madness and became a beggar in order to collect money to build a home for poor children in the city.

fruit, books – unaffected by patents held by private persons. The pretext was to encourage inventions and protect manufactures in their first stages; in fact the system was essentially parasitic, even if it did act as a rudimentary form of excise. The state wanted to impose on the whole sphere of trade and industry the sort of control which a medieval guild carried out in a small specific area; but with its imperfect organization it could only employ this crude method. One monopoly much resented was that of the Saltpetre Men who were entitled to force their way into anybody's house in order to dig up nitrate-laden soil into which the urine had run. No dovehouse or stable was permitted to be paved. The search-warrant was indeed a necessary condition of all monopoly-patents.

The new governmental machine was thus by nature cumbrous, inefficient, corrupt, vexatious; and the more it extended its powers, the worse it became. Yet all sorts of valuable developments were going on, socially and economically, which created a series of deep conflicts both in the political arena and in the minds and emotions of Englishmen. The life of the family shows clearly what sharp stresses were affecting manners and morals: efforts to cling to old attitudes side by side with efforts to find new lines of development. The procedures of marriage were still medieval. Marriage consisted of two parts: the spousal and the marriage proper. Spousals in turn were of two kinds: a promise to marry at some future time, which could be made by parents for young children, and promises made with direct application to the present, which in effect were indissoluble except by death or entry into Holy Orders. Cohabitation as a part of either kind of spousal was censured and punished by the Church, but was accepted as legally binding by both Church and state. A couple could thus be fully married without any intervention by Church or state, though at public spousals a priest was normally present.

The legal age for males was fourteen, for females twelve. We learn of children who had been married, divorced, and widowed before puberty. Juliet in Shakespeare's play is aged thirteen; Manthea in *Englishmen for my Money* cries at the age of twelve, 'Good God, how abject is this single life, I'll not abide it.' Clandestine marriages were those performed by children over seven years, publicly or secretly without parental consent, or by lads of fourteen and girls of twelve. Though condemned, such marriages remained valid. In essence, copulation together with a vow was what constituted a marriage; public acts were advisable because they proved that vows and copulation had taken place. The worst transgressors in child-marriages were the nobility. Becon about 1562 declares:

As touching men of nobility, wee see dayly by experyence that they for the moste parte marrye thyr chyldren at theyr pleasure when they are verye yonge, even to suche as wyll geue them most mony for them, as men use to sel theyr horses, oxen, sheepe, or any other cattel.

Public spousals were held at the bride's house or the church-porch. The main feature, after the vows, was the exchange of gifts. The betrothal ring was worn on the right hand. Marriage itself was in the church-porch, with the blessing inside while the couple knelt under the care-cloth held by four ecclesiastics. Prayers followed, with additional benediction, perhaps also a mass or a sermon. Before leaving, the couple partook of wine, bread and sweetmeats blessed by the priest, who gave the groom a benedictional kiss which he passed on to the bride. Then they went to the groom's house where a feast was held. Often indeed his friends started drinking before the ceremony, with scandalous results. People attended the church half drunk. 'Such folkes', says Bullinger, 'also do come vnto the church with all manner of pompe and pryde & gorgiousnesse of rayment and Jewels. They come with a great noyse of basens and drommes where with they trouble the whole church'. Among the rich, the feast lasted two or three days, with banquets, dances, songs, games (especially of a kissing kind), outdoor sports, even masques and interludes. In *The Changeling* folk from a madhouse are hired for amusement on the third day; in *The Wonder of Women* there is a pageant in the bridal room. Finally a levee was held in the bedchamber, with the couple enthroned on the bed.

Then there is such a renninge, leapinge, and flynging amonge them, then there is such a lifting vp and discoueringe of damesels clothes and of other womens apparell, that a man might thinke, all these dauncers had cast all shame behinde them, and they were become starke madde and out of their wyttes, and that they were sworne to the deuels daunce. Then must the poore bryd kepe foote with all dauncers, & refuse none, how scabbed, foule, dronken, rude and shamels so euer he be. Then must she oft tymes hear and se much wickednesses, & many an vncomely word. And that noyse and rombling endureth euen tyll supper. (Bullinger)

Then came deep drinking and more riot, with 'vycious and naughtie balates' sung outside the chamber door to encourage the couple in bed.

On the basis of these medieval views and practices developed the debate on marriage between Puritans and Anglicans. The former, with their dislike of ecclesiastical controls, often wanted a ceremony wholly or largely outside the church; and so they championed the propriety of feast and merry-making, so long as they were not carried too far. The Independents indeed regarded these elements as the essential part of the wedding rite, since they made it public without recourse to the church. They thus carried on medieval traditions, whilst secularising them. The Brownists went furthest in opposing church-marriages. (These attitudes were carried to America; the first marriage in New England, 1621, was done as 'a civill thing'.)

Again, through their more secular attitude, the Puritans tended to allow divorce, at least for adultery and desertion, with remarriage 'for the innocent party. The Anglican Church, which had never taken in strong Lutheran or Calvinist elements, and which wanted to differ as little as possible from the Catholics (apart from the issue of supreme control), persisted in the Catholic attitude to divorce, with the result that England is still the least liberal of all Protestant countries in this matter. Persons in search of divorce had to go to one of the five Church-courts where, however, many dispensations, licences and faculties were still to be bought for money. Puritans ignored these courts; and after 1603 divorce among them must have been granted by a single minister, some kind of local magistrate or informal assembly. Becon inveighs against the practice: divorces 'now-a-days be so commonly accustomed and used by men's private authority'.

A prolonged controversy between Puritans and Anglicans was the result. Bishop Hooper, the first puritan writing on the subject, allowed divorce for adultery and put men and women on the same footing in matrimonial issues. Many leading puritan writers, including Milton, followed him in this elevation of women. Henry Smith, while allowing divorce for adultery, showed a less pliable spirit:

If they might be seperated for discord, some would make a commoditie of strife; but nowe they are best not to be contentious, for this Law will holde their noses together, til wearines make them leaue strugling, like two spaniels which are coupled in a chain, at last they learne to goe together, because they may not goe asunder.

But as many Puritans accepted the validity of the old impediments, with some modifications, the main argument went on about the question of remarriage. The Church stood firm on the principle of refusing to let people remarry after separation; but in fact paid little attention to what they did in practice. Edmund Bunny, writing in 1595 (though publishing in 1610) mentioned well-known families in his area who had 'gotten divorce, & were married againe.' The Puritans retorted, in this as in all matters, by condemning the bishops and their courts. Robert Brown, who did much to encourage Independency, wrote in 1582: 'It is the Beast and they are the Ryders. It stoupeth as an Asse for them to get vp. The whippe of their sprituall Courtes, and the Spurres of their lawes, and the Bridle of their power, do make it carie them.'

The Puritans were generally opposed to forced marriages, and thus raised the whole question of parental authority. Becon says that when the enforced couple grew up 'and see whom they could finde in theyr harte to fansie and loue better, than many of them beginne to hate one another,' and 'to curse theyr parentes euen vnto the pitte of hel for the coupling of them together.' They try to get divorced, fail, and then 'what frowning, ouerthwarting, scolding, and chiding, is there betwene them, so that the whole house is filled full of these tragedies euen vnto the toppe.' Moreover, this bad example set by the upper classes had a dire effect throughout society. 'The baser sorte of people seeth this vnquiet life that is vsed among the Gentilmen and theyr wyues,' they return home and imitate them. 'If anye thinge (bee it neuer so lytle) displeaseth them, streight they are together by the eares with their wiues, so that shortly after the whole town is in arore.' He asks:

What is the orygynall cause of all these tragicall and bloudy dissencions, but only the cuetous affection of those parentes whyche for lucres sake so wickedly bestow theyr children in theyr youth and yoke them with such as they can not favoure in thyr age.

Fuller later put the matter in an aphorism: 'They that marry where they do not love, will love where they do not marry.' The theme is prominent in the dramas of the period; one play is even called *The Miseries of Enforced Marriage*. In Middleton's *Roaring Girl* a father tries to back out of an arrangement, which is one of love, and the son defeats him by pretending love for a whore. In another play an erring wife is even tenderly treated – Heywood's *A Woman Killed with Kindness*: though the husband shuts her in solitary confinement, he does end by forgiving her.

The idea that children were unregenerate creatures totally at the mercy of the father's will was deep-seated. 'What was thou being an infant, but a brute, having the shape of a man? Was not thy body conceived in the heat of lust, the secret of shame, and stain of original sin?' cries Lewes Bayly in *Practice of Pietie* (1612). Even Francis Bacon thought that parents should choose a child's vocation without any reference to his wishes. 'Let them not too much apply themselves to the disposition of their children, as thinking they will take best to that, which they have most mind to.' Women were generally accepted as immeasurably inferior to men. The writers of domestic books often follow the Church's line that woman was 'made for the man's use and benefit'. She held an inferior position because of her role as the provoker of Adam's Fall, becoming 'a devill to tempt him to eate' (Rogers, *Matrimoniall Honour*); and royalists later used the argument that Eve and her children were completely in Adam's power to justify the absolute power of the kingship. We find the quip repeated that there were two good days in marriage, the wedding day and the day of the wife's death, 'for that beast being dead, deade is the poyson, and that by the death of the woman the husband is out of bondage'. One of the books citing this jest is Nixon's *The Dignitie of Man*, 1612. There is an insistence that wives must always be cheerful and diligent to please, ready to bear even unjust blame; and a tendency to class them as either shrews or sheep. Even when preaching before the Queen, Bishop Aylmer described women as:

fond, foolish, wanton, flibbergibs, tatlers, triflers, wavering, witless, without council, feeble, careless, rash, proud, dainty, nice, talebearers, eavesdroppers, rumour-raisers, evil-tongued, worse-minded, and in every way doltified with the dregs of the devil's dungill.

Though often anguished with a sense of sin, the Puritans did introduce the idea of marriage as an honourable society of man and woman, with children as a proper result but not as the prime cause. Thus at their best they discarded the medieval notion of marriage as essentially inferior to celibacy, and they attacked the common attitude that, since married life was worldly and imperfect by its very nature, a single life of immorality was preferable. The idea of a true married life as a form of chastity, which is met in Spenser, Bacon and Milton, was consciously opposed to the prevailing ecclesiastical position.

The Catechisms give chapters on women, always on the maid and the wife, often on the widow, sometimes on the stepmother and the old woman. Becon sets down nine duties for maids: Fear and serve God. Obey parents. Avoid idleness, 'out of ye which springeth all mischiefe, as pride, slouthfulnesse, banketting, dronkenshyp, whoredome, adoultry, vain communication, bewraying of secretes, cursed speakings &c. to avoid these pestilences, it shall become honest and vertuous exercises, to spinning, to carding, to sweping, to scouring, to bruing, to baking, and to all kinde of labors without exception, that become maides'. Avoid 'the runninge about vnto vain spectacles, games, pastimes, playes, enterludes &c.' Avoid all 'light, vain & wanton persons: whose delite is in fleshly and filthy pastimes, as singing, dauncing, leaping, skipping, playinge, kissing, whoring &c.' Do not be 'full of tonge, and of much babling', and unless for some grave reason or in answer to a question, 'kepe silence'. Further, 'as maides no les then yonge menne after they come ones to xiii yeres of age, are so desirous to be maried', they should be made to 'labor to the vttermost of their power to suppresse that luste and desire in them'. Suppress too the strong desire for 'galante apparell, and sumptuous raiment'. Finally, curb inclinations and accept the husband allotted by parents. Other moralists advise against naughty ballads and 'vaine romances', such as the books of Robin Hood, Bevis of Hampton, Troilus and the like. (Bullinger)

But whatever the theories about women, on the whole they had a fairly free time, even if wife-beating was practised under the sanction of the law. On the Continent England was called a paradise for women, a prison for servants, and a hell for horses. In the 1575 account by a Dutchman Van Meteren we are told:

Although the women there are entirely in the power of their husbands, except for their lives, yet they are not so strictly kept as they are in Spain or elsewhere. Nor are they shut up: but they have the free management of the house or house-keeping, after the fashion of those of the Netherlands, and others of their neighbours. They go to market to buy what they like best to eat. They are well dressed, fond of taking it easy, and commonly leave the care of household matters and drudgery to their servants. They sit before their doors, decked out in fine clothes, in order to see and be seen by the passers-by. In all banquets and feasts they are shown the greatest honour; they are placed at the upper end of the table, where they are first served; at the lower end they help the men.

All the rest of their time they employ in walking and riding, in playing at cards or otherwise, in visiting their friends and keeping company, conversing with their equals (whom they term gossips) and their neighbours, and making merry with them at child-births, christenings, churchings and funerals; and all this with the permission and knowledge of their husbands, as such is the custom. Although the husbands often recommend to them the pains, industry and care of the German or Dutch women, who do what the men ought to do both in the house and in the shops, for which services in England men are employed, nevertheless the women usually persist in retaining their customs. This is why England is called the Paradise of married women. The girls who are not yet married are kept much more rigorously and strictly then in the Low Countries.

Heywood in his *Most Worthy Women* condemns the French saying: 'Let the woman be in the house and her legge broke.' He prefers the custom of 'allowing both their features and fames a liberall freedome to undergoe any publicke censure'.

The traveller Keichel in 1585, like the Venetian ambassador of 1558, thought they painted themselves much less than in Italy, but noted, 'they are somewhat awkward in their style of dress; for they dress in splendid stuffs, and many a one wears three cloth gowns or petticoats, one over the other'. The Puritans however stress the use of cosmetics. In 1583 Stubbes declared that women 'colour their faces with certain oyles, liquors, unguents and waters made to that end, whereby they think their beauty is greatly decored; but who seethe not that their soules are not thereby deformed'. Elizabeth, with her restrictive views, legislated to check luxury. A fine of ten pounds for every month was to be imposed on women wearing silk petticoats, velvet French hoods, or gold chain necklaces – unless the husband kept a horse ready for national service. A woman in Hampshire was reported for a velvet kirtle and others at Winchester for a gold necklace and a French hood with paste of gold. But cosmetics were not cited, and after 1564 no royal commission made inquisition into female dress; though a later proclamation denounced imported ruffs and cloaks, calling on both sexes 'to leave off such fine disguises and monstrous manner of attiring themselves, as are insupportable for charges and indecent to be worn': a characteristic mixture of moral and economic motives. Elizabeth herself had been captivated by silk stockings. Her silk-woman knitted her first pair for New Year's Day, 1559, and promised to make more. 'Do so', urged the Queen, 'for indeed I like silk stockings well, because they are pleasant, fine and delicate, and henceforth I shall wear no more cloth stockings.'

The dramatists and satirists have much to say on female paintings, and complaints are made about the length of time taken in dressing.

Five hours ago I set a dozen maids to attire a boy like a nice gentlewoman; but there is such a doing with their looking-glasses, pinning, unpinning, setting, unsetting, formings and conformings, painting blew veins and cheeks; such a stir with sticks and combs, cascanets, dressings, purles, falles, squares, buckles, bodies, scarfs, necklaces, carcenets . . . that she is scarce drest to the girdle. (*Lingua*, 1602)

Nash in 1593 attacks fashionable ladies:

Their heads, with their top and top-gallant lawn baby-caps, and snow-resembled silver curlings, they make a plain puppet stage of. Their breasts they embusk up on high, and their round roseate buds immodestly lay forth to show at their hands there is fruit to be hoped. In their curious antic-woven garments, they imitate and mock the worms and adders that must eat them. They shew the swellings of their mind, in the swellings and plumpings out of their apparel. Gorgeous ladies of the court, never were I admitted so near any of you, as to see how you torture old Time with sponging, pinning, and pouncing; but they say his sickle you have burst in twain, to make your periwigs more elevated arches of.

He mocks 'your pinches, your purls, your flowery jaggings, superfluous interlacings, and puffings up,' 'flaring frounced periwigs low dangled with love-locks,' and carcenets of pearls. A year before he had derided city wives:

Mistress Minx, a merchant's wife, that will eat no cherries, forsooth, but when they are at twenty shillings a pound, that looks as simperingly as if she were besmeared, and jets it as gingerly as if she were dancing the canaries: she is so finical in her speech, as though she spoke nothing but what she had first sewed over before in her samplers, and the puling accent of her voice is like a feigned treble, or one's voice that interprets to the puppets. What should I tell how squeamish she is in her diet, what toil she puts her poor servants unto, to make her looking-glasses in the pavement? how she will not go into the fields, to cower on the green grass, but she must have a coach for her convoy; and spends half a day prinking herself if she be invited to any strange place?

Patches – stars, crescents, diamonds – were coming in. Glasses were now common. Penny-ware ones came in from the Low Countries, though often made in Venice. In 1558 we find them valued wholesale at 8s. a gross, the halfpenny ones at half that. They were kept in a pocket or attached to the belt or the girdle men wore in their hats. But old ladies, especially in the country, talked indignantly of the way they had had only a tub or pail of water for their reflections. Stubbes calls glasses, 'the devil's

bellows, whereby he bloweth the blast of pride in our hearts'. Handkerchiefs were particularly English. Foreigners noted how widely they were
now used, made from imported linen or silk, and in turn exported. Fine
ones were edged with bonelace of gold and silver.

Unwed girls wore their hair down their backs, and brides were married
'in their hair'. Stubbes attacks the new styles:

Must be curled, frisled, and crisped, laid out in wreathes and bordes, from one
ear to another. And lest it should fall down, it is under-proped with forks,
wires, and I cannot tell what, rather like grim, stern monsters than chaste
Christian matrons. At their haire, thus wreathed and crested, are hanged bugles,
oncles, rings, gold, silver, glasses and such childish gew-gaws.

The poor used bows, feathers or flowers. Hair was combed rather than
brushed. It was tinted with saffron or gold for red effects. Blondes seem the
most popular, though we meet recipes for turning hair back. The whores
of Covent Garden, those 'doves of Venus, those birds of youth and beauty,
the wanton ladies', affected 'golden tresses, which were wont to flag about
their shoulders like so many ensigns in Cupid's regiment'; but no doubt
their coarser sisters of Turnbull street and Southwark did not bother to
dye their locks. Wigs were not uncommon – the Queen had a large
collection – and hair powder was coming in towards the end of her reign.

Homemade preparations were used on the teeth; thus mallow-root was
rubbed on them. There were no toothbrushes, but toothpicks were much
used; also earpicks. Precious stones or 'pure sugar candy' were held in
the mouth for the imparting of 'virtuous properties'. But teeth were often
in a bad way; the Queen's were yellow and irregular and, as Hentzner
noted, had turned black. Baths were used as a cure for gout or rheumat-
ism – though we find the Queen taking a bath at Hampton court, developing a shivering fit, and ending up with smallpox. Normally people rubbed
themselves with a cloth dabbed in water – if possible, fennel-water or
rose-water (considered good for the eyes) or something of that sort. Soap,
in much demand, was made in London; it must have been used mainly
for laundering. The physician Boorde in his *Compendyous Regyment* thus
advised on one's morning routine:

After you have evacuated your body and trussed your points, comb your head
oft, and so do divers times in the day. And wash your hands and wrists, your
face and eyes and your teeth, with cold water; and after that you be apparelled,
walk in your garden or park, a thousand pace or two.

King James's skin was 'as soft as taffeta sarsanet, which felt so because
he never washed his hands, only rubbed his fingers' ends slightly with the
wet end of a napkin'. The general condition of people is illustrated by this
passage from a letter of Sabine Johnson's:

We were at the least four or five hours coming three miles a' this side Graves-
end, and in such company that I had rather five shillings for a telt boat than I

would come among such a company again. For there was cuckolds by their own confession, and both whores and bawds, with so much knavery that it was too abominable, and such a lousy company that they had work enough to pick off lice one off another's clothes.

Every large household made toilet waters as well as herbal concoctions and pomander-balls in the still-room. The Queen prided herself on her fine skin, golden hair, and fine hands; and as she grew older, so she took greater pains to keep up her rôle as Oriana. She gave up dyeing her hair and took to red wigs. (Earlier she had tried to catch out the Scottish courtier Melville in comparisons between herself and his Queen Mary. 'What colour of hair was reputed best; and whether my queen's hair or hers was best; and which of them was fairest?') She washed her brow with posset curds and sent to Antwerp for rose-water. (At court care had to be taken that poisons were not introduced in the guise of perfumes.) She was credited with various beauty-preparations. Near her end she bravely asked for a mirror after using for twenty years

only such a one as was made on purpose to deceive her sight: which glass being brought to her, she fell presently into exclaiming against it, which had so much commended her and took it offensively that some which before had flattered her, durst not come into her sight.

Commercial cosmetics were more dubious than the stillroom waters, as ceruse, a carbonate of lead, was the main ingredient of rouges and lip-salves. Safer but costlier was bear's fat from France. Women used crayons or pencils, face-powder from ground alabaster, perfumed starches, all sorts of dyes and aromatic drugs often fetched from Aleppo in the Levant Company's ships. As there was no fixative, lovers had to beware of being smeared by a woman's paints. Scents were much in demand, not only for purposes of vanity. There was such a stench in the streets that city-fathers in procession bore nosegays, and a pomander-ball hanging from a woman's neck or a nosegay in her bosom was considered to be a preservative against infection. Clothes, especially gloves, were scented; and a Dutchman remarked that

their chambers and parlours strawed over with sweet herbs refreshed me; their nosegays finely intermingled with sundry sort of fragrant flowers in their bedchambers and privy rooms, with comfortable smell cheered me up, and entirely delighted all my senses.

In general, people were still living close to the earth, with time determined by the seasons rather than by clocks. They held to the medieval notion of their rights to extensive festivals and holy-days, with the effortless plenty of the Land of Cockaygne as the ideal. But a different view was held by the Puritans with their sense of sin and by the employers seeking to make more money out of agriculture or manufactures and profit from the rising price-levels rather than be crushed by them. Steadily compulsions of all sorts were gathering round the common man, to drive him from his medieval attitudes, which seemed mere laziness to the men of the new dispensation. But there was still an immense heritage of games, plays, fertility-festivals, and guisings of all sorts.

What shall I say of dancing with curious and rural music, frequently used by the better sort, and upon all holidays, by country people dancing about the maypoles with bagpipes or other fiddlers, besides the jollities of certain seasons of the year, of setting up maypoles, dancing the Morris with hobby horses, bringing home the lady of the harvest, and like plebian sports, in all of which vanities no nation cometh anything near the English. What shall I say of playing at cards and dice, frequently used by all sorts, rather as a trade than as a recreation, for which all strangers much blame us. (Moryson)

The accounts of Stubbes are so full of a vivid hatred that they have the effect of lyrically conjuring up the scenes.

[*Mayday*] Against May, Whitsunday, or some other time of the year, every parish, town and village assemble themselves together, both men, women and children, old and young, even all indifferently; and either going all together or dividing themselves into companies, they go some to the woods and groves, some to the hills and mountains, some to one place and some to another, where they spend all the night in pleasant pastimes; and in the morning they return, bringing with them birch boughs and branches of trees, to deck their assemblies withal.

And no marvel, for there is a great lord present amongst them, as superintendent and lord over their pastimes and sports, namely Satan, prince of hell. But their chiefest jewel they bring from thence is their May-pole, which they bring home with great veneration, as thus. They have twenty or forty yoke of oxen, every ox having a sweet nose-gay of flowers placed on the tip of his horns: and these oxen draw home this May-pole (this stinking idol, rather) which is covered all over with flowers and herbs, bound round about with strings from the top to the bottom, and sometimes painted with variable colours, with two or three hundred men, women and children following it with great devotion. And thus being reared up with handkerchiefs and flags streaming on the top, they straw the ground about, bind green boughs about it, set up summer-halls, bowers, and arbours hard by it; and then they fall to banquet and feast, to leap and dance about it, as the heathen people did at the dedication of their idols . . .

[*Lord of Misrule*] First all the wildheads of the parish, convening together, choose them a Grand-Captain (of all mischief) whom they ennoble with the title of my Lord of Misrule, and him they crown with great solemnity and adopt for their king. This king, anointed, chooseth forth twenty, forty, threescore or a hundred lusty guts, like to himself, to wait upon his lordly majesty, and to guard his noble person. Then, every one of these his men, he investeth with his liveries of green, yellow, or some other light wanton colour; and as though they were not bawdy – gaudy enough I should say, they bedeck themselves with scarfs, ribbons and laces hanged all over with gold rings, precious stones, and other jewels: this done, they tie about either leg twenty or forty bells, with rich handerkerchiefs in their hands, and sometimes laid across their shoulders and necks, borrowed for the most part of their pretty Mopsies and loving Bessies, for bussing them in the dark.

Thus all things set in order, then have they their hobby-horses, dragons and other antics, together with their bawdy pipers and thundering drummers to strike up the devil's dance withal. Then march these heathen company towards the church and church-yard, their pipers piping, their bells jingling, their handkerchiefs swinging about their heads like madmen, their hobby-horses and other monsters skirmishing amongst the throng; and in this sort they go to church (I say) and into the church (though the minister be at prayer or preaching), dancing and swinging their handkerchiefs, over their heads in the church, like devils incarnate, with such a confused noise, that no man can hear his own voice . . .

Then, after this, about the church they go again and again, and so forth into the churchyard where they have commonly their summer-halls, their bowers, arbours and banquetting houses set up, wherein they feast, banquet and dance all that day and (peradventure) all the night too. And thus these terrestrial furies spend the Sabbath day.

The main sport of the gentry was hunting deer or hare. When Elizabeth came to the throne, most of the London militia were bowmen; but by the time of the Armada every man of the 6,000 had firearms. In sport however the bow was still used. When in 1621 the Archbishop of Canterbury shot at a buck and killed a keeper, he was using a crossbow. By then however the long gun was much used for wild fowl, though 'to shoot flying' was still a feat. Thus John Eliot in 1593 set out the typical conversation on a hunt:

I like the pastime of hunting aboue all other sports. – I haue a fine grayhound. – And I a bitch that will kill a hare in her forme. – There is no pleasure in that. – I loue a life to see the beagles hunt and grayhounds run. – You haue a faire mastiffe, what can he do? – Lap, bowle, howle, and barke in the morning. – The barking cur is often fearefull, and biteth not. – One should for all that beleeue the barking of an old dog. – We will couple my Grayhound and your mastiffe together. – My mastiffe will not be led in a lease. – It is a hard matter to vse an old dog to a string. – Let vs vncouple our beagles, they shall follow the tracke, and trace after the footing. – The hare is now in her forme but in the euening she will come to releefe vnder this forrest. – Thrust your Ferret into the burie. – There are no conies in this warren. – This pasturage is full of the dunging of wild boares, stags, hinds, and fawns. – Lets discouer first the heard. – What a fine praie tis, a conie in a brake to enclose. – We shall catch rather a woodcocke at the nose. – Looke what a hearde of wild beasts here is. – Wind your horne, let slip your mastif. Bugle your horne, wind him double. Set your snares, grins, and purs-nets. Where are your beagles? – See a goodly stag with ten hornes. – Behold here his bracke, lets gallop, lets spur cut to catch him with your mastiffe. – Let him go, let him run. – He will scrape from our dogs well ynough, and our horses are almost tired alreadie.

Gambling and dicing we have noted were general. A list of sports in verse, 1600, runs thus:

> Man, I dare challenge thee to throw the sledge,
> To iump or leape ouer a ditch or hedge,
> To wrestle, play at stooleball, or to runne,
> To pitch the barre, or to shoote off a gunne:
> To play at loggets, nine holes or ten pinnes,
> To trie it out at foot-ball by the shinnes;
> At Ticktacke, Irish, Noddie, Maw, and Ruffe;
> At hot-cockles, leape-frogge, or blindman-buffe;
> To drinke halfe pots, or deale at the whole canne
> To play at base, or pen-and-ynk-horne sir Ihan:
> To daunce the Morris, play at Barly-breake:
> At all exploytes a man can thinke or speake:
> At shoue-groute, venter-poynt, or crosse and pile:
> At beshrow him that's last at yonder style.

For the winter, Burton cites:

cards, tables, dice, shovelboard, chess, the philosopher's game, small trunks shuttlecock, billiards, music, masks, singing, dancing, all games, frolicks, jests, riddles, catches, purposes, questions and commands, merry tales of knights errant, queens, lovers, lords, ladies, giants, dwarfs, thieves, cheaters, witches, fairies, goblins, friars.

Football was a violent pastime, played in the street or the countryside. Stubbes gives his usual evocative picture:

I protest unto you it may rather be called a friendly kind of fight, than a play or recreation; a bloody and murdering practice, than a fellowly sport or pastime. For doth not every one lie in a wait for his adversary, seeking to overthrow him and to pick him on his nose, though it be upon hard stones, in ditch or dale, in valley or hill, or what place soever it be he careth not, so he have him down. And he that can serve the most of this fashion, he is counted the only fellow, and who but he? So that by this means, sometimes their necks are broken, sometimes their backs, sometimes their legs, sometime their arms, sometime one part thrust out of joint, sometime another, sometime their noses gush out with blood, sometime their eyes start out, and sometimes hurt in one place, sometimes in another. But whosoever scapeth away the best goeth not scot-free, but is either sore wounded, and bruised, so as he dieth of it, or else scapeth very hardly.

And no marvel, for they have sleights to meet one betwixt two, to dash him against the heart with their elbows, to hit him under the short ribs with their gripped fists, and with their knees to catch him upon the hip, and to pick him on his neck, with an hundred such murdering devices. And hereof groweth envy, malice, rancour, choler, hatred, displeasure, enmity and what not else; and sometimes fighting, brawling, contention, quarrel picking, murder, homicide, and great effusion of blood, as esperience daily teacheth.

Tennis was played by the upper classes. On the court at Hampton Court, Robert Dudley, Earl of Leicester, was playing with the Duke of Norfolk; sweating, he casually took the handkerchief from the Queen's hand and wiped his face. Norfolk, enraged at this familiarity as an insult to the Queen, swore that Dudley was saucy and threatened him with the racket. 'Here vpon rose a great troble, and the queen offendid sore with the Duke' – not with the Earl. Eliot gives us a tennis-conversation.

Shall we play a set at tenise you and I? – Lets go to the great Bracke at Whitehall. – Where is the maister that keeps the tenis? – Here I am sir, what is your pleasure? – Giue vs some soft and gentle shooes here. Rackets and bals bring here ho. – Well, play. – I haue fifteene. – A losse, marke that chace there. – Fifteene all. – This racket is not worth a rush. – Some more rackets ho. – Now giue me a faire ball. I cannot take a ball aboue hand, nor at rebound. – The chace is mine. – I am thirtie. – Thirtie all. – Aske standers by, I touched it not. – Fortie fiue. – At dews then. – A ball, I haue the aduantage. The set is mine. I will bande a ball more then six score paces mounting, with this racket which you refuse. Looke here. – O fiuell! what a firking stroke is that. You have an arme of yron.

Dancing was loved by Queen and milkmaid alike. Elizabeth, nimble in movement, was devoted to it; we find her dancing frequently except when an ulcer above her ankle made her limp. The Spaniards complained that the English idea of a dance was simply to jump in the air; but Elizabeth went on with her leaping. Six or seven galliards a morning, apart from music and singing, was her daily exercise; so we are told, in 1589. (The Earl of Oxford, who was understandably later locked in the Tower, remarked, 'By the blood of God, she had the worst of voyce, and did everything with the worst grace that ever any woman did.') Near the end, almost seventy years old, she is glimpsed 'dancing the Spanish Panic to a whistle and a tabourer, none other being with her but my Lady Warwick'. She liked music too. When she hunted at Bushey Park – that is, when beasts were herded into enclosures and chased out in front of pavilions to be slaughtered – she had musicians hidden in bowers of greenery while a lady disguised as a nymph made a curtsey and offered a crossbow to the Queen who was a Virgin Huntress like Diana.

In England the new individualism working on the medieval heritage had produced an important development in chamber music. Instruments were hung in shops and houses for anyone who had to wait. Peacham in *The Compleat Gentleman*, 1622, remarked that everyone should be able to sing at sight and 'play the same upon your viol, or the exercise of a lute, privately to yourself'. Generally the groups numbered between two and six, with no listeners or only a select few. This English chamber-music reached its height about 1600, when madrigal and ayre were at the height of their popularity.

The uglier side of the period appeared in the passion for cockfights and for bull and bear baiting. 'Brawn of the baiting' was in much demand, being thought a safe way of obtaining beef.

Harrison noted that, apart from the mansions, almost all houses were built in wood, but they were often 'coarse cabins'. In Mary's reign the Spaniards had said, 'These English have their houses made of sticks and dirt, but they fare commonly as well as the king.' The roofs were tiled or thatched; the clay walls of white, red, or blue; on the walls were tapestries or painted cloths. Stoves were coming in for the rich. Chimneys were becoming more popular though in Harrison's young days there had been few. Furniture too was increasing: 'tapestry, Turkey work, pewter, brass, fine linen, and thereto costly cupboards of plate', with carpets and napery on tables. Stools or benches were common, but not chairs: what there were, were of the box type, 'and as for the wainscot stools', Sir John Harrington said they were 'so hard, since great breeches were laid aside, men can scant endure to sit upon them.' Straw pallets and rough mats with a log for pillow were giving way to mattress or flockbed; wooden plates and spoons to pewter, silver, tin, though rush-mats or loose rushes still covered the floor. Court-cupboards (ancestor of the dinner-waggon) had the flamboyance of the oak furniture of the period; the front corner-supports were heavily bulbous and richly carved. We are reminded of the elaborate costumes of the period, in which medieval styles were seen expanding pompously and lavishly, in a fantasy of display. In the same way the architecture of Smythson matured in a complex of 'ingeniouse devices', making the house itself a sort of externalisation of the resplendent magnifico who inhabited it.

Gardens too were growing in variety; compared with them the old ones, says Harrison, 'were but dungills'. 'Strange herbs, plants and annual fruits are daily brought unto us from the far parts of the world.'

The upper classes still had little taste for art in any serious sense. The great houses showed no fine paintings: only genealogical tables, mechanical devices, mediocre portraits. Contemporary portraits were largely judged by the extent to which they showed magnificent clothes and enriched the background with coats-of-arms. The work of art was a prestige-object intended to glorify the subjects' rank and ancestry, while in churches the use of hangings and the desire for a 'decent plainness' instead of murals was disastrous for the artist. The later paintings of the Queen were fantasy cult-ikons. In compensation, the miniature, with its limning as opposed to painting, developed a lyrical affirmation of the individual graces. Hilliard, we learn from his *Art of Limning*, sought to catch the 'lovely graces', 'wittye smilings', 'stolne glances' that are the pleasures of intimacy. Melville tells us of the Queen:

She took me to her bed-chamber, and opened a little cabinet, wherein were divers little pictures wrapt within paper, and their names written with her own hand upon the papers. Upon the first that she took up was written, *My Lord's picture*. I held the candle, and pressed to see that picture so named; she appeared loath to let me see it; yet my importunity prevailed for a sight thereof, and found it to be the earl of Leicester's picture.

The peculiar compromise of the medieval and the new which characterized the Tudor state appears in the new great houses where the Renaissance may be seen in the strong imposition of symmetry, while the type of house itself is that of late medieval turned-in courtyard-houses but without the functional position of such a building in the feudal world. The H-shaped house thus evolved, with the communal Hall dwindling in importance and its rôle usurped by the Long Gallery and the Great Chamber (later called the Saloon). The romanticizing of the past, which, we earlier noted, often found a positive expression as Elizabethan energies gathered and burst out in such poems as Spenser's *Faerie Queen*, in gestures like Philip Sidney's discarding of his cuisses at Zutphen, and in guisings like those of Lord Pembroke and his friends when they dined at Ludlow in the costumes and with the names of the knights of the Round Table.

The age saw a rapid growth of grammar schools where Latin could be learned as a prelude to the university. Previously the upper-classes had shown little interest in education; but now the gentry pressed into schools that formerly had been filled by the poor and the clergy. Education was recognized as necessary in the struggle for post and place. The universities were affected by the new attitudes, but were still weighted down by medieval views and methods, with logic as the main subject. Bruno said that the dons 'knew much more about beer than about Greek'. The statutes provided that any master or doctor diverging one jot from the teaching of Aristotle should be fined five shillings for each offence. But in Puritan circles there was an interest in the challenge to Aristotle by such thinkers as Ramus – though in 1574, Barebones was ejected from Oxford for following Ramus' ideas.

A student or his father contracted privately with a College Fellow to act as teacher or guardian; and such a tutor often had half a dozen pupils, who might all sleep in his room. Attempts were made to impose rigid control on behaviour. In 1571 the Vice-Chancellor forbade all members of the university of Cambridge to swim in any stream or pool. Yet, as Harrison complained,

gentlemen or rich men's sons often bring the Universities into much slander. For, standing upon their reputation and liberty, they ruffle and roist it out, exceeding in apparel, and riotous company which draweth them from their books unto another trade. And for excuse, when they are charged with breach of good order, think it sufficient to say they are gentlemen, which grieveth many not a little.

And Cecil in 1587 was informed that through
the great stipends of tutors, not only the poorer sort are not able to maintain
their children at the University, but the richer be so corrupt with liberty and
remissness that the tutor is afraid to displease his pupil through the desire of
great gain.

On leaving, the richer youths often went to one of the Inns of Court at
London, though only nominally studying law.

The problem of the Church was both to keep the Puritan rebels and
the Catholic recusants under control, and to rebuild the neglected churches.
Buildings were often in bad decay; the Marian exiles, on their return, had
worsened things by much defacing of monuments, breaking of windows,
and melting-down of bells. The level of education among ministers was
low. Lay patrons gave benefices to 'their bakers, butlers, cookes, good
archers, and housekeepers' (Harrison). Weavers, pedlars, and glovers
had been appointed, pleased to get an extra £8 or £10 a year, while letting
the patron take the rest. The Church's lists showed clergy drawn from
day-labourers, servants, ostlers, husbandmen, parish clerks, poor-clerks,
ex-monks, carpenters, glovers, drapers, chandlers, shoemakers, soldiers,
fishermen, clothiers. Thus, at South Hanningfield was found a man
'sometimes a fishmonger, now a buttonmaker, a very careless and insufficient minister, an alehouse haunter'. Many were taverners, dancers,
brawlers, fornicators, card-players.

On 26 May 1576 the rector of Sherington 'wolde have taken away a
mans wief from him by the high waie and used such filthy speech that they
banished him out of their company'. The vicar of Stickford 'beat his wife
in the churchyard, and is a common sower of discord amongst his neighbours; and he has two wives'. A Visitation of 1576 found many parsons
using the vicarage as tavern or alehouse. The rector of Moor-Moncton
in 1567 was 'of verie dissolute lieffe and lewd conversation and useth
verie undecent apparell namelie great britches cut and drawne out with
sarcanet and taffite, and great ruffes laid on with laceis of gold and silke'.
The rector of Worlingham was excommunicated for striking and drawing
blood in his churchyard on Easter Eve 1594. We find parsons in all sorts
of quarrels, dragged from the pulpit, stripped of gowns, beaten-up. A
new class of Readers was established to fill vacancies and cover up the
pluralities held by the richer clergy. The Puritans retorted by taunting
the orthodox clergy as Dumb Dogs, unable to preach. So great was the
confused variety in the Church that in 1581 it was noted that out of 350
parishes in Essex only seven performed identical services.

There were, however, good men like Bernard Gilpin with a large parish
in County Durham, who boarded and kept twenty-four scholars, mostly
poor lads; held open table on Sundays, spent five hundred pounds on a

Religious Troubles

'The fruits of the new Gospel'. This print attacking the iconoclasm and desecrations of the Protestants illustrates the passions aroused by religious controversy.

In 1560 an attempt by a group of Calvinist nobles to kidnap Francis II at Blois was foiled; the plotters were captured at Amboise and hanged from the battlements.

In July 1562 the Protestants of Tours were massacred by Catholics in an outburst of violence.

Above. Procession of the 'Holy League', a militant party, opposed to concessions to the Protestants, that demanded the re-establishment of unity of faith.

Right. Henri, Prince de Condé, one of the Protestant leaders, taken prisoner in 1580. Shortly afterwards he died of poisoning.

The Massacre of St Bartholemew in Paris, 24 August 1572, the most brutal act of Catholic repression during the religious wars in France.

Above. The 'Bloody Entry' of the Spaniards into Antwerp, during the repression of the United Provinces under the governorship of the Duke of Alba.

Left. Spanish soldiers entering Oudewater.

Opposite. Brueghel's painting of the *Massacre of the Innocents* was based on the conduct of the Spanish *soldatesca* in the Netherlands.

Adam Elsheimer, *Narcissus*. A freebooting soldier admires himself in a fountain. The wars in the earlier part of the century had left a large body of professional soldiers, who readily joined in the wars of religion as mercenaries.

A group of wandering peasants, who typify the plight of many left homeless by the wars.

school, remitted tithes when the harvest was bad, and on journeys was liable to give away not only his money but also his clothes. And amiable characters like Alexander Nowell, who as minister at Much Hadham (before becoming Dean of St Pauls) was a keen fisher; once he left some bottles of beer behind on the river-bank, found them much bettered some days later, and after experimenting became the inventor of bottled beer. Psalms were sung in the rhymed version of Sternhold and Hopkins (there were as yet none of the later hymns); and a music of viols and wind instruments might be used in accompaniment.

The Puritans included men who had grown tough in exile or had been used to underground organization in the London Congregation under Mary. They liked long extempore prayers in loud voices, with even louder responses from the people; and at least two sermons on Sunday. In many districts they developed a weekly Prophecy or Conference, where they got to know one another and gained confidence. Many gentry attended as audience, and the meetings flourished especially in Essex, Norfolk and Northants. The Queen finally suppressed them as well as quashing any attempts of the Puritans to bring legislation forward in Parliament. But the ministers then began corresponding and putting into action their own systems (built up from Walter Travers' *Book of Discipline*): denying church-government by Bishops and insisting that discipline be vested in ministers, congregational elderships, classes and synods, provincial and national.

London was more than a large city. If we take it to include Whitehall and Westminster, it was more a nation within a nation. The Mayor and his citizens with their militia formed almost a separate power. At Elizabeth's accession there were about 100,000 inhabitants; at her death the size was doubled. The next important towns, York, Norwich, Bristol, had perhaps 20,000 each. London, then, in trade, in fashion or culture, was the pace-setter, with the rest of the country following, if at all, much more slowly. The dramatists and pamphleteers have left us endless pictures of the lively scene. Here is the *chatter in the Pawne*:

Let vs go aboue to buy some thing of these fayre maidens. – What seeke you, sir? Come here my friend: see here fine ruffes, falling bands, handkerchers, sockes, coiffes, and cuffes, wrought with golde and siluer. – Haue I nothing which likes you? I will vse you well. – Would you haue any fine Holland? Any Cambricke, I haue very fine, and of all prices. – Harke my loue will you take a pint of wine? – Thanks sir, not now. – Fine Venice Glasses, French garters, Spanish gloues, sweet, Flanders kniues, fine Silke stockes of Italie. – What want you Gentlewoman? what lacke ye? – Shew me a Peach colour'd Netherstocke. – There is very fine hose, the price is an Angell, at word. – Will you take a noble? – I cannot truly. There is a pair of incarnate, take them for eight shillings. – You are too deare. – Will you see a good hat sir? Lacke you a good hat or a cap? – I seeke for a Beuer. – There is one which will fit you iust, with the feather. – I weare no plume. – It becommeth you very well. – It is too large and too great for me. – It is after the Babilonian fashion, and the feather after the Polonian slant. It is all the fashion now a daies. Shew me another after the French fashion, with a flat crowne. – Will you see one of Spanish wooll? with a Cypres band, pinkt with taffetas, and finely trimde on the new cut. – Let me see it. Let vs come to a price. – The price is reasonable: giue me a bald-pate. – Hold your hand, you shall haue neither more nor lesse. Take you any double Ducates? Come, I will pay you in Portegues, or in Iackean Apes pense. – Hem! ho: heare yee? – Come hither, buy something of me, Northren man. Ah my loue, I haue not money inough to bestow. – You sir, what want ye? – Is there no high shooes here abouts? – Come here my friend: heres a paire which will fit you iust. – Will you buy a prettie wench to carrie into the North with you? – By my troth I no. – What lackest thou welch boy? – Thou liedst, I am a Pilchard. – Wallon, you honest man of Wales, buy something of me. Softe and faire gallant. – Soft and faire French Pig – You anger my Lords of the Parlement. – What want ye sir? – What would you buy mistresse? – What lackest thou fellow? What will it please you to buy Gentleman? what seeke you honest man? Come hither: come to me. I will sell you a peni-worth.

– I want nothing. I buy nothing. I seeke nothing. I will haue nothing of you. I staie here for one. I walke here for my pleasure. (Eliot)

Dekker in 1608 depicts the jostling of crook and gull in St Pauls:

What whispering is there in *Terme* time, how by some slight to cheat the pore country Clients of his full purse that is stucke vnder his gridle? What plots are layde to furnish young gallants with readie money (which is shared afterwards at a Tavern) therby to disfurnish him of his patrimony? what buying vp of oaths, out of the hands of knights of the Post, who for a few shillings doe daily sell their soules? What layinge of heads is there together and sifting of the brains still and anon, as it growees towardes eleuen of the clock, (euen amongst those that wear guilt Rapiers by their sides) shere for that noone they may shift from Duke *Humfrey*, and bee furnished with a dinner at some meaner mans Table? What damnable bargaines of vnmercifull Brokery, and of vnmeasureable Vsury are ther clapt vp? What swearing is there: yea, what swaggering, what facing and out-facing? What shuffling, what shouldering, what Iustling, what Ieering, what byting of Thumbs to beget quarrels, what holding vppe of fingers to remember drunken meetings, what brauing with Feathers, what bearding with Mustachoes, what casting open of cloakes to publish new clothes, what muffling in cloaks to hyde broken Elbows, so that when I heare such trampling vp and downe, such spetting, such halking, and such humming (euery mans lippes making a noise, yet not a word to be vnderstoode,) I verily beleeue that I am in the Tower of *Babell* newly to builded vp, but presenlie despaire of euer beeing finished, because there is in me such a confusion of languages.

For at one time, in one and the same ranke, yea, foote by foote, and elbow by elbow, shall you see walking, the Knight, the Gull, the Gallant, the Lawyer, the Vsurer, the Cittizen, the Bankerout, the Scholler, the Beggar, the Doctor, the Ideout, the Ruffian, the Cheater, the Puritan, the Cut-throat, the Hye-man, the Low-man, the True-man, and the Theefe.

Dekker too, with his intimate knowledge of London low-life, gives us the picture of a whore's night:

So soone as euer she is rig'd, and all her furniture on, forth she lanceth into those streetes that are not most frequented: where the first man that she meetes of her acquaintance, shal (without much pulling) get her into a Tauerne: out of him she *kisses* a breakefast & then leaues him: the next she meetes, does vpon as easie pullies, draw her to a Tauerne againe, out of him she *cogs* a dinner, & then leaues him: the third man, *squires* her to a play, which being ended, & the wine offred & taken (for she's no Recusant, to refuse any thing) him she leaues too: and being set vpon by a fourth, him she answers at his own weapon, sups with him, & drinks *Vpsie Freese* [Friesland Beer], till the clok striking Twelue, and the Drawers being drowsy, away they marche arme in arme, being at euery foot-step fearful to be set vpon by the *Band of Halberdiers*, that lie scowting in rug-gownes to cut of such mid-night straglers.

But the word being giuen, & *who goes there*, with *come before the Constable*, being shot at them, they vaile presently and come, she taking vpon her to answer al the *Bil-men* and their *Leader*, Betweene whome & her, suppose you heare this sleepy Dialogue, where haue you bin so late?

at supper forsooth with my vncle here (*if he be wel bearded*) *or with my brother* (*if the haire bee but budding forth*) *and he is bringing me home.*

Are you married? *yes forsooth*:

whats your husband? *such a Noble-mans man, or such a Iustices clarke,* (And then names some Alderman of London, to whom she perswades herselfe, one another of the bench of browne billes are beholding)

where lye you? *At such a mans house:*

Sic tenues euanescit in Auras: and thus by stopping the Constables mouth with sugar-plummes (thats to say), whilst she poisons him with sweete wordes, the punck vanisheth. *O Lanthorne and Candle-light*, how art thou made a blinde Asse? because thou hast but one eye to see withal: Be not so guld, bee not so dull in vnderstanding: do thou but follow aloofe, those two tame Pigeons, & thou shalt finde, that her new *Vncle* lies by it all that night, to make her kinse-woman on of mine *Aunts*: or if shee bee not in trauell all night, they spend some halfe an houre together, but what doe they? marry, they doe that, which the Constable should haue done for them both in the streetes thats to say *commit*, *commit*.

This glimpse of low-life reminds us of how widespread was beggary and roguery. The Statute of Artificers had set out the obligation of all (except gentlemen) to work; it involved direction of labour and a system of priorities. Agriculture topped the list, then its ancillary trades, then clothing, then the higher trades and professions. Landwork was rated the most important; the trader or lawyer the least socially useful. Yet it was the latter who were at the heart of the onward-driving forces, and social pressures were all the time reversing the official code of values. The increasing number of workless, described as rogues and vagabonds, meant that hordes of wretched creatures were haunting the roads or slums and seeking to avoid constables or other harrying officials. The Puritans were much interested, and they, together with the later pamphleteers who exploited the picturesqueness of the theme, have given us abundant information on the unemployed, and the road-wanderers, who ranged from madmen (moonmen) or professional beggars, to rat-catchers, tinkers and ochremen or a complicated series of thieves and cheats: rufflers, sharkers, anglers, wild-rogues, clapper-doyens, and the like. Among the beggars were abram-men, whipjacks (sham sailors with gybes or faked licenses), mumpers, dommerers. Horrible ulcers or wounds were fabricated with spearwort and other irritants.

Harman gives us a charming and moving picture of one of the girls:

I chaunced, not longe sithens, familiarly to commen with a Doxe that came to my Gate, and surelye a pleasant harlot, and not so pleasant as wytty, and not so wytty as voyd of all grace and goodness. I founde, by her talke, that she hadde passed her tyme lewdlye eyghtteene yeares in walkinge aboute.

'Fyrste tell me,' quoth I, 'how many vpright men and Roges dost thou knowe, or hast thou knowne and byn conuersaunt with, and what their names be?'

She paused a whyle, and sayd, 'Why do you aske me, or wherefore?'

'For nothinge els,' as I sayde, 'but that I woulde knowe them when they come to my gate.'

'Nowe, by my trouth' (quoth she) 'then are yea neuer the neare, for all myne acquayntance, for the moste parte are deade.'

'Dead!' quoth I, 'howe dyed they, for want of cherishinge, or of paynefull diseases?'

Then she sighed, and sayfe they were hanged.

'What, all?' quoth I, 'and so many walke abroade, as I dayly see?'

'By my trouth,' quoth she, 'I know not paste six or seven by their names,' and named the same to me.

'When were they hanged?' quoth I.

'Some seuen yeares a gone, some three yeares, and some within this fortnight,' and declared the place where they weare executed, which I knewe well to bee true, by the report of others.

'Why,' (quoth I) 'did not this sorrowfull and fearefull sight much greue the, and for thy tyme longe and euyll spent?'

'I was sory,' quoth she, 'by the Masse; for some of them were good louing men. For I lackt not when they had it, and they wanted not when I had it, and diuers of them I neuer dyd forsake, vntyll the Gallowes departed vs.'

'O, mercyfull God!' quoth I, and began to blesse me.

'Why blesse ye?' quoth she. 'Alas! good gentleman, euery one must haue a lyuinge.'

We may then sum up by saying that Elizabeth with her shrewdness and economy was able to hold the difficult situation down, but all the while problems were heaping up, which she bequeathed to the Stuarts. The ceaseless conflict in manners and morals which we can trace throughout her reign had its roots in the attempt to perpetuate medieval ideas and systems while in fact moving away from the roots that had given medieval society its stability. Catholic recusant and stay-at-home squire were at least in many ways logical in trying to live by the old values; the Puritans were struggling in the last resort to find ethical systems and ways-of-life that were more in accord with the realities of the changing world. The sphere of officialdom was too often striving to create some sort of harmony out of all sorts of discordant elements and to face in two directions at once. We are struck both by the aspects of violent change and by the stubborn continuities. This chapter began with an Italian commenting on insularity of the English at about 1500; in 1598 Hentzner was to declare: 'If they see a foreigner, very well made or particularly handsome, they will say, "It is a pity he is not an Englishman." '

5 Germany

In 1555 the Treaty of Augsburg ended a period of wars: the peasants' revolt, part social and part religious, the Hanse's struggle against the Scandinavian kings, the wars of Saxons against Saxons, and of Bavarians against Hessians. When the wars came to a close there were Spanish and Italian mercenaries everywhere in Germany; princes had been deposed, some even imprisoned. Everywhere religion had been changed by coercion, and German affairs were in the hands of the Spaniards Granvella and Alba. When in 1556 Charles v, whose wars to end the religious schism had only led to more wars, abdicated, a long period of peace and prosperity began.

It was also a period of tolerance. Micheli wrote in 1564: 'One party tolerates the other. In villages and towns with mixed populations nobody cares who is Protestant and who is Catholic. It is the same within families. Brothers have different faiths, Catholics and Protestants intermarry.'[1] The German aristocracy was Protestant almost without exception. The Austrian aristocracy studied at Protestant universities, three of its members were rectors at Luther's university of Wittenberg – the world's best university in the opinion of Erasmus of Rotterdam. In 1561 Albrecht v, Duke of Bavaria, attended with his court the sermons of the Protestant Pastor Pfaufer. The monks left the monasteries and married, perhaps one clergyman in a hundred was celibate, and there were no more pilgrimages. The establishment in Rome was held in contempt. The ambassador Tiepolo said in 1557: 'This country will be completely estranged from the Catholic faith in a short time.' And Soriano: 'The Princes and people of Germany are heretics.' In 1582 the archbishop of Cologne tried to convert his archbishopric into an evangelical state, for he wished to marry. This, however, would have resulted in a two-thirds evangelical majority in the Council of Electors who chose the Emperor. Pope and Emperor therefore objected and installed a new archbishop. Clusius, the great botanist from

[1] Ranke.

Arras in the Netherlands, an ardent Protestant whose family had been murdered and whose property had been confiscated in the revolt of the Netherlands against Spain, now found refuge at the Court of Vienna where he supervised the gardens of Maximilian II. The Lutheran Kepler, too, lived at the Catholic Emperor's court. And when Apianus had to resign as professor at Ingolstadt for refusing to take the oath demanded by the Council of Trent, Duke Albrecht of Bavaria invited him to his court and gave him a pension. During the reign of two tolerant Hapsburgs, Ferdinand I and Maximilian II, seven-tenths of the Germans were Protestant, one-tenth Catholic and two-tenths sectarian.

The German towns had reached the height of their good fortune. Danzig was the second or third port of the world, and there were sometimes, as many as 500 vessels assembled in the greatest transit harbour between East and West. The Hanse were still the most favoured traders in Denmark, they had a monopoly of herring fishing in the Sound, and the Stahlhof in London was their most coveted trading post. In 1551 they shipped 44,000 pieces of cloth from England to the Continent as against only 1,100 carried by the English in their own ships. In 1564–6 the Hanse erected a gigantic office building in Antwerp, a veritable palace, and installed an agent in France; whence their ships sailed in big convoys to Lisbon.

Nuremberg was a world famous depôt between the Danube and the Rhine where linen from Silesia, Italian silk, and English wool were made up into finished goods. A Venetian ambassador told of the splendid armour, of 300 cannons, of corn for two years stored in her warehouses. The leading families were traders. Their living standard can be inferred from a bed made for Herr Paulus Scheuerl, a silk merchant, from ebony and alabaster adorned with gables, niches with figures, four corinthian columns and angels with trumpets.

The handicrafts of Nuremberg and Augsburg were world famous. The pocket-watch – the so-called Nuremberg egg – was invented by a Nuremberger. The watch industry had the same significance as the Swiss watch industry today, the toy industry was exporting then as now. Nuremberg exported jewellery and armour to France, Spain and even to Italy. In most museums today one finds the gold and silver jugs, goblets and epergnes made in Nuremberg. It was likewise with ceramics, most famous of which were the great *Steins* of Hirschvogel.

London was a similar trading centre between Danzig and Genova, between Vienna and Nuremberg and Lyons. The Frankfurt fair became a third important centre: where 'Occident and Orient find their treasures and the eternal products of the intellect', wrote Scaliger.

What the pattern books of Chippendale did for cabinet-making or the famous pattern books of Monnoyer (1634–99) for textiles and tapestries in a later period, was done by the pattern books of Peter Flötner and others for the arts and crafts of the sixteenth century.

Not only Danzig, Nuremberg and Lindau prospered. At Breslau a certain Dr Laurentius Scholz, who had studied in Padua, laid out a garden with a labyrinth of rose hedges, a shrubbery, and a flower garden. He gave large garden parties known as Floralia Vratislavia – Roman festivities – on the River Oder. Tiny places like Stendal had 800 cloth weavers; the herring brought wealth to Berlin; Luneburg prospered on salt. Magdeburg was able to spend 4,000,000 florins on her soldiers. The mines – especially the silver mines – brought great wealth. A Venetian records that Dresden was coining 3,000 silver thalers daily. Merten Heidler of Joachimsthal made 100,000 florins by mining, together with his wife. Brass was produced at Buntheim, silver in Saxony, copper in Thuringia, iron at Gittelde. 'Germany has increased the amount of precious metals in the sixteenth century as much as America in the first fifty years after her discovery.'

No wonder that great civic buildings testified to the prosperity and pride of the citizens: the Guildhall of the cloth merchants at Bremen (1619–20), the Wine-house at Munster (1615), new or extended town halls at Nördlingen, Esslingen, Heilbronn, Emden, Minden, Lindau, Halberstadt, as well as the princely residences of the merchants four or five storeys high. And then Augsburg: the new Town Hall built in 1615–20 by Elias Holl contained the 'Golden Hall', the most splendid hall of any German town; the 'Armoury' by the same master already shows a distinctly baroque flavour. Pope Pius II called Augsburg the richest town in the world. Only Milan could compete in wrought iron work with Augsburg or Nuremberg. The famous Desiderius Kolman received 3,000 florins for a suit of chased armour. Augsburg's bankers were the richest in the world, Welser, Paumgartner and, of course, Fugger. Anton Fugger left 6,000,000 gold crowns. Jacob Fugger was apprenticed in Venice – a Venetian ambassador said of him later, 'If Augsburg was the daughter of Venice she had surpassed her mother' – he brought spices from India in his own ships, traded silk and wool to and from Italy, owned mines in Hungary, Spain, Thuringia and Austria. The Fuggers who had remained Catholic in Protestant Augsburg financed the wars of Charles V. They built the first excellent workers quarters, the *Fuggerei*. A garden acquired by them in 1580 was more magnificent than the royal park of Blois, and in 1584 the people of Augsburg complained that the Fugger garden was encroaching upon their vegetable plots. Georg Fugger was the first to cultivate the musk rose. The botanist Konrad Gessner saw the first tulip of Europe in the garden of the Augsburg councillor Herwarth. He listed gardens for five income groups, in contrast to the two, rich and poor, which Crescentius had recognized 300 years earlier. They were:

(1) Simple kitchen gardens with vegetables, vines, fruit and a lawn for man and beast.

(2) Physic gardens with additional medicinal herbs.

(3) Variegated gardens containing also rare plants for contemplation and admiration of nature.

(4) Elegant gardens for pleasure only, with arbours, summerhouses and labyrinths, noble evergreen trees and all the shapes topiary art can produce; the gardens of noble ladies and rich gentlemen and above all of monks.

(5) Gardens of luxury owned by wise men or princes or states, with magnificent buildings, ponds and fountains, artificial hills, gymnasiums and playing fields, thickets for wild beasts and an aviary.

Hans von Schweinichen, the companion of the Duke of Liegnitz, a glorified tramp sucking the European courts, describes their stay in Augsburg:

At Fuggers the meal took place in a hall in which one saw more gold than colour. The marble floor was slippery like ice. A cross-table filling the hall was laid with Venetian glass altogether worth more than a ton of gold. I had to drink the health of the Duke from a most beautiful Venetian glass ship. Taking this from the buffet I slipped and fell recrossing the hall. I poured the wine over my neck. My new garment of red damask was spoiled, the ship smashed. While great laughter ensued I was told afterward that Herr Fugger had said he would have rather lost a hundred florins than the ship. Herr Fugger showed my master over the house which is so large that the Roman Emperor at the Reichstag would have found room therein for his whole court. Then Herr Fugger led my master into a little turret and showed him chains, jewels, strange coins and pieces of gold as large as heads, a treasure valued by himself at a million gold pieces. Thereafter he opened a box containing two hundred thousand florins which he made over to the King of Spain. They say Herr Fugger could pay for an Empire and my master was expecting a substantial gift but got drunk. The Duke owed his innkeeper 1,300 thalers. My master sent me to Herr Fugger to ask for 4,000 thalers. He refused, as he had to lend a large sum to the King of Spain. Next day he sent his steward to me to announce him to my master. He left him 200 crowns, a beautiful jug worth eighty thalers and a fine horse with a black velvet rug. As our plot to obtain a loan from the Fuggers had failed, my duke then sent me to the counsillors of Augsburg to ask them for the 4,000 thalers. They kept me in a waiting room for two hours and then sent four counsellors who delivered a long speech, concluding that they would loan my master 1,000 thalers for one year free of interest, also they would endow him with an excellent horse. I thanked them politely and brought the good news to my master. But as this was insufficient I was ordered to pawn some plate made at Augsburg and Nuremberg which raised only 800 thalers, although its value was 1,200. The innkeeper's bill was 1,470 thalers. We gave him the 1,000 thalers from the councillors, the rest the innkeeper lent for two months. When the duke found the innkeeper so generous he decided to throw a banquet, ordered me to arrange everything at its

F

best and invited six councillors, among them a count and a baronet, two Fuggers and two other persons. There was much merrymaking and chamber music, and when the banquet was over my master left Augsburg, accompanied by the party on sixty horses for the first two miles.

Drinking and feasting were the order of the day. In 1610 the Elector Christian II of Saxony thanked the emperor in Prague 'for having been so well treated that he was not left sober for one hour'. In the Rittersaal of the castle of Riegersburg in Austria chairs were so constructed that a man could not fall off them even when dead drunk, and an inscription engraved on a window-pane reads – 'anno 1635 on the 6 April the drinking started and we were drunk every day till the 26 dto.'

Elias Holl, the architect, praised Jacob Fugger for being drunk at every meal. In 1590 Johann Kasimir of the Palatinate arranged a drinking competition while his Lutheran wife, Elizabeth of Saxony, was dying in prison. Philipp Hainhofer had to place himself in Stettin under the personal protection of the Duke to avoid being pressed to drink. The Count of Hessia, very courageously, started a Temperance Society in 1601. It is only fair to say that heavy drinking was also the fashion in France and England.

Immoderate eating was just as fashionable, and it should not be forgotten that the preserving of food consisted only in salting and smoking. When beasts were slaughtered they had to be eaten at once. The 'slaughter feast' is common in northern Germany to this day. When Hainhofer was invited to dine with the vicar of Stettin, they began to eat at ten a.m. and did not finish until six p.m. Guarionius reported in 1610 that at parties the German middle class served six courses, each of nine different dishes. The upper class served only three courses, but each consisted of 100 items. Tables were decorated with show dishes made from wax or wood. The baker Michael Lochmaier of Donauwörth made a movable Goddess of Fortune and a Pegasus who knocked at the fountain of the Muses. The Elector of Cologne ordered show dishes for 11,000 thalers for a banquet at the meeting of the Princes in Regensburg in 1613. But this had to be cancelled because of an outbreak of the plague.

But this society with all its wealth, its feasting and drinking was abominably superstitious and believed in demons, witches, sorcerers, and alchemists. It is reported that Markus Fugger was greatly impressed by a Jesuit exorcizing seven devils from a maid. To prove his gratitude he went with his wife on a pilgrimage to the Black Madonna at Altötting, dedicating to her a precious golden goblet. Later he lost 400,000 florins which he gave to an alchemist for manufacturing gold.

In the matter of burning sorcerers and witches, there was nothing to choose between Catholic and Protestant. In Neisse, 1,000 persons, among them children of two to four years of age, were put to death over a period of a decade. In Fulda 250 people were burnt in three years; in tiny Ell-wangen 127 persons in one year. Some time later, between 1623 and 1631, 900 people were burnt in Würzburg and a stop was put to it only when the Archbishop himself was appealed to. It was an easy way to get rid of adversaries. The excellent Lord Mayor of Brunswick was tortured to death in 1604 because he was supposed to be in league with the devil. The judges had a financial interest in these trials: 500,000 florins belonging to those killed were confiscated in Bamberg alone. Benedikt Carpzov, a Leipzig professor, boasted of having signed 20,000 death warrants. The dark side of the century is evident when we hear that judge and jury drank seventeen cans of wine and twenty-six cans of beer, whilst watching a woman of eighty being tortured.

The princes meanwhile, found new forms of distraction, and where formerly hunting, drinking and fighting had sufficed them, they now cultivated their gardens, and made enclosures for many novel animals which it became fashionable to nurture. In addition several collected works of art, and the Princess of Bavaria was reproved for her extravagant pur-chases by her councillors of state. From 1531 to 1584 the whole of Bavaria was surveyed. The courts were the only centres of civilization even then, and the country as a whole remained feudal both in political management and in agrarian economy.

Conditions of life were simple. Everybody except a small upper class slept on straw. Chocolate, tea and coffee were unknown. Breakfast con-sisted of beer, or wine-soup, bread and cheese. In Mecklenburg the maids had to rise at four a.m. in summer, at five a.m. in winter; children rose at six, infants at seven. Ablutions were followed by family prayers. This spartan régime was common to all classes, and is recorded in the life of the Duchess of Pomerania. Luncheon was eaten between eleven and twelve in the morning and dinner between five and six in the afternoon. The servants ate their meals earlier. Bedtime was between eight and nine. According to Spanish Court rule bedtime was at nine in winter and at ten in summer. Women devoted themselves to knitting, spinning, weaving and making soap. Every house had its smoking chamber for curing pork. Lighting was by candles or oil-lamps made of tin or clay. Fire was made with tinder, steel, firestone and sulphur, burnt wood and woodcoal. There were many complaints about dishonest, lazy, quarrelsome and immodest servants, who were punished by beatings and fines. Negligence in cleaning silver and tin and dishonesty in pilfering food were common vices amongst them. Manners were still crude: liquids were drunk with a spoon from a common bowl, solid food eaten with the fingers. Montaigne complained of constantly biting his fingers through eating too quickly. Although by 1560 knives were common in Germany, manners were far behind those of Italy, as observed by Thomas Coryat, an English traveller:

'People here hold their food with a fork on the plate and cut it with a knife, something unknown in any other country. It is considered bad manners to put ones fingers into the bowl.'

Earlier democratic ways changed at the beginning of the seventeenth century. Previously, everybody – nobles, councillors, merchants and princes – had sat at the same table in the castle dining room but now a separate table was laid for persons of the nobility. Likewise a redistribution of the land took place with annexation of the bishoprics in Brandenburg, Pomerania, Mecklenburg, Saxony and Brunswick. At the same time small farms were bought up by the gentry, many of whom were not wealthy. Hohberg, a titled Protestant farmer in Lower Austria, had two small estates: one consisting of twenty-four cows, a hundred and fifty sheep, fourteen dependant peasants and ten lease-holders. A cousin of Hohberg had thirty dependant peasants, but large landowners like the Prince of Liechtenstein had as many as 1,800 dependant peasants.

Masks, ballets and brilliant pageants heralded a new age of theatrical display. When Elizabeth Stuart married the Prince of the Palatinate, the gate of the Department of Philosophy in the University of Heidelberg was hung with tapestries and music was played on violins, violas and portable organs. A masque was performed with Pallas Athene, on a wagon of gold and silver drawn by dragons, Roman gods, and other mythical personages including even Don Quixote.

6 Low Countries

The seven Provinces were virtually seven sovereign states, and they were Calvinist. They are flat countries, looking seawards, and most of their wealth was drawn from maritime trade. Calvinism and commerce have often been regarded as the inseperable formations of the modern capitalist state. And the combination of these two agencies also gave rise to the democratic spirit which profoundly marked daily life in the Low Countries; a spirit which was unique in a Christendom as it emerged from the Middle Ages.

In 1585 the sack of Antwerp, the principal centre of commerce in Europe, gave a powerful impulse to Dutch economy; it brought a flow of traders, ship-owners, and bankers with considerable capital to Amsterdam. At this time, the Low Countries were struggling against Spain and they could no longer act as an intermediary between northern and southern Europe. They had to look for new outlets, and these were found in the East Indies and Africa. The creation of the East India Company in 1594 marked the beginning of a great commercial venture. Fifteen years later, the King of Spain signed the Twelve Years' Truce and granted the Dutch the right to trade with the East Indies. The Catholic King, the first sovereign of the world, had bowed before the Protestant bourgeois.

There were considerable repercussions as a result of a social system which was very different from that of any other nation. Until now the social system had been dominated by a military and landholding patriciate, imposed in accordance with its antiquity, its distinction and its alliances; this predominance had been suppressed. The old nobility of the Dutch provinces still existed, but they did so in obscurity. However, since society could not dispense with a hierarchy, it substituted new distinctions for the old ones. The rights of economic success replaced the rights of birth.

At the beginning of the seventeenth century, the tax-rolls of Amsterdam recorded 1,500 fortunes ranging from 25,000 to 50,000 florins; the citizen most heavily taxed was 'worth' about a million. It was an enormous sum, considering that it was a young republic based on purely commercial revenues. In the neighbouring States, only twenty families possessed more, less than a hundred families had as much. However, the general prosperity did not prevent the masses from finding their lives hard. The price index for the most essential products rose from 100 in 1580 to 166 in 1620, and the working classes struggled fiercely for an increase in wages.

Since the bourgeoisie exercised a predominant influence, the Dutch way of life was characterized by democratic simplicity, to which the nobility were obliged to conform. There was, of course, the court of the Princes of Orange (Het Hof), but the Stadtholders had neither the means nor, apparently, the wish to live in the grand manner. They had three 'palaces' at The Hague, the first of which was an old fortress, the second a fine residence which was no more luxurious than other houses in the town; the third 'palace' was a pleasant country seat.

The noblemen whose families had once possessed fiefs were still comparatively well represented in the rural provinces of Guelderland and Overyssel; but they did not count in the North or in Friesland, and in the west they had been greatly reduced in numbers by the wars against Spain. In 1620 the province of Holland had only thirty-five patrician families. This caste had once been preponderant, but was unable to renew itself because the Republic did not grant letters of nobility, and the idleness which gentlemen considered obligatory, led them to emigrate. Some of them were able to staff the army and the administration, provided that their ambitions were limited.

Most of the rural noblemen lived like rich peasants, on the produce of their estates. 'The nobility is in exile in the heart of a nation of tradesmen; it refuses to be concerned with any commerce', noted Paul Zumthor; and the French professor, Jean-Nicolas Pauval, who lived for a long time in Leyden, wrote of these last heirs of feudalism: 'If some of them are violent, proud and haughty, they find themselves scorned in their turn. Honours are only rendered to those who have earned them by gentle, engaging manners.'

The bourgeoisie was divided into several classes corresponding to the different levels of commercial success. At the top of the scale was an élite which exercised political power and controlled the economy. These families were no longer active in business, and generally contented themselves with managing their fortunes. They provided staff for the administration. High functionaries received considerable emoluments, but they could not have obtained their posts if they had not had private means. The women concerned themselves with charity work which was not without its influence on their husbands' careers.

At the end of the sixteenth century, these people led a family life which hardly differed from that of the middle bourgeoisie. Later, they married the last heirs of the nobility so as to form a modern aristocracy which kept only two characteristics of the old one: wealth, and the abstinence from trade. Unlike their predecessors, these gentlemen abstained from bearing arms.

What might be called the middle nobility of the bourgeoisie had no political responsibility. It was entirely devoted to commerce. Most of the families in this class had completed their patient social ascent. The Witsens of Amsterdam were a perfect example: originally peasants, one son became a sailor; they saved up enough to buy a ship and, after several prosperous voyages, were able to buy another. After half a century of thrift and relentless work, the Witsens found themselves the masters of a merchant fleet. The great merchants never specialized, and they had little taste for their work. They passed without transition, as circumstances dictated, from selling wheat to selling jewels.

If they had the reputation of being 'firm and quite honest', they were not unduly hampered by scruples when they had to contend with their rivals. Bankruptcies were not unknown, and liquidations sometimes verged on scandal. In general, the principle that the end justifies the means took the place of the code of chivalry. The liberal professions could not be ascribed to any particular category. Doctors, solicitors, barristers and professors came from the bourgeoisie and maintained its laws. They often formed dynasties.

Face to face with this opulence, the petits bourgeois and workmen lived a frugal life. Foreigners admired the kindness of the working men who were, however, led by poverty to be ruthless in the way in which they earned their money. They were also reproached with being aggressive and quarrelsome. This hierarchy, founded on the inequality of fortunes, presented striking contrasts between the millionaires and the beggars. Nineteenth-century England was to show a similar pattern. Most of the humble lived in hovels. It was accepted that children should work intensively, and working days were up to fourteen hours long. Sometimes a twinge of conscience was felt in the Republic, and in 1597, a decree condemned the practices of those employers who reduced their employees to slavery.

In 1601, the city of Amsterdam forbade pastrycooks to decorate the cakes in their windows too lavishly, 'for fear of depressing the poor, whose greed was excited by the display'. It was a touching attention, but no one thought of ensuring that the poor could taste the cakes.

The first genuinely Dutch Calvinist council met in 1571. The war against Spain had allowed the new religion to cement a unity in the face of the Catholic oppressions, and to hide its internal disagreements. When the danger lessened, the contradictions between the social classes grew more marked, although at the end of the sixteenth century, the patriciate and the petite bourgeoisie were not yet in conflict. But there was a remarkable difference between the relative liberalism of the one and the strictness of the other, between the elegant tolerance of the rich and the austerity of the poor, who were hostile to luxury and art.

These differences did not annul the fact that every action and habit was impregnated with the religious spirit. The Bible was food for conversation, it provided justification for conduct. People often prayed: in the morning, before and after each meal, and again at nightfall; the head of the family presided over religious ceremonies every day. Sunday was kept scrupulously as a day of rest. But in spite of all this, materialism prevailed. The controversies over predestination and grace were to encumber Dutch history for a century, but they were not to affect the prosperity of bankers and ship-owners.

Ministers of religion enjoyed general consideration. Under their black cloaks they were better fed than most of the people whose origins were as modest as their own; they walked on the inside of the pavement, and kept their womenfolk to their left, exposed to the mud of the streets. On solemn occasions they preceded the doctors and other notables in the liberal professions. However, they were badly paid, and could hardly claim the pleasures bestowed by wealth. If they thundered from the pulpit against misconduct, dancing, the theatre, tobacco, coffee, and the persistent custom of celebrating the old feasts, if they showed such severity towards children, it was perhaps because their situation was difficult. The habit of contemplating wealth that was beyond their reach embittered them in the exercise of their important duties.

The Dutch possessed religious scruples and strict principles from their earliest infancy; they were known for their good morals and frugality. Every traveller recorded their scorn for good living. In his *Essai sur les moeurs*, Voltaire tells the following anecdote:

The Marquis de Spinola and President Richardot went to The Hague in 1608 to negotiate a truce, and they saw eight or ten people get out of a little boat, sit down on the grass, and make a meal of bread, cheese and beer, each man having carried what he needed. The Spanish ambassadors asked a peasant who these travellers were. 'Those are the deputies of the States, our sovereign lords and masters,' replied the peasant. And the ambassadors, much impressed, exclaimed: 'Those people will never be conquered, we must make peace with them.'

The story is a little unconvincing, but it shows to what extent the great people of the time could be surprised by simplicity and naturalness.

Part Two

1610–1660

7 Spain

Spain was half way to decadence, but neither the world nor the Spaniards suspected it. Despite the superabundance of precious metals quarried from its American mines, and the huge monopoly of its commerce with the New World the Spanish found it impossible to cure the economic crisis from which they continually suffered. Despite their grandeur a pitiful standard of living was common. The nobles hid their poverty under a cloak of laziness and conceit, the poor people hid their sufferings under a cloak of stoicism in which there was a mixture of cunning, bitterness and fatalism.

The Church reigned supreme, and above the Church stood the Holy Office. Finally, more stringent than the Inquisition itself were the curbs of etiquette and *punctilio*. In Madrid, full of palaces and cloisters, of duennas and assassins, a husband might stab his wife if she was immodest enough to show a glimpse of her feet; failure to greet a nobleman according to his rank brought a fine of 10,000 *maravedis*; attendance at autodafés was counted among the privileges of ambassadors; systematic informing provided victims for the pyres.

And yet these constraints did not stifle idealism or inspiration or amorous frenzy or yet the passion for adventure. This passion was especially lively among those younger sons who did not want to enter Holy Orders; for entailed estates, not only among the nobles, but also among the middle classes, reserved the family fortunes for elder sons so that they could lead lives of idleness.

Philip III was on the throne. He bore small resemblance to the famous portrait (which was posthumous, anyway) in which Velasquez showed him with the flattering appearance of a grave, determined cavalier galloping along the seashore. (One might add that the artist did not resist making a discreet suggestion of stupidity in the royal face.) The King of Spain was German in his fair hair, his pink skin, his Hapsburg lip, his stoutness, slowness and phlegm. The conviction that he was a semi-divine personage and the feeling of his own inadequacy caused an inward conflict which was carefully hidden beneath an attitude of unchangeableness and imperturbability.

The Catholic King divided his time between pleasure and devotion. His pleasures were hunting, dice, ballooning, and the table; wine was forbidden, but the table was covered with incredible quantities of meat. 'He had ruined his stomach with it (and his stomach had been weak since childhood),' reported the Venetian Ambassador, 'and he would have died of it if nature had not given him a necessary relief: the disgusting infirmity of suppurating legs.'

Philip, however, was no philanderer and hardly ever left his young wife, Margaret of Styria; he loved her for her freshness, appetite and religion. They both heard at least two masses every day. The King read the office, asked for blessing of every monk he met, and made his Dominican confessor enter the council to avoid the least uneasiness of conscience. Deeply convinced of the Immaculate Conception, he wished to see this belief established as a dogma; he kept up an enormous correspondence on the subject with the Pope, and even considered making the pilgrimage to Rome on foot. In the meanwhile he treated the court to unheard-of splendours including millions spent on festivities, while the treasury grew emptier.

His inability to govern as his father had done led him to inaugurate a system which was adopted, almost at the same time, by James I of England. A few years later, it was to become the system of Louis XIII of France. Philip III delegated his power to an intimate adviser, a favourite. The favourite, who was to dominate the West for the first half of the seventeenth century, was a sort of intermediary between the royal divinity, the court and the great mass of subjects. Representative, spokesman, guardian of the living idol, trustee of the wishes addressed to him, he also preserved his inviolable character by taking his master's wrongs upon himself. 'If he [the King] has committed a fault,' wrote Bacon to Buckingham, 'you have committed it yourself or you have allowed it and you should suffer for it, you can even be sacrificed to please the multitude . . . You should be a constant sentinel beside him.'

Just as he had entrusted his soul to his confessor, so Philip III entrusted his kingdom to Don Francisco de Sandoval y Rojas, Marquis of Denia, (subsequently Duke of Lerma) who soon had as his own favourite, Rodrigo Calderón, the son of a soldier of fortune and a Flemish servant. 'Of mediocre intelligence, . . . envious, jealous, morbid, sometimes impetuous to the point of madness, he [Lerma] wanted to gather all affairs into his hands, and he succumbed under this formidable burden.' His power was to be such that he was able to have the court transferred to Valladolid, near his own estates. After a long reign, Calderón was to sink into crime and financial scandals, and die on the scaffold, condemning the Duke of Lerma to exile. The Duke, incidentally, was succeeded by one of his close relations.

Philip III, a martyr to ceremonial, died of erysipelas, because one day he was unable to find any nobleman in his palace who was entitled to damp down his fire.

Velasquez has left us a likeness of his successor; a long, pale, blond image which suggests a hot-house flower cultivated in solitude and tedium. This indolent intellectual was undoubtedly the most humane and most sensitive prince of his race. He had a sense of justice and bounty, cared about the welfare of his subjects. Though he was devoid of political talent, he knew how to choose good minister-favourites – Olivares, then Don Luis de Haro; but the first was no match for Richelieu, and the second no match for Mazarin. And so the reign was subjected to defeats and secessions.

Philip IV consoled himself with hunting, gallantry and mysticism. Unlike his father, he had both mistresses and bastards. About 1640 he fell in love with a very pretty nun, and managed to get a secret door opened in her cell so that he could meet her. But the abbess had been warned and the King found his beloved laid out between four candles on a catafalque, a crucifix in her hands. He fled, in terror. A scandal followed, and the Inquisition refused him absolution until he earned their forgiveness by an expiatory novena. His first wife, Elizabeth of France, daughter of Henri IV, was not hard on his escapades. She was also his best and most energetic counsellor. It was she who extorted Olivares' dismissal by appearing like Nemesis in the royal cabinet, having forced the door. Spain lost much by her premature death.

In a century, the ceremonial of Their Catholic Majesties had lost none of its rigour. It is piquant to find considerable traces of orientalism in it. For example, no man, except the King, slept in the same palace as the Queen and the Infantas. Philip IV, when he gave audience, assumed expression so hieratic that the pupils of his eyes did not move. The House of Austria took a pride in caste which was all its own. The Infanta Maria Theresa, who married Louis XIV, was convinced that only princesses could touch the heart of a king. It took Mlle de la Vallière and many others to disillusion her.

After 1660, a close relationship developed between Philip IV and the mother superior of a Franciscan convent, Maria de Agreda. This rival of St Theresa, whose *History of the Virgin* had been censured at Rome, was tormented by visions, though she lost none of her native good sense. The belated publication of the correspondence between the sovereign and the nun dissipated any suspicion about the nature of their relationship, and showed the faith, the humility and conscience of this prince who witnessed the disintegration of his empire.

The equestrian statue of Philip IV at Madrid is decorated with bas-reliefs on which no trophies or victories are to be seen. The sculptor, Pedro Tacca, preferred to show the King handing Velasquez the anchored cross of the Knights of St James. He thus recalled the King's true glory: not the glory of a conqueror, but that of a humanist and a patron.

Philip himself wrote comedies and translated the works of Guicciardini. Like François I of France, he did not simply protect and pension artists, sculptors, writers, musicians and architects, he also liked them. He commissioned several theatres to be built, and liked to go there and watch performances, sometimes surrounded by his court, but more frequently alone, disguised by a black velvet mask. It was on one of these escapades that he met la Calderona, who became the mother of his natural son, Don Juan of Austria.

Under his impulse, Madrid was transformed. With his own hand he improved the plans for the Plaza Mayor in which 20,000 people could watch processions, carrousels and bullfights. The old Alcazar was abandoned in favour of the Buen Retiro, and magnificent gardens were liberally opened to those who wished to stroll. Fêtes and great public rejoicings multiplied, with their masquerades, their illuminations and their processions. The love of the arts spread among the Grandees and the taste for enriching life reached even the lowest classes of society. Luxury increased to such a degree that the King's conscience was disturbed, and he promulgated strict but ineffective sumptuary edicts. In the middle of the streets, to the great delight of the onlookers, *alguazils* might be seen cutting out farthingales and starched ruffs with their scissors.

Thanks to the artistic magnificence of his reign, Philip IV holds a place of honour in this golden age. When, from an armchair set in front of the master's easel, he watched Velasquez painting, perhaps he contributed more to the renown of his country than Philip II, who launched his Invincible Armada against England.

8 France

Louis XIII was not a fashionable king. The high nobility, more impatient, more arrogant, more extravagant, more pugnacious, more debauched than they had ever been, looked with some disdain on a prince who was his own executioner: a prince who was chaste, uncommunicative, taciturn, stammering in his speech, strained in his movements, and readily clad as a soldier. They thought of him as a sort of schoolmaster determined to forbid those things which represented the joy of living: splendour, disorder intrigue and wantonness.

This crowned stoic was passionately fond of hunting and travelling, and (when he had to stay at home) of childish amusements: knotting nets, making preserves, forging weapons and money. He would willingly have dispensed with the Court, like Louis XI. Only duty and tradition, the necessities of government, obliged him to live in the middle of a crowd of 1,300 people (not counting the 10,000 men in his guard) and to review parades which he detested. The Code of Etiquette of 1585 remained theoretically in force, but the ceremonial was reduced to a minimum.

If the King did not hold a court and hardly let the Queen do so, the court existed, none the less. It was composed of a multitude of noblemen and noblewomen who crowded the Great Hall at the Louvre or Saint-Germain throughout the day in autumn and in winter. In the fine season, His Majesty waged war, and the gentlemen delightedly returned to their unique occupation on the battlefields.

When they had had a good fight, and even while they were fighting, they thought of nothing but *appearance*. *Appearance :* that meant following the slightest decrees of an ever-changing fashion, speaking a language in reverse. The Duc de Chevreuse was to order fifteen carriage and reject fourteen so as to have the most sumptuous in town. Costumes were streaming with feathers and lace, with gilt and precious stones. The excessively beautiful Marquis de Saint-Mars was to leave fifty-two such costumes on his death.

As the courtiers gambled excessively, they nearly all lived in acute financial difficulties. Their creditors beset them. At first they were simply shown the door, like Molière's Monsieur Dimanche; and then a public office had to be sold, an estate had to be let, jewels had to be pawned, one might even resign oneself to a *mésalliance*. But the vanity which ruled these people never let them dispense with a golden tassel or a plume.

The most unfortunate were certainly those who often came from the proudest families, but only possessed the incomes of their offices. ... They secretly summoned assistance from cunning merchants who provided them with new materials, hats, ruffs, collars, shirts, silk stockings, and constant new pairs of shoes, for four écus a month and the return of their worn clothes. Outside the royal palace these poor 'braggarts' ... took a good many meals without dirtying napkins or crockery, for they lived on nuts and apples and dry bread.[1]

Among the great entertainments with which he still had at times to regale his people, Louis xiii, composer and dancer, enjoyed only the ballets. 'Royal Majesty is not always found in lofty severity,' wrote the *Gazette de France* after one of these diversions, during which the 'hypochondriac' appeared in an unexpected light.

Was it really the Court of the most parsimonious of monarchs? At the Louvre, and sometimes at the Hôtel de Ville, a multitude whose fine clothes had been their passport showed tumultuous admiration of a spectacle which our miserly epoch could not conceive. The flower of the royal family and the nobility shone among more than a hundred artists. There were extraordinary machines, disguises in which gold and jewels were used like common stuffs; there were giants, dwarfs, funambulists, fabulous animals, mythological divinities, valiant knights, enchantresses, solemn displays and, most important, comic fantasies. But who was that burlesque Mahomet, who was the clown who hid himself under that turban and false beard, under the mask of that horned devil, under the rags of that beldame who was dancing three-quarters of an hour without a break? The King, the austere and sombre King, who was one day overwhelmed by his puritan indignation, and spat a mouthful of wine down a young lady's over-generous cleavage!

Louis xiii did not look on writers with a favourable eye. He left Richelieu the task of protecting them and, as soon as the cardinal died, he stopped their pensions. On the other hand he was interested in town-planning, and authorized building opposite his palace, on the Left Bank of the Seine. He fully appreciated his two painters-in-ordinary, Georges De La Tour and Nicolas Poussin. Though he was always anxious to save, he still permitted to others the expense of building. It was Marie des Médicis who built the Luxembourg, Anne of Austria who built the Val-de-Grâce, Richelieu the Palais-Cardinal and the restored Sorbonne.

The French Court was no longer the centre of radiance which it had

[1] Emile Magne: *La vie quotidienne sous Louis XIII.*

The Seats of Power

Cosimo II de Medici, 1619. Politically Florence was now of little importance, but Cosimo lavished money on public festivities, and was the protector of Galileo.

Opposite. Cardinal Richelieu, prince of the Church and brilliant politician, who laid the foundations of absolutist policy in France.

Right. Donna Olimpia Maidalchini, sister-in-law of Pope Innocent x. Her influence at the papal court was so strong that her favours were sought even by ambassadors and cardinals.

Bottom left. Urban VIII with his nephews. The Barberini Pope was famed for his magnificent rebuilding of Rome, notorious for the 105 millions lavished in nepotism during his twenty-year pontificate.

Bottom right. Father Joseph of Paris, Richelieu's adviser and confidant, the 'red-haired unkempt Capuchin'.

Marie des Médicis, regent of France during the minority of Louis XIII, and Richelieu's rival for power in France. Painting by Rubens.

Charles I and Queen Henrietta Maria welcome Marie des Médicis (the Queen's mother) on her visit to England in 1639, and offer her the symbols of their power.

Below. George Villiers, Duke of Buckingham, and his family. Buckingham was the minister of James I and Charles I, and exemplified the dangers of rule by 'favourite': increasing unpopularity for his master and his own assassination.

Print celebrating the marriage of Louis XIII to Anne of Austria. Buckingham had created a scandal in the year of the marriage by his chivalric declaration of love for the Queen of France.

Firework display to celebrate the triumphal entry of Louis XIII into Lyon in 1623.

Bottom. Carnival carriages for a princely celebration designed by Jacques Callot.

The power in Holland: the States General. Parliamentary control in the Low Countries, after they had broken free from Spain, contributed much to their commercial supremacy in Europe.

been under the Valois. It was the Hôtel de Rambouillet and certain other houses in Paris which inspired the way of living and thinking; it was there that consecration had to be sought; it was there that the aristocracy learned the manners on which they would pride themselves until modern times.

To be accepted by Mme de Rambouillet, or, to a lesser degree, by her rival, Mme des Loges, conferred 'a brevet of fashion'. For a long time these two houses accepted only people of quality. If Malherbe and Racan shone there it was because they were gentlemen, not because they flirted with the Muse. Only in 1625 did the young poet Vincent Voiture, 'master of the trifling arts', enliven the receptions at the Hôtel de Rambouillet, while Guez de Balzac was presented by Mme des Loges as the god of eloquence. The two ladies had understood that literature could assist their own glorification. Henceforth, in their *hôtels*, talent was to be worth almost as much as a coat-of-arms.

Mme des Loges, a Protestant, liked the gravity of scholars, historians and moralists. She also dabbled in politics, which earned her the enmity of Richelieu, and forced her to close her salon after the Siege of La Rochelle. Vicomtesse d'Auchy then re-opened her salon which her late husband had formerly obliged her to abandon. She was 'avid for readings, comedies, letters, harangues and speeches, and even sermons'.

But she did not shake the prestige of the Hôtel de Rambouillet, any more than Mme des Loges.

Its doors were open to visitors every day after the mid-day and evening meals. Some of these visitors came intermittently, some came daily . . . Resting in the blue room on her bed of state, dressed in rich clothes of taffeta, or tabby, or flowered damask with gold lace, majestic, revered like an idol, Mme de Rambouillet reserved a place of honour for conversation. This conversation was enriched, in the first place, with items of news on which everyone made comments as he pleased . . . It also bore on general topics, one day on war, another on the sun-spots recently discovered by the astronomers, another on marriage, a brilliant subject at this period . . . Mme de Rambouillet wanted her alcove to be a place for pleasure, not a school that was ruled by pedagogues. That was why she let the young enjoy themselves as the fancy took them . . . She encouraged them by her example, for she herself liked to mystify her friends . . . From 1638 to 1643, the Hôtel de Rambouillet became the place where daily life offered more delights than anywhere else in the world. It was spent in balls, collations, entertainments mingled with conversations pearled with laughter. (Emile Magne)

By 1648, when the Fronde brought about the disappearance of this 'paradise of wit and gallantry', a great work had been accomplished. It is not true, as people are too ready to believe, that Mme de Rambouillet had been a bluestocking; it is still less true that she had inspired that preciousness which originated in several bad novels and a manual of conversation, the *Marguerites Françaises ou fleurs de bien dire*, which appeared in 1625. On the other hand she had allowed writers to win public esteem; she had imposed on behaviour and language that *bienséance* which was to transform the manners and even the mentality of the French élite.

Although the social classes had changed little since the preceding epoch, they all found themselves, by a singular phenomenon, in opposition to the power of the monarchy and to its formidable representative, Richelieu.

'To humble the pride of the Great' was one of the three main points in his programme, from the time when the Cardinal entered the Council. Two years later (1626), the nobility hatched their first plot and began a struggle which was to continue even after the death of their enemy.

Richelieu retorted by delivering three cruel blows in the form of three Edicts: the first prohibited luxury of dress; the second, remarkably strict, was aimed at the duel, and thus deprived them of their favourite sport, which was also a perennial exhibition of strength and audacity; the third ordained the destruction of the strongholds, so to take from them, as it were, the cuirass and palladium.

The noblemen took up the challenge. They redoubled their magnificence, and the most famous duellist, Montmorency-Boutteville, came back specially from Flanders to fight the Marquis de Beuvron in the middle of the Place Royale. Public opinion was all on his side, but his head fell all the same in the Place de Grève, and so did that of his second, des Chapelles; however single combats only became yet more fashionable now that they had been outlawed.

The strongholds crumbled and were never restored. Throughout the provinces a long line of ruins replaced the fortresses which had perpetuated feudalism. Deprived of his towers, the nobleman lost his protective authority over the countryside, his powers of jurisdiction, the means of intimidating the King and declaring war on him. He lost the ability to set himself, armed and threatening, outside the sovereign state. It was the end of an age, and people were to regret it, as they always regret a glorious past.

Some leading critics have claimed that the origins of decadence lay in the destruction of the secular framework, the withering-up of local life and in the death of particularism.

Whilst it is true that centralization, carried to extremes, was to have unfortunate consequences, the real fault lay with the patricians, who, unlike the more constructive English aristocracy, had not ceased, since the Hundred Years' War, to foment troubles, discord, and foreign interference.

The nobility rebelled again and again during the reign of Louis XIII, and the scaffolds where so many of them perished still did not daunt them. On the death of Richelieu, they hoped to achieve their revenge; but then, finally disillusioned, they joined the parliamentarians in the Fronde, a last struggle against the régime.

The Fronde, which was to devastate France and lead the Spaniard to the gates of Paris, was conducted with astonishing frivolity. The nobility showed itself ineffective, selfish and trivial. The ladies played a capital part: La Grande Mademoiselle, Mmes de Longueville, de Chevreuse and de Chatillon, the Princesse Palatine, among many others, enjoyed themselves grotesquely at the expense of the State, thanks to the freedom accorded to aristocratic behaviour. Reviewing troops, in unbelievable costumes, firing cannons, joining their love-affairs to their politics, dragging their lovers first into one camp, then into another, they gaily created incredible havoc. Thus the nobility stood self-condemned and in them a vital stream of energy dried up.

Richelieu has been accused of favouring lawyers to the detriment of swordsmen, but this was not altogether true: he had to struggle against a bourgeoisie among whom protestants had disseminated republican ideas. The bourgeois controlled the administration of Paris, and had a veritable army at its disposal, the bourgeois militia, of sixteen regiments comprising 30,000 men. Parliament was a formidable power, and it did not countenance absolutism.

Richelieu's tactics consisted in destroying the unity of the bourgeoisie by establishing distinctions between the functionaries and the tradesmen. The urban magistracies ceased to be elective, and became venal. Richelieu was careful how he dealt with the bourgeois for he intended to keep them out of politics. He did not altogether succeed, since it was the parliamentarians and the people of Paris who later gave the signal for the Fronde. The austere red-robed Councillors showed themselves little wiser than the lace-collared dandies. There was naturally discord between them, and it was the Prince de Condé who finally ordered a massacre of parliamentarians.

As for the peasants, the death of Henri IV had been a disaster for them. After the demands of the regency of Marie des Médicis, they had had to bear the crushing burden of politics conducted in the grand manner. Louis XIII and Richelieu did not hesitate, in fact, to inflict real martyrdom on them in order to set France at the head of the Western world. Every year, war and the massive expenses of diplomacy required an increase in taxes and, nearly every year, provoked revolts in the provinces. Richelieu ordered the intendants and 'all-purpose judges' to repress the rebels without pity. Men were broken on the wheel, hanged, their goods confiscated, or imprisoned, but still they did not submit. In 1639 a particularly stringent measure, the joint fiscal liability of the inhabitants of each parish, set Normandy ablaze. The 'Barefooted' cut the throats of the tax-collectors and committed other misdeeds. They had to be suppressed by arms before the survivors were passed to the executioner. Corneille, writing *Cinna*, pleaded in vain for clemency in his province.

In 1640, France was great and victorious, but most citizens knew only the depths of poverty. Gaston of Orleans, the King's brother, wrote to him:

Less than a third of your subjects in the provinces eat ordinary bread, another third lives solely on oat bread, and the remaining third is not only reduced to begging, but languishes in such lamentable want that some actually die of hunger, the others just sustain themselves on acorns, grass and such like as if they were animals. And among these the least to be pitied eat only bran and blood which they pick out of the streams in the slaughter-houses.

The Frenchman of the years 1600–60 would have disconcerted us by his small stature, his precocity, his physical and nervous stamina, his love of fighting, his prodigious appetite and unshakable convictions. If we follow him from his birth to his death, he will give us some surprises.

Though the birth of a child occurred almost yearly in most families, it was still celebrated extravagantly. In her scented, sumptuous 'childbed room', the noble mother lay on a bed of antique style decorated with paintings; she wore a garment embroidered with gold, and lined with sable. Every Sunday before her churchgoing, she changed her attire. Visitors abounded. The 'gossip parties of women in childbed' had become proverbial, they had already furnished material for a book.

During this period the nurse rocked the new-born child in its cradle and sang it ditties which were often bawdy. If the child had teething trouble she rubbed its gums with a finger coated with honey, butter and the brains of a hare and a viper. The remedy for bed-wetting was more alarming still: it was porcupine meat. Children who survived their infancy were strong indeed.

Sons of the nobility were privately baptized at their birth, commoners made the ceremony a pretext for feasting which ended in a carousal at the tavern, where they soon forgot the unfortunate baby who sometimes paid very dearly for such rejoicings.

Boys remained in the hands of the women until they were seven, but even so their treatment was not gentle. Parents were careful to avoid pampering their children, who were submitted from infancy to rigorous discipline, and taught absolute obedience. Girls were sent to a convent. After a few years the adolescent learned that either she was to marry a stranger, or that she had to take the veil in order to preserve intact her eldest brother's inheritance. The life of nuns was usually quite short.

Schoolboys suffered in the colleges. They rose at four in the morning, and worked until eight o'clock at night. Two recreations and one mass were their only respites. Little heating, little food and that little very bad. Discipline was barbaric: Montaigne had written, and it was to remain true until the eighteenth century: '[In the colleges] you hear nothing but the cries of tortured children and the cries of masters drunk with anger, guiding them with a terrible face, and with whips in their hands.' Such discipline was of course relaxed in the case of the heirs of great families.

The colleges in which Latin was taught were able to obtain brilliant results. There was no lack of boys who, like Henri de Mesmes, could 'dispute and harangue in public' from the age of twelve and recite their Homer from end to end. Thus the humanities and the cult of the Ancients prepared the generations of the Great Century.

Young noblemen who were not destined for the Church would leave the university at the age of fifteen, and enter the Academy of M. de Pluvinel, later that of M. de Benjamin. There they learned equitation and fencing (the pillars of patrician education), tilting at the ring, the quintain, the subtle art of the courtier.

Children were often betrothed to each other at the age of seven, in every class of society. The marriage of the time was essentially a *mariage de raison*, a business marriage dependant upon the future bride and bride-groom's submission to their parents' choice, and upon the woman's submission to marital custom. However, there also existed secret marriages, about which Church and Parliament argued for a long time. In 1639 the victory of the clergy was marked by an ordinance which codified the somewhat fluid rules. It demanded publication of the banns by the curé, and the presence of four witnesses who were entrusted, with him, to receiving the consent of both parties. The Church did, however, admit the binding nature of the contract, the nullity of which could mean the nullity of the marriage. The dowry, rarely comprising real estate, always included furniture and a trousseau. Since the end of the sixteenth century the legal mortgage had become general; this was designed to protect the dowry against the future husband's extravagance.

The woman found herself, according to the Latin phrase, 'in the hands of her husband', who was to 'cherish' her, but also 'keep her in fear'. Often, in the provinces, she addressed him in the third person, served him at the table at which she would not dare to sit. The husband had the same rights over her as he had over a daughter who was under age, among them the right to strike her, to silence her, and even to relegate her to the convent. And yet the Frenchwoman of the time was not a feeble creature. She appeared an Amazon to the eyes of Italian and Spanish women, who were prisoners of an inflexible jealousy. Many women hunted tirelessly, broke horses, handled the rapier, the boar-spear and the arquebus with skill. It is recorded that there were not more than three happy marriages in Brittany. Unhappy marriages were unhappy to such a degree that the sudden deaths of the husbands were often considered to be crimes committed by their wives.

Love remained extra-marital.

In spite of the civil wars the splendour of interiors had constantly increased since François I. A bourgeois whose grandfather hardly owned two silver cups could boast of a mass of goblets, plates, ewers and basins made of the same metal. There were many houses whose furniture would dazzle us today. On the other hand few of us, even among the humble, would accept their lack of comfort.

Both in the castle and in the one-roomed lodging the bed was the centre of the house. There were still huge 'couches', about four yards broad, but most of them were less than three yards. These monuments, raised on two steps, flanked with pillars and curtains, surmounted by a 'ceiling' or pavilion, heightened by a headboard, were made for receiving a numerous company. The master, receiving a guest of distinction, would readily ask him to share his bed, even if his wife was also to lie in it. And often the dog came and joined them. There were occasions when a bed gave shelter to a whole plebian family.

However, the bedroom and the bed were, first and foremost, the wife's domain. It was there that a woman spent the best part of her time, for the salon, like the dining-room, was unknown. From the height of her couch the lady reigned supreme. She received the visits and compliments occasioned by the consummation of her marriage, the births of her children, and her widowhood. At less solemn moments, she listened to poems and prattled with the beaux, who could hide quickly, if need arose, in the folds of the curtains. The big *ruelle* was distinguished from the little one, which was kept for intimate conversations and for the servants.

Near the patrician bed stood the dresser, proudly laden with the principal riches of the family: silver plate, goldsmith's work, treasurers of every kind. The dresser was carried from room to room as each one became the reception place, as a guarantee of family and fortune. On certain religious festivals it even shone in front of the house. The bourgeois contented himself with a sideboard in which he hoarded his treasures.

Seats were very high and hard, and were used mainly for decoration. They were set out against the wall, and hardly ever moved. The armchair was a stately exception. People used stools and footstools, without backs or arms. At court it was only the duchesses who had the honour of stools. The other ladies sat in the oriental manner on cushions and hassocks.

The commode was not the least elegant piece among all this furniture. Sometimes it was decorated, and edged with rich materials. Mme d'Albret's was covered with green cloth, that of the Duc de Guise with crimson satin, Mme de Montglat's with red serge, and the princes' commode was surmounted by a canopy. So were the 'perforated stools' and the 'pissing chairs' of the Duc de Lorraine and his wife, which were covered with velvet which bore their coat-of-arms. This is not surprising, since the nobility readily gave audiences while they were occupying this seat. Such was the case at the fatal interview between Henri III and Jacques Clément. The custom was to continue until the days of Louis XIV.

The chamber-pot was rarely found. There were none in the hostelries, or in the colleges, or in the majority of castles where the fireplace would fulfil the purpose. Possessing a 'retreat' of one's own was a luxury one was careful not to hide.

How can one talk of the pleasures without beginning with those of the table?

Joseph Duchesne, a doctor, forbade the morning *déjeuner*. He recommended that dinner should take place between ten and eleven and that the company should then 'remain at table for a good half-hour at least in pleasant talk. Supper at six. Then, at nine in summer, it will be time to light candles and to think of going to bed at ten'.

This relaxation, this moment of pleasure which every busy man was supposed to enjoy each day, was provided by the meal: the meal which, even among the peasants, kept a kind of solemnity. The pictures of Le Nain are eloquent in this respect. The naturalist Belon admired the 'majesty' of the French at table.

As everyone knows, the menus were alarming. What would they include? Let us forget the wretched bread-soup of the country-folk, the distasteful whale fat with peas, called *craspois*, or *Lenten blubber*, the principal food of the poor at this time. The rich favoured thick soups, made of meat and fish boiled with vegetables (there were four kinds under Henri II, one hundred and twenty-three at the time of the Fronde); stews were hardly less numerous. If gourmets generally avoided peacock, swan and heron, which had been promoted to the rank of decorative elements, they delighted in guinea-fowl, turkeys, chickens (discovered during the sixteenth century), crows with cabbage (a much-prized dish), innumerable birds, and, from about 1560, young game which had long been disdained (partridge, hare, etc . . .). They ate most kinds of fish; salmon, soles, turbot, turtle, skate, herrings (which were much sought-after), and prawns. Also they ate snails, fried and boiled and skewered; frogs, snakes and hedgehogs; oysters but rarely. Vegetables were scorned except for aphrodisiac truffles and artichokes, turnips, and cabbages which were said to prevent baldness, give milk to nurses, and to cure asthma, rabies, gout and paralysis.

The cheeses – over which *brie* maintained its supremacy – were much appreciated, and so were plums and apricots (both were popularised in the course of the century), cherries, strawberries, peaches, pears, and apples which housewives also used to scent their linen; however it would have been considered unseemly to munch an apple on Christmas Day, because of the misfortune of Adam and Eve.

The vines of the rue Beautreille bore a wonderful grape similar to the famous vineyards of Thomery. Raspberries, those 'fruits of the briar', were left for the peasants.

There were countless different kinds of cakes, but no puddings, except for 'snow cream', the ancestor of *oeufs à la neige*. Sugar remained a luxury. When it figured on some noble table, even the meat was sprinkled with it. The poor knew only honey.

Let us look at the order of a dinner with people of quality. Before the guests arrival, the table was set with food, which was laid out in covered dishes (not to keep them warm, but because of the old fear of poison). Hence the expression 'lay the table'. The custom of washing one's hands was hardly respected, except on the occasion of solemn feasts. Scented water was then passed round. If this were lacking it was replaced by wine.

> At this point people wash themselves according to their rank,
> And each sits down upon a chair or settles on a bench
> According to his merit, or his office, or his birth[1]

The host took his place at the head of the table, as he does to-day, and the chaplain blessed it. The benedicite was recited.

Silver plates had quite recently taken the place of trenchers. A spoon was provided for each person, but two or three knives had to suffice for the whole company. There were no forks, and glasses were arranged on a sideboard. Anyone who wished to drink would call a valet who filled a glass, presented it, and replaced it when it was empty, so that it did not change hands.

If hand-towels belonged to the future, table-napkins were in regular use, cunningly folded in the shape of fruits, birds or ships. The guests all tied them round their necks. 'Knotting the ends of one's napkin' presented serious difficulties: hence the expression to be applied to a precarious financial balance: 'making two ends meet'.

The napkin was changed with every course. At the *entremets* the table-cloth was changed, too. Very understandable customs among people who were used to eating with their fingers. The Prince de Guéméné usually made the sauces spurt up to his diamond-studded hat. Gluttons were known sometimes to bite their fingers.

Knives had ebony handles in Lent, ivory handles on Easter Day, half-ebony, half-ivory at Pentecost. The gold- and silver-plate, admirably wrought, bore the family coat-of-arms. It represented the 'reserve', the 'safe investment' to guard against financial surprises. Alas, the needy kings did not hesitate to requisition it.

[1] Mathurin Régnier: *Satires*

The Domestic Scene

Frying pancakes on Shrove Tuesday.

Above. The fashionable courtier bathes, and has his hair cut and curled.

Left. Wide-brimmed boots, huge hats and extravagantly cut clothes were the height of elegance in the 1620s.

Below. A German cartoon of 1628 attacks the *A la Modo Monsiers* and their mistresses, who ape French and Italian fashions.

Top. The schoolroom. The girls play with their toys, while the boys repeat their lessons encouraged by the master's admonitions, and his birch.

Bottom. Spring, in the castle of the rich, and in the farmer's cottage.

Frances Howard, Duchess of Richmond, after Van Dyck. She was celebrated for her beauty and her vanity, and was married three times. One of her suitors, Lord Seymour, Earl of Hertford, killed himself when he was rejected.

Rubens's painting of Hélène Fourmont in a fur wrap. Rubens married her when she was sixteen, and he was fifty-three.

Venetia Stanley, 'a most beeautifull desireable creature', who became the mistress of the Earl of Dorset, and later married Sir Kenelm Digby. Painting by Van Dyck.

Rembrandt, *The Rat Catcher*.

Above. Dutch painters frequently drew
attention to the miseries of patients
undergoing medical treatment.
Engraving after A. Brouwer.

Below. Velazquez's painting of a woman
frying eggs.

A peasant woman with a distaff, and children who have returned from a bird-nesting expedition, painted by Louis Le Nain.

Georges De La Tour, *Woman with a Flea*.

Henri IV encouraged the making of earthenware and instigated many factories both in Paris and in the provinces, and gave statutes to the corporation of earthenware-makers. In the last years of his reign there appeared whole services in earthenware. Unfortunately they were largely destroyed by the carelessness of pages and the brutality of lackeys.

There was no fixed order for the procession of dishes. In principle it began with the soups, fricassés, hashes and salads. Then followed the roasts and the boiled meats. If it was a feast, there came the *entremets*, that is to say a great bird decorated with its feathers, and resplendent with gilt beak and claws. There followed dessert, fruits, cheeses and sweet-meats.

People commonly challenged each other to drinking contests and failure to respond was considered an unforgivable offence.

A custom which was very widespread consisted in putting a toasted crust of bread at the bottom of the glass. It was called toasted, *toustée* or *tostée* (from the verb *torrere*). The glass was passed from hand to hand until it reached the guest in whose honour they were drinking. It was he who ate the toast. Hence the modern expression 'drink a toast'. By 1600 people had already stopped speaking of carousing and carousals, they spoke instead of clinking glasses and drinking hard.

When death arrived, there were no papers or funeral letters, and criers went round the city announcing the news. If the deceased was a man of importance, they 'cried the body', mentioning the day and time of the funeral service. Since the sixteenth century, the criers had formed a corporation which corresponded more or less to our funeral companies.

The poor had to be content with the common coffin which came back empty from the cemetery and received another corpse the next day. Even worse was the destiny of the poor wretches who had died in the workhouse: they were buried during the night, sewn up in a coarse cloth. Their cemetery, the *Cimetière de Clamart*, belonged to the Hôtel-Dieu and was situated in the Faubourg Saint-Marcel.

The nobility and the rich made their final journey with great pomp and circumstance. The criers provided the hearse which, in the days of Henry IV, was called a *corbillard* because the undertakers' men were called *corbeaux*. Until then the word *corbillard* meant the barge that went to Corbeil. A multitude of poor followed the funeral procession, torch in hand. The family dressed them in black from head to foot, but no woman ever appeared at a burial.

After the funeral ceremony a banquet was held, even amongst the poor. At the feast which followed the obsequies of one distinguished bourgeois, his desolate friends drank 160 pints of wine, and devoured twenty dozen rolls, six carps, six perch, three large pike, five soles, 200 mussels, 150 crayfish, thirty-five fresh eggs, twenty pounds of butter and innumerable cakes.

9 Italy

As Venice grew increasingly decadent, the political rôle of Italy became more and more restricted, but she remained an occasional battlefield for France and Spain. No social movement, or evolution in manners disturbed the sleep into which the country had fallen since the eclipse of her former brilliance. Artistic achievement, whilst still lively, was only a shadow of its former self, and great as her prestige still was, it was founded on the works of the Renaissance, which continued to attract pilgrims from the rest of Europe.

In the face of increasing opposition, the Popes continued to intrigue, both at home and abroad, for the extension and safeguarding of their spiritual domain. Matters were further complicated for them by the system of nepotism which characterized the Holy See, and from which the individual popes obtained great personal benefit. It was in fact accepted that the Pope's family should govern the Church and gain great wealth from it. The cardinal-nephew was entitled to exercise the functions of a prime minister. Each pontificate therefore created its own dynasty whose interests were identified with the church.

In spite of the purity of his life, the elevation of his mind and the scrupulousness of his religion, Pope Paul v Borghese, elected in 1605, gave remarkably full rein to dynastic abuses. A former lawyer and advocate, he had determined to keep what he called 'the immunities of the Church, the privileges of God'.

Yet Paul v had certain merits. He grew anxious about the poverty in the Roman countryside and he improved the lot of the peasants. He fought against crime and tried to keep the dependants of great families close to the land, even although those families committed, with impunity, many excesses. He was much concerned with the religious instruction of the faithful, and kept a close watch on the recruitment of the clergy; he tried to force the priests to live according to the rules laid down by the Council of Trent (but his success in this was only partial).

He obliged each religious order to create a chair in Hebrew, Latin and Greek, and at the same time considerably enriched the Vatican Library. It was his especial glory to complete the work on St Peter's Basilica, a task which he had entrusted to Carlo Maderna. His name shone on the frontispiece of the great temple of Christianity in which the spirit of the Renaissance was embodied.

Gregory xv Ludovisi, assisted by a cardinal-nephew of twenty-five, left considerable achievements after a reign of only two years (1621–3). It was he who, in the *Æterni Patris Filius* bull, settled the election of Popes according to the rules which are still in force, at least in essentials. For centuries the Papacy had struggled to free itself from imperial domination. Up to the twelfth century the election had been valid only with the consent of the clergy, the people and the Emperor. The third Lateran Council had declared that the vote of two-thirds of the cardinals was sufficient, but this measure had not prevented the deplorable compromises of the period of schisms, and the influence of these still persisted. Gregory xv defined the three possible ways of election: by inspiration (adoration or acclamation), by compromise, or by scrutiny and accession. He would have liked to free the Sacred College from external influences, but he could not prevent the Catholic powers from exercising a right of veto which was not to be abolished until early in the twentieth century.

Since Paul iii, successive Popes had created numerous institutions for the purpose of training missionaries to meet the expansion of the Old World into the New. Gregory xv founded the Congregation of Propaganda (*De Propaganda Fide*) and a College of Propaganda. The 'provinces' placed under the jurisdiction of the Congregation included not only lands abroad, but European countries pledged to the Reform. The Capuchin Jérôme de Narni, a fiery preacher, was the apostle of this enterprise.

Gregory xv, a former pupil of the Jesuits, canonized St Ignatius Loyola and St Francis Xavier. He did likewise for St Helen, St Philip Neri and St Isidor. The example of this debilitated old man, tortured by his liver and touching in his piety, greatly enhanced the prestige of the Church.

One could not say as much for Urban viii Barberini (1623–44). His nephews and other relations made such use of nepotism that even the Romans, who were thought to be inured to this abuse, found their indignation roused. '*Quod non fecerunt Barbari, faciunt Barberini* (what the Barbarians did not do, the Barberini do),' became a popular saying. The Pope was not afraid to satisfy his avid relations by laying hands on the Duchy of Castro, a fief of the Farnese, and excommunicating the Duke (1641). There followed a war which ended with the mediation of France and of Mazarin, whose protector Urban viii had been. The Pope was forced to surrender Castro. This completed the ruin of a temporal authority already shaken after many defeats; it carried the unpopularity of the Barberini to its extreme, but it did not humble their pride.

It may be said, in their defence, that the bees on their armorial bearings decorate some of the finest monuments in Rome. The Barberini Palace, erected at such great expense, was a centre of intellectual and political life. Bernini had begun to build the colonnade of St Peter's Square with its gigantic canopy on bronze columns to shelter the tomb of the Prince of the Apostles. Rome was more than ever a land of the arts from which a Nicolas Poussin or a Claude Lorrain could hardly tear himself away. Urban VIII himself was both an aesthete and a scholar, and commissioned a reform of the breviary which satisfied the humanists better than the theologians.

It has been remarked of this imperious and indecisive Pontiff, that he was the most unfortunate of all the Popes; the advent of Galileo during his term of office was characteristic of his ill-luck.

On 19 February 1616 the Holy Office had condemned two of the famous astronomer's theories. The proposition according to which the sun remained stationary was 'foolish and absurd as philosophy, and strictly heretical'; the theory which denied that the earth was the centre of the world 'deserved the same censure from the philosophical as from the theological point of view'. Galileo submitted, but the controversy continued.

Urban VIII, who was a friend of the learned man, overwhelmed him with honours. This emboldened Galileo to publish *The Dialogue*, in 1632, in which he blamed his detractors. In spite of a promise in exchange for which he had obtained the *imprimatur*, he failed to correct certain passages, and these provoked the Holy Office into action. Once again it was a question of the movement of the earth. Galileo was summoned to Rome, and he made the journey in the Grand Duke of Tuscany's coach, unescorted by the myrmidons of the law. So far from being thrown into prison, he stayed at the Florentine Embassy. He submitted to the tribunal as he had done in 1616. He was sentenced to recite the seven penitentiary psalms for three years and to suffer imprisonment; the Pope commuted this into house arrest, first at the Embassy, then at Siena, and finally in the Villa Arcetro near Florence. Galileo continued his work and on his deathbed he received the papal benediction. As for the tortures which the Inquisition inflicted on him, and the famous phrase: '*E pur si muove!* (But it *does* move!)': they belong to legend.

It is none the less true that the Church was irrevocably opposed to the new Enlightenment in which it, rightly, discerned a grave threat to its authority. Just as it had laid an interdict on Galileo's theory, the Holy See protested against the Treaty of Westphalia, and condemned Jansenism. But in vain: and equally vain was the hope of the reformers to eradicate nepotism in the body of the Holy See.

Innocent x Pamphili, whose election was due to the Barberini, began well, by dispossessing the former favourites, who fled to Mazarin, but then himself fell prey to the intrigues of his sister-in-law, Olimpia Maidalchini, who soon inspired the aphorism: *'olim pia, nunc impia'* ('once pious, now impious'). No effort to remove her succeeded. Donna Olimpia dominated the Holy Father; she distributed the funds of the Church; cardinals and ambassadors, not to mention lesser personages, had all to win her good graces. This scheming woman, who was above all determined to grow rich, held all the strings of papal politics in her own hands.

When Innocent died on 7 January 1655, Donna Olimpia, who had been charged by the Curia with making the necessary arrangements, abandoned the body for three days, failed to order a coffin, and refused to pay for the funeral, protesting that she was only a poor widow. A canon had to pay the bearers of the coffin out of his own pocket. 'A great lesson for the Pontiffs!' the chronicler Palladivini was to write. 'It teaches them what they can expect from relations for whom they have compromised their conscience and their honour!'

Whilst the other European countries were being revolutionized by the new Enlightment, Italy stagnated except in the field of art. Caravaggio, a duellist and frequentor of gaming-houses, had astonished and even scandalized people with his intense realism, and his novel use of light in the composition of his paintings. A whole new school derived from his work, including such disciples as the brothers Le Nain, and Georges De La Tour. In architecture and sculpture, the Cavaliere Bernini, having imposed his mark on the Eternal City, continued to instruct the Western world.

10 England

When James came south as Elizabeth's successor, he was struck by the country's prosperous look after his rougher Scotland. He thought he could be as lavish as he liked, but soon learned his error. Within a year he was in trouble, and decided to abandon direct administration and return to the system whereby private contractors bought up the right of customs-collection, repaying themselves from receipts and keeping any surplus as profits. A new schedule (excluding some previously sold items such as wine and currants) was drawn up and sold in block to a London syndicate. Meanwhile, Cecil set himself to reduce the Crown's debt. In 1610 James almost succeeded in making a bargain with Parliament, agreeing to end the Court of Wards and certain impositions such as Purveyance in return for £200,000 a year; but the scheme broke down, partly through his demand that officers of the Court of Wards be compensated. Next year Cecil tried forced loans from individuals; commissions took up the task of retrenchment. Cranfield, a London apprentice who had married his master's daughter and risen through trade and usury, entered the court-service and worked hard to eliminate corruption. He found that of forty-three ships in the Navy only twenty-nine were fit for sea and fourteen were completely rotten; he advised James that it was better to pay people to take the ships away than send them to the naval depots for repairs. He became Lord Treasurer in 1621; but in 1624 his economies annoyed James and his favourite Buckingham, and he fell. National debts were now a million.

By 1640 money had declined to a third of its 1540 value, but only very well-managed estates had been able to treble their income. Food-prices went on rising, wages were kept low, pauperism increased. Yet trade was active. British shipping expanded tenfold in thirty years; and even under Cromwell excise and customs revenues went on growing.

The hard-up gentry tried to rack-rent and enclose commonland. This led to the revolt of the Midlands peasantry in 1607 under Captain Pouch.

They filled the ditches, cut down the hedges, and laid open the enclosures. A pamphlet of the time declares:

The world with us of the country runs upon the old rotten wheels. For all the northern cloth that is woven in our country will scarce make a gown to keep Charity warm; she goes so a-cold. Rich men had never more money, and Covetousness had never less pity. There was never in any age more money stirring, nor never yet more stir to get money. Farmers are now slaves to racking young prodigal landlords. Those landlords are more servile slaves to their own riots and luxury.

Later Laud tried to oppose the landlords who 'devoured the people with a shepherd and a dog' (enclosed arable land and put sheep on it), but he had no effective alternative. The country-folk were often sullenly depressed or rebellious. 'I care not for constable or the King,' said a labourer in Yorkshire in 1616; at Thirsk in 1611 a constable told a Justice of the Peace that he would not go into a man's house to serve any warrant, and a tanner agreed with him, taunting the infuriated Justice that he 'would commit a pudding'; in 1633 a village blacksmith remarked, 'The Devil go with the King and all the proud pack of them, what care I?'; George Nelles of Danby was tried for 'the slanderous speeches against the Justices'.

After the Essex revolt, Cecil tried to placate both the great nobles and the gentry; he succeeded with the first, and James carried on the policy. But the lesser gentry, still largely frustrated, began idealizing the Good Days of Queen Bess. The old Queen was 'ever hard of access and very covetous in her old days', but after her death 'the Queen did seem to revive; then was her memory much magnified – such ringing of bells, such public joys and sermons in commemoration of her, the picture of her tomb painted in many churches, and in effect more solemnity and joy in memory of her coronation than was for the coming of King James.' Her Day was long kept up:

Monday being Queen Elizabeth's coronation day there were vast quantities of bonfires about town, but chief of all was at Temple Bar, over which gate Queen Elizabeth was dek't up with a Magna Charta and the Protestant religion; there was a devil in a pageant and 4 boys in surplices under him, 6 Jesuits, 4 bishops, 4 archbishops, 2 patriarchs of Jerusalem and Constantinople, several cardinals, besides Franciscans, black and grey friars; there was also a great crucific, wax candles and a bell, and 200 porters hired at 2s. a man to carry lights along with the show, which came from the Green Yard, in great order thro' Moor (or Cripple) Gate, and so along London Wall, then up Houndsditch, and so on again to Aldgate, from whence to Temple Bar, when they were disrobed and burnt. 'Tis believed there were above 100,000 spectators, and most say the King was at Townes' the goldsmith's; £10 was an ordinary price for a room at Temple Bar. (John Verney, 20 November 1679)

Here the Day was used for a political demonstration, but that could happen only because it was still cherished.

Though the City welcomed the peace with Spain that James made in 1604 and the courtiers enjoyed the influx of Spanish gold in pensions, one of the gentry said, 'Peace and law hath beggered us all.' They tried to circumvent the peace through joint-stock companies which were in part privateering ventures. The cult of Drake and the martyred Ralegh also appeared. Ralegh's *History of the World* was a best-seller, and one of Cromwell's favourite books. In 1632 Sir T. Roe, who had stood for an Elizabethan foreign policy, failed to gain the Secretaryship of State; feeling that he was now thrown back into private country-life, he compared himself to Drake's ship lying idle at Deptford.

Under James the court expanded as a place of bustling courtiers and the centre of profitable posts. Here we meet the court of the absolute monarchy in England at its fullest and most topheavy point of development. Very different from the dignified Elizabeth, James had weak legs, ungainly body, goggling eyes, and a tongue too big for his mouth. Slovenly, he wore heavy padded clothes for fear of daggers. Though shrewd and learned he lacked self-control and made an exhibition of his love of handsome young men. The terms of his self-defence are revealing:

You may be sure that I love the Earl of Buckingham more than anyone else, and more than you who are here assembled. I wish to speak in my own behalf, and not to have it thought to be a defect, for Jesus Christ did the same, and therefore I cannot be blamed. Christ had his John, and I have my George.

Once, in 1618, the dancers in a masque had become tired; James shouted, 'Why don't they dance? What did they make me come here for? Devil take you all, dance.' Buckingham restored his good-humour by springing forward and cutting a caper. The level of amusement at the court was low indeed: James would leave his dining or supping room

to witness the pastimes and fooleries performed by Sir Edward Zouch, Sir George Goring, and Sir John *Finit*. The first sung indecent songs and related tales of the same description, the former of which were written by *Finit*, who procured fiddlers as an accompaniment to Zouch; and Goring was master of the game for fooleries sometimes presenting David Droman and Archee Armstrong, the King's Fool, on the back of other fools, to tilt at one another, till they fell together by the ears; sometimes antick dances; but Sir John Millisent, who was never known before, was commended for notable fooling, and so he was the best extempore fool of them all.

Queen Anne bored an intellectual like Lady Arabella Stuart by spending her time in playing with her ladies games like *Rise, pig, and go*, or *One penny follow me*. Arabella says, 'persuaded by the princely example I was to play the child again'.

161

H

But the court was still the centre of the nation. Its function was to minister to the needs, comfort, and recreation of the king and his family; to show the world – and especially ambassadors and visiting notables – the wealth and greatness of the kingdom, and demonstrate the king's magnificence; to supply posts, prestige, rewards; to carry out the central government and provide its machinery. The great officers were the Lord Chamberlain, Lord Steward, and Master of Horse. Daily meetings of the Board of the Green Cloth ran the household, with a huge staff of sergeants, clerks, grooms, pages in such offices as the Kitchen, Pantry, Buttery, Spicery, Wafery, Ewery, Larder, Catery, Scalding House, Scullery, Bottlery, Bakehouse, Cellar, Pitcher-house, Chandlery, Confectionery, Laundry, Boiling-house, Poultry, Pastery, Woodyard.

Purveyors had the right to requisition supplies below market-prices, often on credit. Tradesmen hid their best stocks and charged high prices, as they were in danger of not getting paid at all. The Apology of the Commons in 1604 stated that the purveyors 'have rummaged and ransacked since Your Majesty's coming-in far more than under any of your royal progenitors'. The other great curse lay in the Court of Wards. Wardships were 'the ruin of almost all men's houses once in three descents'.

The courtier's first aim was a lucrative office. Most appointments were buyable. In France there was regular market for offices, and the English system worked out much the same. Unless dismissed in disgrace, a man sold his post on retiring. There were never enough posts to go round, so new posts were devised. Others were divided up, so that they were held for only a quarter of the year; but there were still not enough; so the king promised reversions, which again were saleable. A man could sell even a share in a reversion. When a functionary seemed likely to die, his office increased in price. And still the pressure of demand kept driving prices up, even to uneconomic levels.

After the offices came the monopolies. Even the Fool had one: on the clay for making pipes. Search-rights continued to cause trouble: thus, when Heron in 1619 got the patent for salting fish, he had power of entry on any suspected premises and the right to stop foreigners from fishing in adjacent seas. Even when lighthouses were needed, men were empowered to build them and exact a charge of a penny a ton on all passing ships. Another way of making money was to collect crown-debts, or to get a benevolence (an order on the Exchequer for cash), or first charges on revenues like those from the Court of Wards. A courtier could even petition for a title to sell to someone else. Failures could be forced into exile on the Continent. To take away a man's offices was to ruin him; for besides being disgraced, he was more than likely to be penniless. When Sir John Winthrop lost his post in the Court of Wards, he could not bear the shame of being unable to maintain his servants, so he sold up, and migrated to America.

James on his part raised funds by creating new knights – 838 in his first year. In Webster's comedy, Sir Fabian Scarecrow borrows the price of his title from his landlady. In April 1623 the College of Arms had to admit in a proclamation that they had lost track of the new creations. The heralds indeed were thriving on the sale of countless coats-of-arms, and pseudo-heralds enraged them by setting up in country-towns while they themselves were fighting over the allocation of duties and the division of fees. The squabbles grew so bad that the Garter King of Arms and the York Herald were locked in the Marshalsea while commissioners threw their wives and children out of Derby House. The position of Earl Marshal was revived and a Court of Chivalry convened in 1623 in the Painted Chamber at Westminster. Among the knights were an earl's barber and a man who had married one of the Queen's laundresses; the goldsmith uncle of the poet Herrick was knighted for 'making a Hole in a great diamond the King doth wear'. The principle that a man was knighted for services in the field was given up, and the carpet-knight was born. To raise yet more cash, James invented a new kind of knight, the baronet, whose title was inherited. The original cost was £1,095, but later the price sank to a quarter of that. For a while there was a pretence that the money was to be used for colonizing Ulster.

James also reversed Elizabeth's attitude to the nobility. He readmitted the nobles on whom she had frowned. In the years 1603–29 the peerage was doubled by the elevation of seventy-two commoners (forty-six by James, twenty-six by Charles). Almost all were office holders. 'I can make a peer,' James jested, 'but I cannot make a gentleman.' Most of the great lords still aimed at a medieval status, keeping little courts of their own, entertaining grandly, and hunting on their parklands. In the whole court-area there was no ethic of thrift. To attempt to save was to 'live like a hog'. The correct thing was to 'maintain a port to the height' of what a man's income permitted. Heirs wanted, not a well cared-for estate, but the chance to rise through education, influence, and patronage. Sometimes parents went too far. The ninth Earl of Northumberland said that on his father's death he was

so well left for moveables that I was not worth a fire-shovel or a pair of tongs; what was left me was wainscot, or things riveted with nails; for wives are commonly great scratchers after their husband's death, if things be loose.

Sons likewise could be hard towards parents. When in 1633 the Countess of Suffolk absconded to get out of paying her debts:

Sergeants-at-arms seek her daily, but she cannot be found. Her eldest son is so far from taking care of her, though it be his own case, that he thinks not of freeing her, no, nor of paying his own debts, which will eate out his inheritance.

Let us glance at a courtier's day under James. Most people rose at six, swallowed some beer and meat stew, and set about their work. But our courtier rose some four hours later, dressed, frizzled and curled his hair, powdered and turned it 'this way and that, about his eares, continuing thus in his bedchamber, even till noone at least'. Then he went to dine at a table, with friends or at least with the gentleman who acted as his paid companion and lickspittle. In fine weather he might be rowed by some of the rowdy watermen who thronged the Thames over to the south bank to watch baitings or see a play: showing himself on a stool on the stage and rising at the moment most likely to disturb the performance. On rainy days, he might go to Whitehall Palace: snatching a chance to bow to the King in the Presence Chamber or slipping off to the western section to watch birds fight and kill one another in the high-roofed octagonal Cockpit, to play tennis in a covered court, to bowl in an indoor alley; to lounge and chat in the Matted Gallery, or to try some gaming. Then if possible he found a friend with a court-post who took him to sup free at his mess, at about half past five. Again he tried gaming, with the groom-porter keeping records of wagers. At nine began the Order of All Night. The King went to bed, the doors of the Privy Chamber were locked, the guard was mounted in the Great Chamber and the pass-word for the night given out. Our courtier hurried out, perhaps to his Westminster lodgings, more likely to the chamber of his perfumed mistress or to a *bagnio*. Then he staggered home, lighted by a page with a burning link.

Whitehall was a rambling warren of royal Chambers, privy rooms, galleries, and quarters for games and amusements including tennis, bowling, tilting and baiting. James had the Earl of Montgomery and his bride bed in the Council Chamber so that he could stroll in next morning to tease them. Beefeaters in the Guard Room did 'nothing but tell Tales, savoure the beaverage, keepe a great fire, and carry up Dishes, wherein their fingers would bee sometimes before they came to the King's Table'. The Terrace, a balustraded wooden roof, looked down on the Preaching Place with a pulpit in the middle: here in December 1604, during a masque, a lewd lady was 'surprised at her business' and carried to the Porter's Lodge. It was so rotten that some years later it collapsed as the Spanish Ambassador was being ushered out from the Council Chamber; some lords were injured, but he was dragged to safety by yeomen of the guard. Gaming was high. In 1623 Lord Howard de Walden lost £500 and then two days later £1,500. Bets were laid on everything possible. When Cecil died, large sums were laid on his successor.

No bailiff could make an arrest for debt in the precincts; indeed nobles could not be arrested for it anywhere. Law at court was the concern of the Knight Marshal with his Marshalsea Court. Thefts however were common, made by servants and hanger-bys. As life grew less honourable, so an obsessive concern with honour grew up. The King was the fountain-head of honour and to lose his presence was to be damned. Lords made their own honour-fetishes. Viscount Montague instructed a Clerk of the Kitchen to see that no servant insulted his lordship by turning his back on the joint roasted for his table. Lord Sanquhar went to much trouble in arranging the murder of a fencing-master who accidentally put out one of his eyes. There were continual affrays after drink, with no qualms about taking advantage of an unready man. Sir Jermyn Poole attacked an inmate of Gray's Inn before he could draw his weapon, injured him in three or four places, and cut off three of his fingers; the other man then leaped on him and bit off part of his nose, which he carried off with him. Courtiers scorned the citizens and often fought with the watch.

James, timid at weapons, prohibited duels in the precincts. The duel itself was a recent innovation, replacing with a certain code and equality of chances the power of the grandee to beat or kill a poor neighbour with his bullies and retainers – though offended husbands still often hired desperadoes to thrash a wife's lover near to death. In 1618 Sir H. Tufton was fined £4,000 for bastinadoing a man suspected of being his wife's paramour. Defenders of the duel argued that it remedied insults and injuries not covered by law; and some determined duellists even went abroad to fight. However, there were duels enough at home. James instructed his attorney-general to start a campaign against them and two proclamations were issued, threatening with death even those who went to fight on Calais Sands. This was some deterrent to the higher ranks. Court ladies had their own way of attacking one another. The Earl of Worcester remarked that 'the plotting and malice among them is such, that I think envy hath tied an invisible snake about most of their necks to sting one another to death'.

Every day twenty-four dishes were served for the King and Queen, with a minimum of thirty when dining in state. Great officers lived almost as well. Lord Hay introduced the ante-dinner: a tall board loaded with choice viands. Seven dishes a day were served in the mess of the Clerks of the Signet and to those of the Privy Council. Clothes were heavy and finicky: immense pleated breeches hanging from a wasp-waist into which the doublet curved, heavy brocaded cloak, stiff elaborate ruff, tasseled earrings and shoe-buckles hidden under a mass of lace-roses. We can imagine such a gallant taking 'a full survay of himselfe, from the highest sprig in his feathers, to the lowest spangle that shines in his Shoo-string'. Display was everything. At the banquet for the Emperor's Ambassador there was represented in sugar-works 'a complete army of horse and foot, with drum, ensigns, &c.' Six cartloads of plate worth £700,000 came from the Tower. When the Countess of Salisbury lay in, £14,000 was spent on white satin embroidered with gold, silver, and pearl for the room.

Questions of precedence were paramount. When the Queen died, the funeral was long delayed, in part through fights between three countesses as to who was to be the chief mourner; (there was also a shortage of money, her French gentleman and Danish maid were said to have made off with huge sums, and the King had given Buckingham handfuls of her jewels). Sycophancy also was ingrained: Cecil told Parliament that James was not only the wisest of kings 'but the very image of an angel, that doth bring good tidings and puts us in the fruition of all good things'. When James backed the Court of High Commission in its claim to be entitled to force witnesses to answer all questions whatsoever, the Bishop of London cried out, 'Almighty God, of his singular mercy hath given us such a king, as since Christ's time, the like hath not been seen.' When James disputed with the Puritan Dr Reynolds:

he rather used upbraidings then arguments; and told them they wanted to strip Christ again, and bid them *away with their snivelling.* Moreover he wished those who would take away the surplice *might want linen for their own breech*! The bishops seemed much pleased and said his Majesty spoke by the power of inspiration. I wist not what they mean; but the spirit was rather foul-mouthed. (Harrington)

Behaviour was often disorderly. More than once we hear of courtiers rushing from a masque and crashing banquet-tables down. The Danish visit of 1606 was a time of hard-drinking, of which Sir John Harrington has left a lively account:

The sports began each day in such manner and such sorte, as well nigh persuade me of Mahomets paradise. We had women, and indeed wine too, of such plenty, as would have astonished each sober beholder . . . The ladies abandon their sobriety, and are seen to roll about in intoxication.

[After dinner one day a representation of Solomon's Temple and the Coming of the Queen of Sheba] The Lady who did play the Queens part, did carry most precious gifts to both their Majesties; but, forgetting the steppes arising to the canopy, overset her caskets into his Danish Majesties lap, and fell at his feet, tho I rather think it was in his face. Much was the hurry and confusion; cloths and napkin were at hand, to make all clean. His Majesty then got up and would dance with the Queen of Sheba; but he fell down and humbled himself before her, and was carried to an inner chamber and laid on a bed of state; which was not a little defiled with the presents of the Queen which had been bestowed on his garments; such as wine, cream, jelly, beverage, cakes, spices, and other good matters. The entertainment and show went forward, and most of the presenters went backward, or fell down; wine did so occupy their upper chambers. Now did appear, in rich dress, Hope, Faith, and Charity: Hope did essay to speak, but wine rendered her endeavours so feeble that she withdraw, and hoped the King would excuse her brevity: Faith was then all alone, for I am certain she was not joyned with good works, and left the court in a staggering condition: Charity came to the King's feet, and seemed to cover the multitude of sins her sisters had committed; and in some sorte she made obeysance and brought giftes, but said she would return home again, as there was no gift which heaven had not already given his Majesty. She then returned to Hope and Faith, who were both sick and spewing in the lower hall.

The King's year was much taken up with hunting and progresses. Whenever possible he rushed to his lodges at Royston and Newmarket, often inconveniencing his ministers. He hunted in a suit as 'green as the grass he trod on, with a feather in his cap, and a horn instead of a sword at his side', and loved beasts 'better than men, and took more delight in them', we are told, 'and was more tender over the life of a stag than a man'. When in 1604 the Archbishop of York wrote to Cecil against the harsh treatment of poachers, 'both that poor men's corn may be less spoiled, and other his Majesty's subjects more spared', the King cried in fury, 'it was the foolishest letter he ever read'. The ladies were given their chance to kill with crossbows the deer that were chased across screen-ambushes; and once the Queen, shooting at a deer, hit the King's favourite hound. He raged, but on learning who had done the deed sent her a message, saying 'he should love her never the worse'. In hunting, as in all matters, betting was general.

In May and June the King was at his riverside manor of Greenwich, where were many mechanical toys, such as a maiden that sang in the sun and was dumb in shadow, and a perpetual-motion device. Late in spring the Progress began. King and courtiers rode on horseback, with liveried running-footmen; the ladies were jolted in the big square springless coaches that had come in under Elizabeth; then came a huge rumbling train of two-wheeled carts with six-horse teams, tents, baggage, and a host of menials. Not much more than a dozen miles a day was possible, and so the area to be covered in six or seven weeks was limited, to the South or to the Midlands. When no house or inn was near, a dining-house was set up in a field. Houses on the route were painted and repaired, streets were sanded and repaved, city-recorders penned florid orations, while gentlemen-ushers rode ahead to check the plans of welcome and the towns hastily handed out gratuities to various officials. Then the King entered, took and handed back the freshly gilded town-mace or sword, and passed through the streets behind the Sword of Estate. In the night a banquet was held. Such a progress was a heavy drain on the areas visited. In 1615 the counties that had been marked out for visiting sent a petition against being so favoured, on account of a bad season which had played havoc with their cattle.

In early September the court resided at Windsor, then at Hampton Court. Here everyone turned out and there was not enough room for the many rows of tents. Whores and hanger-bys plied their trades, and the filth was liable to beget a plague. With October the King was back at

Whitehall, thinking of the hunt, with winter evenings of hard drinking, bawdy tales, fooleries. The Christmas Revels involved plays, masques, big gambling to which no one was admitted without £300 in hand. James would watch while a favourite placed his money.

Many squires and their ladies tried to avoid a dull country-winter by hanging about till in 1620 a proclamation ordered them back home 'to attend their services, and keepe hospitality, according to the ancient and laudable custome'. It must have failed for another came out 'even upon Christmas Eve'. Next year the authorities of London and Westminster were bidden to make a speedy certificate of all nobles and gentry in their jurisdiction, and persons disobeying the proclamations were to be brought before the Star Chamber.

The great men were building lavishly. Bishop Goodman says, 'No kingdom in the world spent so much in building as we did' under James. Renaissance styles had come into vogue and their full impact was now felt. Gardens expanded. Tradescant travelled France and the Low Countries for the garden of Cecil's Hatfield; a kinsman sent 400 sycamores from the Netherlands; the French ambassador gave 30,000 vines, and 500 mulberries were ordered, as James was interested in starting a silk-industry. There was a predisposition for the contrast of plain walling and large areas of glass, and we find decorative brickwork returning, the colour sometimes heightened by pencilling or russeting. Puritans, being against Italian styles as papistical, tended to seek an uncompromising continuation of the national (medieval) tradition. So at Cambridge, where Puritan influences were strong, we do not find the great Jacobean frontispieces of Oxford. The sudden shock of the confrontation of Classical or Renaissance styles is illustrated by the exclamation of Bacon, accustomed as he was to coloured medieval effigies, when he first saw the white marble of Arundel's Roman statues – 'The Resurrection'.

The use of tombs as display-memorials for others than the artistocracy had begun in the late sixteenth century, and was now greatly increased. By 1600 it was a matter of pride for every landed family to boast a splendid series of tombs in the local church. Sir T. Caryll's epitaph at Shipley notices that he was a man 'who but for fashion needs no stone'. Weever, looking back, comments: 'Sepulchres should be made according to the quality and degree of the persons deceased, that by the tomb everyone might be discerned of what rank he was living.' (1631) The desire to emphasize the dead person's rank and occupation leads to scenic representations; a soldier at a siege (Sir M. Dormer at Great Milton, 1616), a maid of honour before the Queen (Blanche Parry at Bacton, looking back forty years), an organist at Exeter Cathedral. Dorothy Selby's at Ightham reproduces two of her best pieces of embroidery; Capt. A. Wood's at St Mary's, Rotherhithe (died 1625) omits the effigy and merely shows his

Recreation and Dissipation

The stag hunt at the Ducal court of Lorraine. Drawing by Jacques Bellange.

'Scenes of Academic Life':
fighting, drinking, dancing,
wenching and other
distractions, but little studying.

Right. 'Where Helen is there
will be Troy'. Husband and
lover fight in the street below
their lady's window.

Opposite bottom. The demand
for money. Engraving after
Adriaen Brouwer.

Above. The day of reckoning for the student: gambling debts, tennis coach's bill, his mistress's child and the proctor from the university.

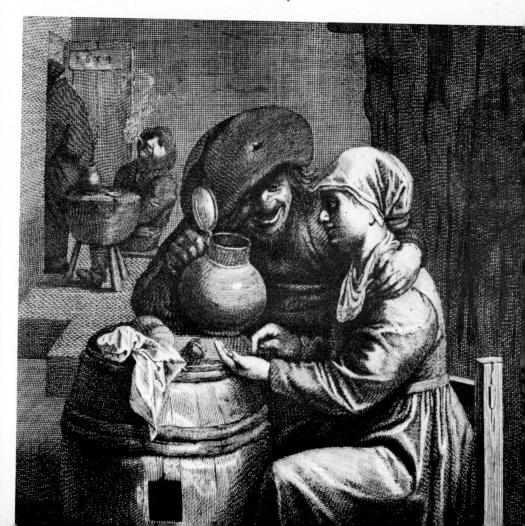

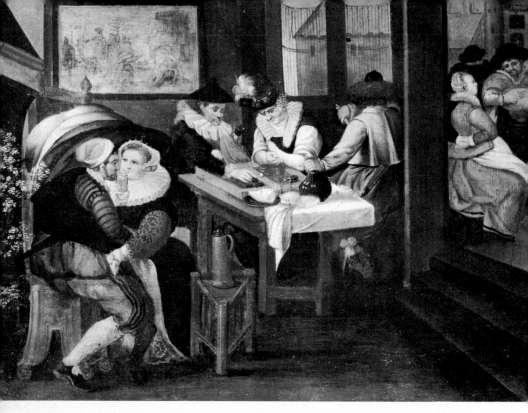

Interior of a tavern with scenes of dancing, backgammon and pickpocketing.

The musician, the whore and the bawd.

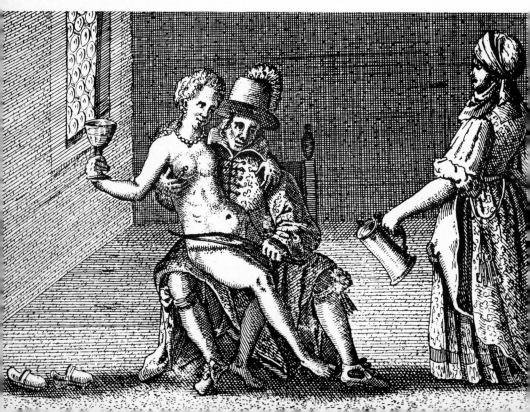

French gallants and their companions.

Card-players in a Dutch tavern.

Above left. Costume of the Roman courtesans.

Above right. Venetian courtesan, her bleached hair heaped up into two peaks on her head, walking on high leather-covered blocks, and lifting her skirts to reveal elaborate underwear.

Below. A more elegant brothel, where visitors to a town in Holland would always be taken by their hosts for entertainment.

Above. Touch, from a series of the five senses by Abraham Bosse.

Below. Georges Lallemant, *The Procuress*.

Entertainment in Italy
by a group of
Wallachian and
Transylvanian acrobats.

Below. Georges De La
Tour, *The Fortune-
Teller*.

ship. Sir Thomas Lucy (died 1640) reclines in armour among his books and rides a horse before a house and landscape (Charlcote Park). At Lydiard Tregoze the Mompesson monument (*c*.1633) is a seated conversation-piece.

Charles I's court was discreet and orderly compared with his father's; but it was in vain for him and Laud to attempt absolutist control (with exacerbations such as Ship Money, extracted even from the peasant who sometimes lost his only cow) and to impose order on the Church. When finally the alliance of the court and the big City-merchants broke down, a violent collision was inevitable. In 1612 two heretics had been burned at the stake; James, in conflict with the Catholics, had wished to prove his own orthodoxy. But there had been an outcry, and thereafter he commuted death-sentences for heresy to life-imprisonment. Charles took over from James the use of the Star Chamber to enforce policies, and extended its power. Judges supported the kings with servility; they upheld James in increasing customs dues without consulting Parliament; and Charles, in applying Ship Money and imprisoning men without showing just cause. The Court of Wards was never so exacting as in the eleven years of personal rule. So that in 1640 the gentry could stand up against the King with disgruntled peers to lead them, and the City to back them with funds.

After the failure of the Hampton Court Conference the Puritans lost hope of changing the establishment and turned to Parliament. Their services were long and devout. At Boston in the afternoon they took five hours: a two-hour sermon, a catechism of the youth, an explanation of the questions and answers. 'There were as many sleepers as wakers, scarce any man but sometimes was forced to wink and nod.' Later, How, Cromwell's chaplain, began at 9 a.m. and ended his service some time after 3 p.m. The vicar of Stamford was deprived of his living by Laud for saying that a man who could hear two sermons on Sunday and did not, committed 'a greate sinne'. As more Anglicans took over livings, Puritans inaugurated afternoon lectureships endowed by well-off laymen; and there, in a Geneva cloak and needing no surplice or prayer-book, they preached and prayed as they willed, and dealt with the deep points of doctrine that Laud forbade the clergy to handle. Dissenters were liable to cause trouble to the orthodox clergy. The vicar of Market Harborough was accused by the vicar of Great Bowden of being a 'lowsie roge, cogging companion and scurvie rascall and did challenge him to the feilde and did laye waite for him for using the rites and ceremonies of the church'; he also 'said he would incense the parishioners of Great Bowden againste their minister, whiche hee did indeede, and they expostulated at him thereof. And also did call this minister puppie'. At Sydenham the churchwardens seemed in league with the abusers.

Canon Law had been codified in 1604; pluralities were reduced and the general level of the clergy raised, though there were still many complaints. Several ministers were accused of ill-treating their wives. At Great Blackenham, the rector 'hunge his wife upp by the heels and tyed her to the bedposts and whipped her'. Perhaps he was recalling the country-adage: 'A wife, a dog, and a walnut-tree, the more you beat them the better they be'. The rector of Fen Ditton entertained his parishioners so well after the morning service that at the afternoon one they 'spewed most shamefully'. At Harby the minister frequented alehouses with cobblers and pedlars, who mocked him, so that he had 'the backside of his clothes besmeared over with creame by those that keepe him Company'. Others drank, brawled, abused people. Many were fighters. The curate at Snarden was often found lying drunk in the street muck, he struck 'both men and women; and that even att the churche door'. Many ministers seemed to be farmers first and clergymen second. A Devon vicar kept a tavern; at Stamford the vicar played stoolball in the street near his own door; at Uggleshall the minister disgusted folk by guzzling custard with sack in it 'after a scandalous manner' and 'with great greediness'. Others were greedy about tithes. The man at Leysdown exacted them for working-horses or the least fish caught by the poor. At Sowerby the minister hunted in his surplice after hare, and when he tore it in taking a gate the parish had to buy him a new one – the old one still being used for hunts. The vicar of Brandeston was arraigned for witchcraft; aided by six imps, he was said to have sunk a ship near Harwich with all hands, and was executed in 1645.

Tithes caused much discontent. Claims were made even on fallen apples and wild cherries. New crops like turnips, hops, saffron, tobacco led to costly disputes, but were finally adjudged to the vicar as small points were fought over: the rector's right to drive his sheaf-loaded waggon from the land of one farmer to another, or his right to force the farmer to reap the tenth he claimed. Many churches were still in bad disrepair. The church, however, still performed its medieval rôle as a meeting place where all sorts of business could be transacted and where schooling was often carried on. Vestrymen, overseers of the poor, justices, coroners, archdeacons, all used it; armour and powder-barrels were kept in the vestry; and all manner of announcements were read from the pulpit. The parson still had many secular rôles, from recording the whippings of sturdy-rogues to making sure his parishioners ate fish on fast-days. Children played in the church after dinner on Sundays and festivals; and the porch, because of its many secular uses, tended to have its own architectural tradition.

Church-bells were rung for all national or local celebrations. Hentzner had noticed the English love of noise:

Vastly fond of great noises that fill the ear, such as the firing of cannon, drums, and the ringing of bells, so that in London it is common for a number of them, that have got a glass in their heads, to go up into some belfry, and ring the bells for hours together, for the sake of exercise.

The church bell thus became a symbol of the union of Church and state. Bunyan records the complex struggles that gathered round his practise of bell-ringing, and George Fox continually states his horror at the sound of the bell: 'It struck at my soul.' But one of the main points at issue between Puritan and Anglican was the use made of Sunday. The Puritan wanted the day to be taken up with church-going, private devotion, visiting of the sick, collection of alms for the poor; and the Justice of the Peace was likely to dislike the laxities that led to drunkenness, brawls, fornications. We find assize courts from 1615 on trying to check jollities, including church-ales, clerk-ales, bid-ales (for raising money for church, clerk, poor). The Lancashire magistrates went too far and provoked the Declaration of Sports, 1618, which, while making church-attendance compulsory, encouraged harmless sports and games, including dancing, to take place afterwards. It was however loosely worded; and we still meet the baitings of bear and bull on Sundays, the carrying of offensive weapons, and drinking at ale-houses regardless of the hour. No attempt was made to stop Sunday labour; and tradesmen still cried their ware, carts rattled over the cobbles, cattle were driven to market and slaughtered.

The authoritarian attitude to children was still strong. We are told it was still the custom under James 'for every child on first meeting his parents each day to kneel and ask their blessing. This happens in the public streets and in the most frequented and conspicuous places of the city, no matter what their age'. Aubrey, looking back, declares:

The gentry and citizens had little learning of any kind and their way of breeding up their children was suitable to the rest. They were as severe to their children as their schoolmasters, and their schoolmasters were as severe as masters of the house of correction. The child perfectly loathed the sight of his parents as the slave to his torture. Gentlemen of thirty or forty years old were to stand like mutes and fools bareheaded before their parents, and the daughters (well grown women) were to stand at the cupboard-side during the whole time of the proud mother's visits unless (as the fashion was) leave was forsooth desired that a cushion should be given them to kneel upon, brought them by the serving man, after they had done sufficient penance in standing.

But a change was occurring. About 1630 Sir Henry Wotton in *A Survey of Education* recommends a careful observation of children as creatures with a character of their own; and letter-writers begin to give admiring accounts of the doings and sayings of children. The church-monuments tell the same story. Instead of lines of stereotyped kneeling figures we find individualized images of parental or filial sorrow and groups aware of a

179

common loss, not merely of a common authority. We note the change especially in effigies of women who have died in childbirth.

Elementary schools were growing up in various ways, through a vestry or private charity. Even a few grammar-schools formed 'petties' where an usher taught. The poor, driven by need, often wanted to get their children away even when the parish paid. Grammar-schools steadily expanded in the years 1603–60; the gentry had not forgotten the value of education. There were some 1,400 of them, though many were quite small. Poor women often taught in the petties. As for the country-master:

He looks over his scholars with as great and grave a countenance as the emperor over his army. He will not at first be over busy to examine his usher, for fear he should prove, as many curates, better scholars than the chief master. As he sits in his seat, he must with a grace turn his moustachios up; his sceptre lies not far from him, the rod; he uses martial law most, and the day of execution ordinarily is Friday: at six o'clock his army all begin to march; at seven they keep rendezvous, and at five or six at night they take up their quarters. (D.Lupton, 1632)

Amusements continued much as under Elizabeth. Every village had its cockpit. The court had its tiltings and its mock-battles on great occasions. In 1609 a courtier tried to astonish the gathering by bringing an elephant with a castle on its back into the tilt-yard, but 'it was long a coming, till the running was well entered into, and then as long a creeping about the tilt-yard, all which time the running was intermitted'. Among events used for betting, the races of running-footmen were popular.

Fairs were occasions for revelry, and London had its great fairs like that of St Bartholomew:

Here a Knave in a Fool's Coat, with a trumpet sounding, or on a drum beating, invites you and would fain persuade you to see his puppets; there a Rogue like a Wild Woodman, or in an antic shape like an Incubus, desires your company to view his motion; on the other side, Hocus Pocus with three yards of tape or ribbon in's hand, showing his art of Legerdemain to the admiration and astonishment of a company of cockaloaches. Amongst these you shall see a gray goose-cap (as wise as the rest) with a What do ye lack? in his mouth, stand in his booth shaking a rattle or scraping on a fiddle, with which children are so taken, that they presently cry out for these fopperies; and all these together make such a distracted noise, that you would think Babel were not comparable to it. Here there are also your gamesters in action; some turning of a whimsey, others throwing for pewter, who can quickly resolve a round shilling into a three-halfpenny saucer. (1641)

Jacobean drama had been losing its popular basis and often drawing for themes on problems of honour; under Charles the basis grew yet narrower, and the theatre, which the Puritans closed, was in decay, a meagre court-form. Under James the masque, a genre born of the Italian *masquerie* and the English *disguising*, had reached its lavish height in the collaborations of Ben Jonson and Inigo Jones, with proscenium arch and elaborate scenic effects. The Commonwealth saw the birth of English Opera and a considerable expansion of music. Wood tells us that the viol went out with the Restoration, being displaced by the violin. The first English newspaper proper, *The Weekly Newes from Italy, Germany, etc.*, appeared in May 1622.

The country-idyll or pastoral, which we meet in one form in Walton's book on Angling and which the Caroline court at times tried to imitate, was not without an element of reality. Dorothy Osborne wrote to her lover in June 1653:

The heat of the day is spent in reading or working, and about six or seven o'clock I walk out into a common that lies hard by the house where a great many young wenches keep sheep and cows and sit in the shade singing of ballads. I talk to them and find they want nothing to make them the happiest people in the world, but the knowledge they are so. Most commonly when we are in the midst of our discourse, one looks about her and spies her cows going into the corn, and then away they all run as if they had wings at their heels.

Under James there were many pimps and bawds living at Court, such as Lady Grisby, a retired Lady of Pleasure turned 'House-keeper to such as herself had been.' Round such characters revolved the cunning-men, who used calendars of unlucky days to cure diseases, advised on bets and card-playing, contraceptives or abortions, found lost property and sold love-charms. A superior example, the astrologer Dr Lambe, a creature of Buckingham, was murdered by the London mob; Charles fined the City £6,000 for taking no steps to find the killers, then after a few arrests reduced the fine to £1,000. Dr Forman used obscene lead figures and incantations said to be written in blood; at his trial, as a parchment bound in human skin was being examined, there were loud cracks from the scaffolding, so there was a great scare. People thought the angry Devil was present. Such characters gave aphrodisiacs more potent than the usual 'eringoes, artichokes, potatoes, and your buttered crab'.

At court the loose women ranged from the laundresses who could be had any time at a minimum charge of sixpence to costly ladies like Venetia Stanley.

She was a most beeautifull desireable creature, and being *matura viro* was left by her father to live with a tenant and servants at Enston-abbey (his land or the earl of Derby's) in Oxfordshire; but as private as that place was, it seemes her beautie could not lye hid. The young eagles had espied her, and she was sanguine and tractable, and of much suavity (which to abuse was great pittie).

In those dayes Richard, earle of Dorset (eldest son and heire to the Lord Treasurer, vide pedigree) lived in the greatest splendor of any nobleman of England. Among other pleasures that he enjoyed, Venus was not the least. This pretty creature's fame quickly came to his Lordship's eares, who made no delay to catch at such an opportunity.

I have now forgott who first brought her to towne ... The earle of Dorset, aforesayd, was her greatest gallant, who was extremely enamoured of her, and had one if not more children by her. He settled on her an annuity of 500 *li* per annum.

Among other young sparkes of that time, Sir Kenelme Digby grew acquainted with her, and fell so much in love with her that he married her, much against the good will of his mother; but he would say that 'a wise man, and lusty, could make an honest woman out of a brothell-house.' ... Once a yeare the earle of Dorset invited her and Sir Kenelme to dinner, where the earle would behold her with much passion, and only kisse her hand. (Aubrey)

Another woman of Dorset's was Elizabeth Broughton, who, 'a most exquisite beautie, as finely shaped as Nature could frame, had a delicate Witt'. She grew cheap and died of venereal disease, becoming a byword. 'From the Watch at Twelve a Clock, and from Bess Broughton's buttoned smock, Libera nos Domine.'

The court-ladies under James had low reputations. 'It was grown a scandalous place,' said Anne Clifford. Necklines grew lower. Lady Lettuce Lake, daughter of the Earl of Warwick, died of pox after bearing a bastard girl. Mrs Overall, wife of the doting Bishop of Coventry (who wedded her when Dean of St Pauls) was repeatedly forgiven for infidelities. A jingle of 1608 ran: 'The Deane of Paule's did search for his wife, and where d'ee thinke he found her? Even upon Sir John Selbye's bed, as flat as any Flounder.' Bastards were accepted as part of the system. Anne Clifford, herself a good wife, provided for the illegitimate daughters of her husband, the Earl of Dorset; what she objected to was his bringing a mistress, Lady Penistone, into the house. We see the morals of the upper classes at their worst in the tale of how Frances Coke, aged fifteen, was forced, after all the struggles of her mother, to marry Buckingham's unpleasant brother. Her father, Lord Coke, tied her to a bedpost and whipped her till she surrendered. The King gave her away. Drunk with toasts, he staggered about the palace, playing jokes such as tying sheets together and dragging off Frances' left stocking, and insisting that the couple stay in bed till noon next day so that he could visit them there.

On Shrove Tuesday the London apprentices had the custom of demolishing brothels. Unchastity, lewderies, oaths, drunkenness, sabbathbreaking, unlicensed teaching, were matters dealt with by the Church. Unless the accused could clear themselves by compurgation or otherwise, they were admonished or did penance (which could be commuted for a few pence). The unchaste however had to appear in church with bare feet and legs, clad in a white sheet, with a white rod in hand, and publicly confess the fault. Failure to attend court or carry out a penance meant the lesser excommunication (excluding from service and sacrament) or the greater one (entailing something like the condition of an outcast from society). The church-courts could not fine or fail, but in fact extracted large fees before granting absolution and invoked the local magistrate to supplement penalties. There was no jury, and the courts worked through spies and informers. The Long Parliament abolished them, and their functions were taken over by JPs.

The estimated average size of a family was four and a half persons. Many more were born, but died as infants. Commoners could not afford to marry young, and the parish authorities took care that a couple did not marry before they were assured of a house and unlikely to come under the poor rate. There was thus much temptation to fornicate. But even persons who offered shelter to women with bastards were liable to be taken to court and fined. Unmarried women of twelve to forty could be forced to go into service, and parents who kept their bastard children at home were fined.

William Dobson of Tarleton, husbandman, shall keep Alice his bastard daughter until she is 12 years old. He and Anne Wildinge to be whipped this day at Ormskirk. Henry Dobson of Tarleton becomes surety for William. Anne Wildinge is to be flogged. Before she is released she must find surety for a moiety of the expense of keeping her child.

We find fathers paying maintenance to the women who had borne their children: '4d. a week until the child be 7 yeares old.'

Women on the whole give the impression of being tough and strong-minded.

She will not sell anie of her ale forth of doores except it be to those whom she likes on, and makes her ale of two or three sortes nor will let anie of her poore neighbours have any of her drincke called small ale, but she saith she will rather give it to her swyne than play it for them. (Easingwold)

Many warrants are presented for 'seditious words'. A yeoman and his wife assault a constable in 1656. At Bagby in 1632 the constable was too frightened to serve a warrant on Elizabeth Simmondson.

The satires and moralizings about women's cosmetics went on without any effect. James I remarked, 'I wonder not so much that women paint themselves as that when they are painted, men love them.' The page in *The Silent Woman* says, 'My lady kisses me with her oil'd face and puts a peruke on my head.' Richard Crashaw seems the first to use the term *make-up*:

> A face, made up
> Out of no other shop
> Than that which Nature's white hand sets ope.

By mid-century mirrors of all kinds were made in London and the makers wanted a ban on imported ones. Starch was much used despite its association with Anne Turner, a widowed blonde, who, condemned for her part in the Overbury murder, went to the gallows in dress, cuffs and ruff treated with the yellow starch she had introduced. Patches grew ever more extravagant until Bulmer declared, 'some fill their visages full of them, varied in all manner of shapes and figures'. A coach-and-horse was specially popular across the brow. Amid all the ceruses the still-room was much used. Henrietta Maria disapproved of the ornate styles she found at court and brought about something of a return to simpler costume and make-up. Charles had good taste in art, and his court was far from the boisterous disorder of James's. But the general principles we noted under James still ruled.

Four-fifths of the countryside were still agricultural and pastoral, though many families divided their time between tillage and weaving or spinning. One way or another a very large number were connected with the sea. From 1620 there was decline in the demand for wool. Generally the provinces were highly individualized and the gentry spoke the local dialect. Roads were bad and many magnates even preferred a second house in the country-town to one in London. The large country houses remained medievally self-sufficient, like that at Claydon belonging to the Verneys, where the family lived on its own produce and had a host of craftsmen at work. The women spun wool and flax; did fine and coarse needlework, fine cooking, curing, preserving, distilling; prepared herb-medicines and made all sorts of syrups and wines.

Medieval laws against forestalling or engrossing were enforced. No one could buy goods except in open market on the appointed day, and no middleman was allowed unless he held a licence granted by the court of Quarter Sessions. When yeomen tried to augment their income by trading, they were thwarted. Vagabonds of all kinds were herded off to the House of Correction. Every village had to keep its stocks in order, and it was against the law to take any wanderer into one's house without informing the constable. Presentments for harbouring vagrants, however, often occurred. A woman of Hutton Rudby, found to be a wandering beggar, was ordered to be whipped by the constable at Thirsk and handed on to be whipped till she reached her own parish: this meant that she would be whipped in at least seven places. We find a mad woman sent from constable to constable to be whipped in the same way from Thirsk to Sandbridge. If a hue and cry was raised, all the inhabitants of a township had to turn out on horse or foot, with knives, bows, and arrows, crying, 'Out, Out', and blowing horns. 'The hue will be horned from vill to vill'. If a murderer escaped, the town was fined for negligence.

London went on growing. A Dorset gentleman said, 'I thought that long ere this we should have the trade dispersed all the nation over; and this City, it seems, must have all the trade.' But it was medievally packed and cramped. Davenant mocked it:

Sure your ancestors contrived your narrow streets in the days of wheel-barrows, before those greater engines, carts, were invented. Is your climate so hot, that as you walk, you need umbrellas of tiles to intercept the sun? Or are your shambles so empty, that you are afraid to take in fresh air, lest it should sharpen your stomachs? Oh, the goodly landslip of Old Fish Street, which, had it not had the ill luck to be crooked, was narrow enough to have been your founder's perspective. And where the garrets, (perhaps not for want of archi-tecture, but through abundance of amity) are so made, that opposite neighbours may shake hands without stirring from home . . .

Here stands one [house] that aims to be a Palace, and, next it, another that professes to be a hovel; here a giant, there a dwarf: here slender, there broad: and all most admirably different in faces as well as in their height and bulk. I was about to defie any Londoner, who dares pretend there is so much ingenious correspondence in this City, as that he can shew me one house like another: yet your houses seem to be reverend and formal, being compared to the fantastical looks of the modern: which have more ovals, niches, and angles, than are in your custards, and are inclosed with pasteboard walls.

In 1600 a bill had been brought in to restrain 'the extensive use of coaches', and things became much worse with the advent of hackneys. The first were in the Strand in 1621; within twelve years there were fifty; 200 by 1652; 700 by 1694. The sedan-chair came in 1634, and litters were still used – Evelyn travelled in one in 1640 with his sick father. Glass began to supplement the metal shutters of coaches about 1617; Lady Peterborough forgot and put her head through a glass window. Sanitary conditions were bad. Industries like soap-boiling and the increased use of coal to heat houses produced a pall of smoke and dust over the filth flowing in the open sewers. Plague broke out in the first years of both James and Charles; in 1634 there was a smallpox epidemic; in 1638 plague and smallpox; shortly before the Civil War, typhus, smallpox and plague; plague persisted in the years 1642–6, in the south and west as well as in London; a quarter of the people in Chester died. In times of plague special watches were set up to cordon off infected houses and prevent stricken persons from entering the parish. Thus, in 1637 a constable was charged for putting on guard 'a poore old blinde man not able to see the light of a candle, to the great dainger of the inhabs of Gillinge.' Dead persons were still buried inside churches, for a fee, if the churchwardens agreed; churches stank, and juniper, benzoin, and frankincense were burned there on festivals. At Houghton-le-Spring in 1657 an order was made for the repair within fourteen days of pavement and seats damaged through grave-digging, 'and the rubbish remayning to be cleane carried forth of the Church'. Skin-diseases were common on account of the salt-diet; salads were only beginning to be widely used. Smallpox ruined many beauties. Lady Suffolk had the small-pox at Northampton House, which 'spoiled that good face of hers, which has brought to others much misery, and to herself greatness, which ended in much unhappiness'. (Lady Anne Clifford in her diary, 1619) With crude surgery, diseases like the stone could be terrible. Thus, Nicholas Byfield, a devout preacher, died after groaning for several years in the most excruciating pain; he was found to have a stone weighing thirty-three ounces in his bladder.

There were as yet no banks. Brokers and scriveners took deposits and arranged loans. Merchants used to put cash in the Tower Mint; but after Charles siezed it all, they preferred the goldsmiths, whom landowners also used. But the magnates often still used primitive methods. The Earl of Bedford had a big trunk in his Strand house, into which went the money from rents, fines (for renewed leases), sales of wood, malt, tallow, hay, sheepskins, with the key held by his chief steward. Mounted servants brought up money from East Anglia, guarding it from highwaymen. A steward at Exeter collected money from western estates; but instead of sending it along all the way to London, he arranged for a bill of exchange to be drawn on a goldsmith in Lombard Street. The Earl however did not spend money only on display; he did much to help along the drainage of the Fens where the *Slodgers* lived in huts of wattle.

Under the Commonwealth the Puritan way-of-life was to a large extent put into action. Thus, in the matter of poor relief we find the first signs of a genuine care for the poor. In Warwickshire the Major-General Whalley wrote to the Protector praising a judge for 'his justice to all, and in a speciall manner takeing care of poore men in their causes, without which some had suffered'. The month before, in Leicestershire he had ordered that the poor be 'amply provided for; for upon these terms I hope God will not be provoked, the poor not wronged, depopulation prevented and the state not dampnified'. We find in 1656 a cottage ordered to be built against the wishes of the lady of the manor, who was bidden 'not to hinder the same being so charitable a work as the providing an house for a poor man'. In contrast the orders issued by Charles about the poor were dry, verbose, detached. Punitive measures were now less prominent, and aid for beggars, vagabonds and others was stressed. Generally efforts were made to reform taxation; there was more discipline in proceedings; overseers and constables were held more strictly to account. Many Justices of the Peace had been officers in the Parliamentary Army; we find a commission of the peace 'renewed according to a New Model'. Many nuisances were ended; thus, in 1656, the saltpetre-men were forbidden to dig without permission in a household, and the baiting of animals was forbidden.

In matters of marriage the moderate Puritan view mainly prevailed. Independents certainly had marriages performed by magistrates, but the 1645 law stated that it was expedient to have the union 'solemnized by a lawful minister'. In 1653 an Act made the vows alone the ceremony.

Milton supported this Act, but wanted further to see authorized the Brownist position of divorce without the intervention of magistrates (as must have been going on among many Independents and others). Cromwell however put divorce in the hands of civil magistrates, though nothing seems to have been done to build up a code of rules and principles.

But the essential thing was the upheaval among the people, which brought about a turmoil of thought, often confused, often grappling vitally with important issues. From 1640 the Puritan movement began to spread to the lower classes; and it was this awakening of what Clarendon called the 'Dirty People of No Name' which provided the character of the period. Dell, an educational enthusiast, was accused after the Restoration:

He has entrapped the gentry of the county into discourses and then given false information against them; he has declared in the public congregation that he would rather hear a plain countryman speak in the church, that came from the plough, than the best orthodox minister that was in the county. Upon Christmas day last one Bunyan, a tinker, was countenanced and suffered to speak in his pulpit . . .

Baxter, one of the conservative Presbyterians, thus expresses the horror he felt when he encountered the Independents:

When I came to the Army among Cromwell's soldiers I found a new face of things I never dreamt of. I heard the plotting heads very hot upon that which intimated their intention to subvert both Church and State.

Clement Walker explains what these discussions in the Army were about:

They have cast all the mysteries and secrets of government before the vulgar, and taught the soldiers and the people to look into and ravel back all governments to the first principles of nature.

And when the hackwriter Roger L'Estrange took over the censorship after the Restoration, as Surveyor of the Press, he especially wanted the suppression of the 'great Masters of the Popular Style', who 'strike home to the capacity and humour of the Multitude'. What was born was a new form of expression, which had roots in both the realistic narrative of a Bunyan or a Defoe, and in the consciously simplified, concise, and scientific approach of men like Sprat, who recorded of the men of the Royal Society that they aimed at bringing 'all things as near the mathematical plainness as they can', preferring 'the language of artisans, countrymen, and merchants before those of wits and scholars'. Bunyan put the same point: 'Words easy to be understood do often hit the mark, when high and learned ones do only pierce the air.' Thus out of the Puritan approach, in its deeper aspects, came a new mode of apprehending reality, which embraced what seem at first glace diametric opposites: an

187

evangelical down-to-earth sense of dedicated purpose and a scientific economy of statement which sought to get at grips with clearly isolated problems.

In 1653 the parish churches were shared out among the Independents, Presbyterians and others – with the more extreme sects such as the Quakers, Fifth Monarchists and the like left unmolested though unsupported, and Anglicans, at least in a place like London, holding private services. On the restrictive side the Puritan Sunday was enforced and attempts made to check festivities, such as Christmas, associated with the Church. The Commonwealth failed in part because groups like the Levellers and Diggers, who stood out for more complete democracy and equality, had been put down, and because the Independents had no clear programme beyond a desire to decentralize as much as possible. Presbyterians and others of their kind feared any appeal to the people. The way was opened to the return of the monarchy, with many old forms and attitudes revived, but on a new level of development which made the whole situation substantially different from anything which had existed under James I and Charles I.

11 Germany

The Emperor Rudolph II still belonged to the Renaissance. A humanist, a passionate collector, interested in everything, he accumulated art treasures in Prague, where he lived among sycophants, sorcerers, astrologers and scientists (including Tycho Brahe and Kepler). Unfortunately he grew sick both in body and mind, suffered attacks of delirium and finally lost all interest in government. On his death in 1612 he was succeeded by his brother Mathias, who had forced him to abdicate his kingship of Bohemia the previous year.

Mathias was fundamentally good-natured, despite his roughness of manner. He was a great hunter, jouster and warrior. His coronation was made the occasion for brilliant festivities. He rode in procession, surrounded by pikemen and followed by the German princes, resplendent in their various costumes. Together with the Empress he opened the ball accompanied by two torchbearers who danced about them. There was a giant firework display and a tournament in which the noblemen took part. The populace were served with roast meat in the squares, and drank their fill from fountains of wine. The festivities culminated in a masquerade, *The Country Wedding*, which would have been considered vulgar in Paris or Madrid, but enchanted the Germans by its realism. Standard-bearers brandished gigantic spits which were hung with interlarded chickens. Bacchus, sprawling on his cask, abandoned himself to drunkenness. Pork was served from a waggon, and a great wicker ox spat fireworks and petards.

Few people supposed that these rejoicings were to mark the end of the peace which had begun in 1555 with the compromise at Augsburg.

Germany at this time was remarkable for two reasons: she had withdrawn into herself and yet kept her frontiers open, whilst the other European states each formed a self-contained economic unit. As she was unable to export her products any more, Germany had paradoxically grown poor during the peace. Whilst the princes struggled to find new resources, various of the towns fell into decline and the bourgeoisie lost much of its splendour and pride.

Such was the situation when the religious conflicts, quiescent in Spain and Italy, resolved in France and England, were renewed in the Empire.

The Peace of Augsburg was between only Catholics and Lutherans; but the Calvinists, who had imposed their dogma on the Palatinate, were still eager to form foreign alliances. These aggressive newcomers were determined to suppress the Catholics who by means of the Counter-Reformation had won greater strength, resolution and intransigence.

The explosion occurred at Prague; and soon afterwards Mathias died. Protestant historians claim that his successor, Ferdinand II who had been educated by the Jesuits, continued to serve them blindly. Ferdinand, in fact wished to champion the Church, but also pursue his personal interests and his grudges. He was a mediocre politician, but attractive as a man who combined Austrian affability and a Spanish sense of grandeur. Few people were as devout as this prince who was obsessed by anxiety and determined to exterminate the heretics. In this he surpassed even Philip II, fasting, walking in processions in foul weather and elevating his confessor almost to the rank of prime minister. This piousness was to be the cause of his downfall. The 'heretics' of Prague were horrified by their sovereign, and elected a Calvinist as King of Bohemia: the Elector Palatine, son-in-law of James I, King of England. And thus began the Thirty Years' War.

For a whole generation Germany, or rather the various states of Germany, suffered the scourge of war. Certainly a few states, like Austria, escaped it completely, and some towns who were equipped to defend themselves against marauders. And some merchants were able to turn the war to their advantage. But the country as a whole suffered martyrdom. According to Gustav Freytag, its population was reduced by two-thirds; modern historians reckon a half but, as Voltaire said of the massacre of the American pagans, 'it was none the less admirable for that'.

Schiller likewise was to deplore the catastrophe.

The burnt castles, the ravaged countryside, the villages reduced to ashes presented the spectacle of an appalling devastation, while their inhabitants, condemned to poverty, helped to swell the number of incendiary bands: and barbarously delivered to their compatriots the misery which they themselves had suffered . . . All the vices flourished in the shadow of anarchy and impunity, men became as wild as the countryside . . . The soldier was lord.

He was lord to such an extent that Wallenstein, the greatest condottiere of the war, managed to found *an empire of soldiers*, an empire

with uncertain limits, extended by recruiting and reduced by desertion. But such was the prestige of the victorious, prodigal leader, that his army finally numbered a hundred thousand men. The larger it became, the less he was concerned about its upkeep ... The more enormous his exactions, the more it grew, the more it was assured of impunity ... The commander-in-chief was surrounded by royal luxury. Generals and colonels grew rich *en route*: they requisitioned the most of the capital they had put into it ... The army was the native land of the mercenaries. To their minds, it was not the Emperor who had given them Wallenstein for a general, it was Wallenstein who had given them the Emperor as a master, and it was Wallenstein, alone, who attracted them to his banners.[1]

In fact the war was fought by mercenaries, and they were very expensive. The belligerents had no permanent or regular army. They addressed themselves to colonels who were granted commissions in exchange for the promise to provide the required contingent. The colonels themselves treated with courtiers. But forced recruitment was not uncommon. An army collects adventurers of all kinds, peasants for the infantry, gentlemen of small means for the cavalry. All nationalities mingled together: German, Danish, Swedish, French, Spanish, Italian, Hungarian, Slav and sometimes Lappish. The Cossacks and the Croats won the worst reputation. The soldiers were grouped according to their ethnic affinities. Their language was a military slang based on Low German and enriched by foreign words.

An army hardly ever exceeded 40,000 men because of the expense which included enlistment premiums, courtiers' commissions and the colonel's bonuses. Also as pay rates rose, pillage began to replace gratuities. However the gentleman did bring his horse and his armour, and the footslogger his pike and musket.

'As soon as a soldier is born,' said a proverb, 'three peasants are affected: one to feed him, another to offer him his wife, and the third to go to hell in his place.' A tacit code of behaviour existed among the mercenaries. They bought prisoners back from each other, because it was less onerous than recruiting all over again. Every regiment published its tariffs in advance. Prices rose as effective strength decreased.

The cudgel, the gallows and the rack ensured discipline. By way of compensation pillage was permitted whenever a town was sacked, and the soldier was permitted to keep his wife by his side. Every regiment was followed by chariots laden with families, prostitutes, livestock and loot. Occupied countries were ravaged systematically. On the other hand, courtesy forbade that a military operation should begin before it had been proclaimed by the drum.

The fate of towns depended on the solidity of their walls. Woe betide them if the rampart gave way! In Magdeburg, three-quarters of the population perished. The villages lived in terror while watchers scanned the horizon from the tops of bell-towers. If the trumpet sounded, the inhabi-

[1] Pierre Gaxotte: *Histoire de l'Allemagne*.

tants rushed towards the forests and sought refuge in a *schutzdorn*. These were enclosures designed for refuge: dense thickets, almost circular, shut in by an inextricable web of brambles and shrubs. They proved almost impenetrable and most difficult to discover, they could withstand assaults, but they could not give protection against hunger or cold, from which causes many unfortunate people met their death.

When they did fall into the hands of the soldiers, their fate was terrible. The fugitives were forced to crawl over braziers, were dragged behind horses, their thumbs were crushed, they were thrown into bakers' ovens: sometimes for amusement and sometimes for their money. 'The devil take anyone who shows pity'! cried a character in *Simplicissimus*.

All the same there came a moment when the soldier himself stood in need of pity: when a truce, bad weather, political or financial considerations forced a belligerent to disband his troops: a carousal to start with, followed by a pitiful pilgrimage. Some of the troops who had enriched themselves wore golden plaques and chains under their clothes, but revengeful peasants now ambushed their former torturers, killed them without mercy and stripped them. The wounded and the unemployed soon found themselves without resources, and were obliged to beg. Naturally they were jeered at and were left to lie down and die by the roadside.

Considering the relatively few effective forces, the devastation was immense. In 1618 the little town of Lowenburg had 6,500 inhabitants: in 1650 she had only 850. The generals, incapable of achieving victory, seemed wantonly to prolong the horrors of war. As time passed, the ferocity increased. The peasants in turn formed armed bands which raided other villages and attacked convoys. Epidemics and typhus were widespread.

Christoph von Grimmelshausen has recalled this terrible tragedy in the *Simplicissimus*, and Jacques Callot (of Lorraine) in his engravings, whose precise details emphasize the horrors of war more poignantly even than the cartoons of Goya.

The disasters of the Thirty Years' War did not prevent the continuance of civil life. The good humour of civilians was not unduly affected by the war. The same could not be said of manners which were both coarse and brutal. Husbands beat their wives, wives beat their servants. At an aristocratic gathering, it was not uncommon to see women slap each other's faces and tear off their headdresses. The Emperor poured wine into the cleavage of an opulent beauty just for a joke. When Louis XIII of France spat on a young lady's breast, he did at least demonstrate his indignation at immodesty.

Peace brought new developments. The translation of *L'Astrée* had a good influence, and manuals of civility grew in number. The appearance of

'Death is the cure of all diseases'

French cavalrymen on the march, painted by Jacques Courtois, who had soldiered as a boy in the 1630s.

Scenes from Jacques Callot's *Grandes Misères de la Guerre*, 1633: (*top*) soldiers plunder a farm, (*centre*) malefactors are hanged, and (*bottom*) cripples returned from the wars beg in the streets.

The Musketeer. Improved hand-guns greatly increased the casualties of war.

The Preacher: 'For the world, I count it not an inn, but an hospital, and a place, not to live, but to die in.'

Below. The Dying Man, by Abraham Bosse. The doctor has given up hope, and devils wait to claim the soul at the moment of death.

Prisoner led before the Inquisition. In the background are the torturers, and two men on the gallows.

John Donne, preacher and poet of the joys and miseries of the human condition.

Marguerite Perier, Pascal's niece, on an *ex voto* painting, dedicated in thankfulness for her miraculous recovery from illness.

Below. François Duchastel, *The Dying Nun*.

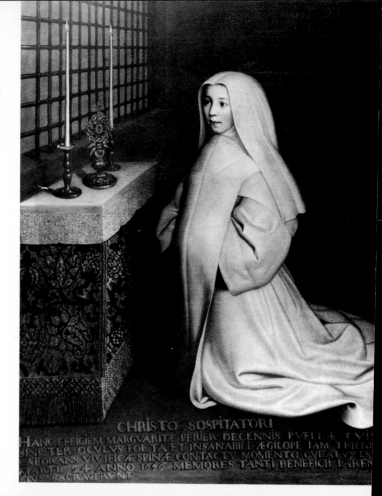

CHRISTO SOSPITATORI
HANC EFFIGIEM MARGVARITÆ PERIER DECENNIS PVELLÆ CVI
SINISTER OCVLVS FOETA ET INSANABILI ÆGILOPE IAM TRIENN
LABORANS VIVIFICÆ SPINÆ CONTACTV MOMENTO CVRATVS ES
MARTII 24 ANNO 1656 MEMORES TANTI BENEFICII PAREN
RIS SACRAVERVNT

Death with the hour-glass, from the tomb of Urban VIII Barberini by Bernini.

Charles I at his trial.

Below. The execution of Charles I, an act which shook the foundations of European monarchy.

society did not change as it did in France, but hyperbole became popular, together with the attendant complexities of ceremonial address. Fiancés wrote to each other: 'Madam, my good angel' – 'Sir, my well beloved'.

The negotiations settled by the Treaty of Westphalia lasted for eight years. And during this period, the ambassadors vied with one another in luxury and pretentiousness. They even vied with their own compatriots; so much so that the Comte d'Avaux squandered his whole inheritance in order to eclipse his less wealthy colleague, Servien. France and Sweden demanded a footing of absolute equality. This was done at the cost of the imperial diplomats who were forced to go to and fro between two towns nearly ten leagues apart: Munster, the French headquarters, and Osnabrück, the seat of the Swedish envoys. Each delegation maintained a body of counsellors and secretaries, sported a dazzling array of carriages and liveries, and gave banquets. The Swedish Ambassador announced the hours of his rising, his retiring and his various meals by the sound of trumpets. The French Ambassador made an even more imposing gesture by refusing to speak Latin.

Naturally, a peace which had been won by such labour was celebrated with exceptional festivity. A huge banquet was held under a canopy which was decorated with foliage, gilded fruit and thirty kinds of flowers. The tables were set out in six compartments, according to the precedent of the guests. There were triumphal arches, towers, and mythological figures. Four choirs accompanied the procession of the four courses, each of which consisted of a hundred and fifty dishes. Incense was burned. When they drank the health of the sovereigns, the cannon never stopped thundering. The banquet ended with a retreat in the light of flambeaux. And the common people were not forgotten either, they were given food, and allowed to drink from a fountain of wine for half a day.

The popular schools which had promoted culture in the time of Luther fell into decline. Likewise the universities, where dogmatism killed the scientific spirit. Germany, drawing further away from the sources of her own genius, now took her inspiration from abroad: the Catholics turned towards Spain and Italy, the Protestants towards France. The result was an artificial literature which had little influence and disappeared at the first reawakening of the national spirit. One must, however, record that academies were founded to 'preserve and practise the mother tongue'. They were presided over by princes (Anhalt, Weimar) and they recruited their members from the nobility and the bourgeoisie. If they did not achieve any useful reforms of the language, at least they formed a bridge between the aristocrats and the men-of-letters.

Mention must again be made of the *Simplicissimus* which was written at this time though not published until 1837. In it the author Christoph von Grimmelshausen draws an incomparable picture of the period.

If various different countries contributed to literary influence, Venice alone exercised an influence on architecture. It was to her that the towns of the Empire largely owed the introduction of the baroque style.

By some paradox, the cities of Bohemia, where the Thirty Years' War originated, were spared the scourge. Vienna had the same good fortune, but it remained exposed to the danger of a Turkish advance, and it kept its medieval appearance. Those people who had escaped and those who had benefited from the War therefore delighted in Bohemia. They summoned Italian artists for the purpose of enriching Prague with chapels, churches and palaces. Wallenstein, at his apogee, decided to create a décor which was worthy of his fortune. While he was having the Charterhouse of Valdice built in his principality of Friedland, he demolished an old quarter of Prague and commissioned three Italians, Spezza, Marini and Campione, to build his sumptuous residence in the city.

The work was finished in four years. Greatly admired was the façade which had no pillars, the state room two storeys high (with a ceiling painted by Baccio Bianco), the huge chapel and its altar-screen with the twisted columns, its bronze statues (by the Fleming de Vries), the stucco panels, the shell-shaped niches, the arches of the *salla terrena*, and, beyond, the splendour of the gardens.

But the fortunes of adventurers are fickle. Five years after these works were completed, Wallenstein himself was assassinated. His palace was abandoned and became the symbol of a departed glory.

12 The Low Countries

The Thirty Years' War which ruined Germany, saw Holland emerge, with a huge increase of wealth, to take her place among the great powers. The rise of Holland was partly due to the military talents of the Stadtholders, who guarded the country against a Spanish invasion; partly to the daring, skill and conquering spirit of her sailors and statesmen. At the time of the Treaty of Westphalia, when England was convulsed, and all the continental states suffering from financial distress, the Republic, mistress of the seas, possessed an unrivalled fleet, vast gold reserves, rich colonies, and enjoyed a thriving industrial life. The excursions of privateers and the enterprises of capitalist companies had given her a virtual monopoly of commerce with the East Indies. The size of her empire assured her a unique position in Europe.

When England recovered, she was to rise against this rival as did also the other European Powers, including France. But, after some reverses, Holland recovered her supremacy, the Baltic remained her fief, and her navy continued to protect the vast maritime traffic centred on Amsterdam.

The profits of the principal companies totalled seventy-five per cent of the capital invested. The East India Company paid the unheard-of sum of 2,500,000 florins a year in salaries for its Dutch agents. In France the interest on money rose to five or six per cent; in the Low Countries it fell to four and then to three per cent. The whole of the West bought Leyden cloth, Utrecht velvet, Haarlem linen, and Delft pottery.

It was the first example of a state which drew its strength exclusively from its economic prosperity. The Stock Exchange, the banks and the fleet were its vital organs. The Burgomaster of Amsterdam kept the keys of this citadel as he kept the keys of the town itself. The Frenchman, Parival, marvelled at the secrecy which 'made it impossible to determine or even to conjecture what ratio there was between its actual treasure and its credit'. He had, however, been able to note the 'prodigious number of gold and silver nuggets'.

Every six months the bank closed for a fortnight. Those who had deposited funds gave the department concerned a recapitulation of their account. If they made a mistake they received a fine in proportion to their error. Another bank specialized in loans. Its work must have been very complex because of the number of currencies, and the somewhat illogical diversity of weights and measures.

Since the middle of the sixteenth century there had been a system of maritime insurance. In about 1650 the premium varied between five and one. Twenty-five per cent of the value of the product was added to its cost. When a ship had sailed from a port in Europe or the Levant, it was considered lost if it had ceased to send news after a year and six weeks. In the case of the East Indies, it was considered lost after two years.

In his *Treaty of Political Economy*, Antoine de Montchrestien apostrophized the miracle of the Netherlands as that 'of human effort in a country hardly suited to human life'. Both the state and the citizens lived within their income. In every citizen's family budget there were always four headings: household expenses, household improvements, taxes, increase of capital. This system caused large fortunes to increase faster than the others. In general, the average businessman devoted his reserves to the acquisition of luxuries, but the wealthiest businessmen invested in lands and state securities.

The influx of wealth had in no way changed the virtuous simplicity of homes or the austerity of behaviour. The instinct for enjoyment was given collective rein in the *kirmesses*, which lasted from one to three weeks. The *kirmess* at the Hague enjoyed particular prestige. William of Orange, now King of England, declared that he would willingly have paid 200,000 florins for the pleasure of attending it. Nothing came as a surprise at these merrymakings, where statesmen chatted together by a waffleseller's stall, where everyone ate, drank, danced, and sold everything from cakes to masterpieces of painting. Acrobats and dwarfs and giants, rat-catchers and horoscope-readers jostled one another in the booths of itinerant showmen. The diversity of the population was more apparent here than anywhere else.

All the races of Europe mingled in Holland as in a later age they were to do in America. This was the country where fortunes could be made, an asylum for the persecuted, the only country which gave complete freedom to religious beliefs and to trade. And so the great towns and the universities were genuinely cosmopolitan, and attracted refugees from the rest of Europe – especially France. Often quoted was the case of a German from Holstein, Jacob Poppen, who had arrived without a florin and had died burgomaster of Amsterdam and a millionaire. And merchants were known to come from as far as Cirencia to trade on the shores of the Amstel.

In 1644 the Archimandrite of Cephalonia and the Metropolitan of

Ephesus settled in Leyden: the Patriarch of Jerusalem had ordered them to translate the Heidelberg catechism into Greek.

The unique character of Dutch culture of this period arose from the attempt to reconcile two conflicts: first the conflict of Humanist enlightenment with religious obscurantism: secondly the conflict of the desire for material expansion with the habit of reinstatement of capital wealth.

Poetry was greatly honoured among the merchants. In every town and in many villages there was a 'chamber of rhetoric' which had grown out of medieval associations of a religious nature. The chamber had its patron, its seal, its motto and its banner: its symbolic flower or tree. Leyden boasted three chambers of rhetoric: they were called The White Columbine, The Orange Lily and The Palm-tree. It was in these chambers that people learned the rules of versification. The members composed rondels, ballads, songs and sometimes even scabrous poetry. On certain festive occasions these works were read aloud.

For a long while Amsterdam was the only town to have a theatre. The Hague did not dare to open one until 1638, and it was not until 1645 that a woman appeared on the boards. The authors did not collect any profits – this was no doubt in order to avoid censure.

The Dutch read a great deal: The Bible, of course, the old tales of chivalry, and travel books. An adaptation of the *Meditations* of Marcus Aurelius by the Spaniard Guevara was highly successful, and even more successful was the illustrated edition of the *Poems* of Jacob Cats of which 50,000 copies were sold, a stupefying figure for the time. At the beginning of the century, 244 booksellers were listed in the guild of Amsterdam. By 1650 their number had risen to 476. Dordrecht and Utrecht had owned their paper mills from the end of the sixteenth century. The Elzevirs imported French paper, but the 'Holland' outclassed its rivals. It was the publisher Jean Le Maire of Leyden who ensured the printing of the *Discours sur la Méthode*. He and Descartes signed a contract in the presence of a notary. The author agreed to collaborate in disseminating his work in France. The publisher granted himself the privilege of making two printings, one of which was to be printed outside France, and this to the number of three thousand copies. Descartes received in payment . . . two hundred personal copies.

The genius of the Netherlands produced nothing memorable in the arts of sculpture and architecture: no monuments or statues to compare with those of other countries. On the other hand the Dutch genius was apparent in everything which concerned domestic life.

Music was popular, and singing formed a kind of social link, indispensable at festivities. Utrecht boasted the Society of St Cecilia. In Amsterdam there were similar groups where the standard was very high, and the members worked at sacred and profane song. A group of notabilities, admirers of Swelinck, the organist at the Old Church in Amsterdam, conceived the idea of giving him 200 florins, not in cash, but in the form of shares in their business. Henceforwatd they scrupulously kept him informed of events on the Stock Exchange. Wandering musicians played the whistle-pipe, the *bombas* (a tall, one-stringed violin with a pig's bladder as the case) and the barrel-organ.

Dutch painting of this period drew its principal inspiration from the 'interior' which was the main focus of attention of all classes of the Republic. Calvanism forbade religious representation, but secular portraiture was popular amongst the successful burghers, and even the humbler bourgeoise enhanced their prestige by collecting paintings.

This practical people, little given to dreams, parsimonious, very busy, not mystic in the least, these people anti-Latin in spirit, a people with broken traditions and a religion without images: such people could only offer themselves something very simple and very bold: they could only demand to have their own portraits.[1]

The Dutch liked to see the record of episodes in daily life, they liked to contemplate pictures of towns and ships, and landscapes which enabled them to reach the highest acceptable point of lyricism. Realism was born of this state of mind, of the close alliance between the artist and the society from which he drew his subsistence. Hence the astonishing homogeneity of the works of the Dutch School.

The painters belonged to a modest guild. The bourgeois considered them as tradesmen, apparently without being aware to what degree of perfection they took their art. It was not a question of patronage, they simply paid for what they had ordered: all of Vermeer's forty known canvases were commissioned. At most, the client advanced the money, but woe betide the painter who did not repay it! Rembrandt and Seghers were made bankrupt. Ruysdaël and Hobbema fell into the care of charitable institutions. Vermeer, when he died, owed 600 florins to his baker.

Rembrandt was able to recreate round Biblical themes a religious painting adapted to Calvinism, but that did not recover the prestige he had won early in his career. His compatriots preferred Rubens, who, in some respects, was his antithesis. The painter-ambassador charmed them by his wealth, his happiness and that tireless genius which was exempt from anguish and from metaphysical misgivings. As with Caravaggio and Bernini, Rubens may be considered as the representative figure of his period. Like 'an Indian god who ... relieves his fecundity by creating worlds',[2] he attracted both extravagant noblemen like Buckingham, and the most prosaic bourgeoisie in the land.

[1] Eugène Fromentin: *Les Maîtres d'Autrefois.*
[2] R. Mousnier.

Part Three

1660–1715

13 France

The France of 1661 found herself leading the nations as Spain had done in 1560, but it was not the Frenchman who served as a model and set the tone, it was his king. Louis XIV was to impose his personality and his tastes not only on his own subjects, but also on the other European powers, for the duration of his reign.

When, to the general surprise, he himself assumed the reins of government, he embodied a nation at the height of its power: renewed, over-flowing with vigour, enamoured of splendour and glory. Richelieu had been execrated, Mazarin despised. Louis XIV was hence to deliver France from the corruption and intrigue, both at home and abroad, which had characterized the previous era. France fell in love with her king. The nobles, fresh from the civil war, the people – among them the precursors of Gavroche and the *tricoteuses* – did not suddenly become servile; they yielded to a movement of enthusiasm, to an infatuation. Hence their obedience resulted from inspiration rather than from compulsion.

Nobody would have thought of contradicting the monarch when he maintained: 'He Who has given kings to men wanted them to be respected as His lieutenants, reserving for Himself alone the right to examine their conduct ... There is no maxim whatever more clearly established by Christianity than this humble submission of subjects to those who are set over them.'

After the follies of the Fronde, the subjects accepted submission. They did so, however, on condition that they were to be guided by a vigorous hand. Louis was at ease on his throne and took great joy in governing. 'I do not know,' he said, 'what other pleasure we should not abandon for that ... The calling of a king is great, noble and delightful.'

From the moment of Mazarin's death, he showed that simultaneous appetite for work and pleasure which he was to keep until extreme old age. Having 'divided the hours of the day and night between his business and his pleasures, his devotions and his duties',[1] he regulated his existence like

[1] Primi Visconti.

a clock that never faltered, a clock that would govern the movements of several thousand subjects who were obsessed by the obligation of 'paying their court'. A look, a smile, an expression on his face was sufficient to provoke calm or tempest. Personages who certainly could not be reproached for their excessive sentimentality fell ill when they had *displeased*.

The King demanded the continual presence of the nobility, whom he obliged to desert their estates and châteaux for the uncomfortable apartments in Versailles, exile from which, however, became the most dreaded of all punishments. The nobility trembled at the thought of exile (*to their own homes*) as their fathers had trembled at the thought of the scaffolds of Richelieu.

Louis XIV, the great-grandson of Philip II, believed like him in the virtue of the ceremonial; and, like him, he made it an essential to his system. But, unlike his ancestor, he did not make himself inaccessible, still less invisible. Petitioners spoke to him more easily than they spoke to ministers. They gave their petitions to him in person. No barrier prevented the humblest of his subjects from admiring him when he walked in his gardens.

And yet the King deliberately encouraged idol worship such that the smallest function performed in the service of his person took on a quasi-sacramental character. Princes alone had the honour of presenting him with the shirt and towel. The office of cotton-bearer conferred nobility!

The *petit coucher* [wrote Primi Visconti] is the moment when the King has undressed and said good-night to the courtiers, donned his dressing gown and installed himself on his commode. The only people who can then be presented are those who hold the office of Gentlemen of the Bedchamber or brevets which are bought for as much as 60,000 écus (many people would pay 100,000). And so you can see what value the nation sets on everything that comes from the King, even the most repugnant things. It is true that this particular King is very honest, and puts himself in this position for the sake of ceremony rather than necessity.

And this was deliberate. Apart from the fact that the sale of Court offices allowed him to raise a considerable tax on vanity, the King was better assured of the public peace if the nobility were vying for his candlestick instead of fomenting plots. Within the court a spirit of intrigue prevailed, but this was limited to designs for personal aggrandizement, and exclusive of political issues.

This glittering, dissolute world, avid for precedence, overwhelmed with attentions from the most attentive master of the house, was subject to a shadowy police terror. The King had invested his court with a network of spies. No letter could conceal a secret. Every morning Louis was informed of the acts, and even the thoughts, of those about him.

He intended to preserve himself, for all time, both from the enterprises of other people and from his own emotions. He is reported to have said: 'People attack a prince's heart as if it was a stronghold . . . While we abandon our hearts, we should remain masters of our minds.' For a long while this maxim allowed him to lead the life of a libertine without falling into licentiousness. The man who had chosen the sun as an emblem clearly judged himself above the laws which applied to ordinary mortals. It was not enough to 'declare' his mistresses and to legitimize his bastards. Two of his favourites, Louise de La Vallière and Mme de Montespan, shared his wife's carriage on expeditions, and the common folk were not at all astonished, but asked one another if they had seen the three Queens. The two rivals shared a single eight-room apartment at Saint-Germain; it was locked with a single lock. In the meantime Molière was desired to justify the double adultery and to make M. de Montespan see reason – for he was ostensibly wearing mourning for his honour.[1]

Mme de Montespan enjoyed practically the rôle of a queen. The Church attempted several times to break this liaison. Bossuet once succeeded. When the marquise returned to Court after rather a long absence, the two lovers saw each other again in the presence of a group of respectable ladies. But, a moment later, they left the matrons standing and withdrew into a 'little room'. A daughter was born nine months later.

Such an example was not wasted. Bourdaloue thundered from his pulpit: 'It seems that there are different religious principles for the court and for the rest of the world, and that the courtier is entitled to fashion himself a conscience which differs in kind and quality from that of other men.'

Monsieur, the King's brother, made no mystery of his tastes, which were called Italian, nor of his passion for the Chevalier de Lorraine. The gentlemen who, like him, disdained women, had formed a brotherhood which was not only numerous, but distinguished, and among them were enrolled one of the natural sons of Louis XIV, the Comte de Vermandois, and his cousin the Prince de Conti. Bussy-Rabutin wrote in *La France Galante*: 'The easy virtue of all the ladies had made their charms so worthless to young men that one hardly remembered at court what it was like to look at them.'

The passion for gambling, which the King encouraged (it was an excellent distraction from the preoccupations of politics), assumed incredible proportions. It sometimes lent to the great apartments the appearance of gambling dens.

Worse was to come. The zest for life, the absence of scruples, the need to display extravagant splendour, drew these courtiers, who dazzled the world, to the extremes of perversion. Did you need to win a heart, rid yourself of a rival, hide a pregnancy, hasten an inheritance, reach the

[1] 'There is nothing at all dishonourable in sharing with Jupiter.' Molière: *Amphitryon*.

summit of favour? You had recourse immediately to magicians and sorceresses, who sold philtres of love or death. For those willing to pay, the devil himself could be invoked by means of the black mass accompanied by sacrifices of children.

The trial and execution of the Marquise de Brinvilliers, convicted of exterminating her family, served as a prologue to the Affair of the Poisons (1680). The King created a special tribunal, the *Chambre Ardente*, which discovered the traces of unimaginable crimes. The kingdom trembled. Birth and rank and genius were no protection for anyone. The Comtesse de Soissons fled from France, the Maréchal de Luxembourg was imprisoned in the Bastille, Racine was suspected. Several sorceresses were burnt, among them the famous La Voisin after which the others systematically accused Mme de Montespan.[1] The King suspended the *Chambre Ardente*, in terror.

This scandal was to mark a turning-point. Louis XIV, now past forty, found himself at his apogee. Breaking with the tradition of the Capetian prince, who always entered the life of his subjects, he represented himself as a quasi-divine being, and claimed from his subjects an intensified idol-worship. An actor constantly on stage, he had an actor's bearing, an actor's grace and an actor's tricks. He could terrify, or intoxicate. Absolute master of himself, he would lose his temper only thrice in fifty-four years.

At last, warned by the Affair of the Poisons, and fearful for his future both on earth and hereafter, Louis decided to conform to religious orthodoxy.

The visible instrument of this conversion was the former governess of his illegitimate children, the widow Scarron, since become Marquise de Maintenon, whom he had secretly married after the death of Maria Theresa.[2] The climate round the sovereign was radically changed. Splendour did not disappear, quite the contrary, the fêtes continued to follow one another. But an official puritanism stiffened people's attitudes, strained conversations, froze wit and gaiety. 'The Court was sweating with hypocrisy.' It was the court which Saint-Simon recorded in a picture too often coloured by personal malice, but none the less unforgettable.

Idolized till the day of his death, the King still received the insults of pamphleteers and sometimes vehement reproaches from his immediate entourage. Even his grandson's preceptor, Fénelon, was not afraid to write to him in 1692:

[1] It seems certain that the crimes imputed to the Marquise were invented by poor wretched women who were anxious to prolong their own lives. However, it is true that Mme de Montespan frequented La Voisin, practised magic, and made the King swallow dreadful mixtures which were designed to revive his failing love.

[2] It is not too clear if this marriage took place in 1683, 1684, 1686, or even 1697. But in fact the relationship between the King and Mme de Maintenon had begun in 1673. It was to last for forty-two years!

You have been raised to Heaven ... because you have impoverished France in order to bring incurable, monstrous extravagance to Court ... Your name has grown odious, and the whole French nation has been made intolerable to our neighbours ... But the whole of France is only one great poorhouse, desolate and without sustenance. Even the people who have so loved you are beginning to lose their friendship and their confidence, and even their respect.

Louis XIV had the good fortune to have among his contemporaries a pleiad of incomparable artists; but, far from accepting their influence, he imposed his own vision of nature and beauty upon them. It is permissible to criticize his remarkably clear and determined taste; but one cannot deny that he inspired the creation of a style, and that this style, adopted in every court, became the symbol of French grandeur.

The great cities were finally emerging from the Middle Ages, from which the Renaissance had hardly freed them. Monumental fortifications relegated the old fortresses to the rank of curiosities. The countryside was modified, a number of marshes disappeared, trees, lakes, rivers, plains and hills, even forests were ordered in the grandiose plans of the nobles' estates. Indoors, the change was equally perceptible. The new motif was light: streaming through the enlarged windows, reflected by inumerable mirrors, increased by candles, by fire and by sparkling water. Only hygiene was forgotten. The filth and stench which had taken possession of France with Henri IV remained.

Louis XIV, like Philip II, wanted to give the monarchy a permanent abode, stamped with his personality. However, if the Escurial was centred round the chapel, Versailles was centred round His Majesty's bedroom. 'The King would give all the women in the world for Versailles,' wrote Primi Visconti. Never was an enterprise more unpopular. Many people declared that it would never be finished, they exaggerated the cost. Preachers vituperated against the extravagance. Virtuous men, from Fénelon to Saint-Simon, veiled their faces. Versailles ruined and bled the nation. In addition, in turning up the soil, the putridity of the waters caused epidemics.

Louis XIV refused to listen. Until the last day of his life he laboured at this work which was to rank him with the great builders of antiquity. Versailles cost about the same as a modern aircraft-carrier and it still earns considerable sums through the admiring curiosity of tourists. And still we cannot imagine it when it really did represent the temple of the sun, with its silver furniture, the profusion of gilt bronzes, the gold of the hangings, the gold of the curtains, the gold of a thousand everyday objects, the gold of the tubs for the orange-trees, the gold of the roofings, the leads, the statues, the fountains, the carriages, the embroideries on the brilliant-coloured costumes.

It is still more difficult to imagine a vanished Marly, 'a vast drawing-room dedicated to Neptune'. Between the walls and the pilasters of greenery, were jets of water, cascades, allegorical images, water theatres and liquid thickets.

The memories of the Fronde had made Paris odious to Louis XIV. But, as he wanted order and splendour in all things, he commanded Colbert to transform his capital, which stood in singular need of it. Sauval groaned: 'There is no muddier or dirtier city in the world; its mud is black and stinking, with a stench intolerable to foreigners, it is so penetrating that you can smell it for several leagues around'. In summer this magma turned into a black, greasy dust, a carrier of lethal germs. Along the streets flowed fetid streams which smelt horribly when it rained. 15,000 horses and 800 coaches obstructed the streets, which were sometimes crossed by herds. The famous Court of Miracles, which was to last until the eighteenth century, gave shelter to a starving and ferocious mob, who committed crimes daily. Vagabonds and beggars constituted seven per cent of the population. Guy Patin wrote: 'People steal and kill here day and night . . . We have come to the dregs of the centuries.'

Colbert was not content to make new streets and squares, to build quays and monuments, factories, palaces and triumphal arches. He entrusted one of the greatest officials of the reign, Nicolas de la Reynie, with the task of forming a modern police force. In thirty years La Reynie accomplished a vast work. He assured the security of Paris, the lighting of the streets, public hygiene, the struggle against epidemics, the regular provisioning of the inhabitants. He created a police force to watch finance, a police force to watch over morals, gambling, entertainments and traffic, and he invested the criminal police with unheard-of efficiency.

If Louis XIV's taste and passion for unity and magnificence produced these admirable results, they produced their most unfortunate effects in the domains of religion and finance. The King, who had a horror of disparity thought that, like any tyrant, he could settle metaphysical problems, and he persecuted Protestants and Jansenists alike. Today we find it hard to credit that the Revocation of the Edict of Nantes was acclaimed with enthusiasm by the great majority of Frenchmen, who at the same time condemned the creation of Versailles. The kingdom thereby lost an irreplaceable élite and offered a scandalized Europe 'the spectacle of a most prodigious people proscribed, naked, and fugitive, vagrant and yet innocent, seeking asylum far from its native land'.[1]

Concerning finances, they had deteriorated to such an extent that in 1708 the King was duped into believing that his first physician, Boudin, knew a man who could make gold and silver, by the use of the philosopher's stone. 'Boudin set up this charlatan in a little house which he had at

[1] Saint-Simon.

Montreuil. The man was given furnaces, crucibles were taken to him . . .
He stayed like that for two months, during which Chamilart, then Con-
troller of Finances, the other ministers and even the princes and noblemen
of the court went to watch him at work and let themselves be seduced by
his speeches. In spite of that he could not succeed . . . This charlatan was
put away for having made a fool of the court.'[1]

Here are some eloquent statistics: in the time of Colbert, the state
collected 112 million livres a year and spent 116 million. The debt rose to
160 million. At the end of the reign the revenue represented 50 million, the
expenditure 220 million. The Sun King left a debt of 3,000,000,000.

This epoch witnessed considerable social ferment and the decline of
the highest orders in the kingdom. 'Never, perhaps, were the recruitment
of the clergy, the morals of the priests, the softness of the prelates, the
frivolity of the abbés, the grossness of the country curés the subject of
such vehement censure as they were in the seventeenth century, and it
was often the clergy itself that made the hardest comments and gave the
most precise information.'[2] Bourdaloue wrote: 'How many interested
priests, ambitious priests, vain, presumptuous priests, lazy and voluptuous
and worldly priests do we see?' Ecclesiastical livings, considered as sources
of income, 'allowed those who never served at the altar to live off the altar',
to quote Père de La Roche. The Bishop of Troyes was nicknamed 'the ladies'
favourite'. The Bishop of Clermont 'had lapses which made him almost
contemptible'. All the balls were held in his house, and the house which
should have been 'a house of prayers and penitence was a house of rejoicing
and feasting'.[3] A curé in his diocese, 'taking the Holy Sacrament to a farm
which was rather far from his presbytery, would get his clerk to bring a gun,
and, if he discovered some game or other in the countryside, he would
abandon the Holy Sacrament'. Many convents took great liberties with
their rule and allowed 'the spirit of the century' to enter.

The Church of France also displayed considerable disorders. The
Unigenitus bull, aimed by the Holy See at the suppression of the Jansenists,
roused the Ultramontane bishops against the Gallicans, divided the high
clergy from the low, and scandalized the faithful. Certainly, there existed
eminent prelates, illustrious preachers, and dedicated monks but the
criticism which they themselves levelled at the church served to weaken
the faith of the laity, and prepared the ground for Voltaire and the critics
of the ensuing age.

The nobility was equally discredited. Bourdaloue said bluntly that it was
'piling up a treasury of wrath for the dreadful day of heavenly vengeance'.
The great noblemen, who were more or less confined to the court or

---

[1] Pierre Narbonne, Commissioner of Police for Versailles, quoted by Gilette Ziegler.
[2] Félix Gaiffe: *L'Envers du Grand Siècle*.
[3] Fléchier.

the army, no longer played any part in the functioning of the state. Strangers to economic life as they were to political life, they became increasingly parasitical. Acquiescence gave way to indignation at their haughtiness, their insolence, their lack of conscience. Now, in company with the lesser gentry, the dukes and peers had the constant anxiety of paying for their magnificence. They were all deep in debt, and they paid as rarely as possible; and many of them were not above cheating when they gambled. 'Her audacity in stealing was inconceivable,' wrote Saint-Simon of the Princesse d'Harcourt. The Duchesse de La Ferté opened a gambling den in her house where she fleeced her servants and her tradesmen. 'Yes, I cheat them,' she used to say, 'but that is because they rob me.' Dangeau had made gambling into a profession, and he practised it assiduously every day.

Absorbed by their anxiety to flatter the monarch and to profit by their flattery, most of the nobles remained far from their estates. Those who continued to reside in them fell into disrepute. Some of them behaved like brigands. The urgent need to raise money brought the nobles closer to a class of people whom they would once have ignored: those people of low extraction who had profited from the financial confusion and the poverty of the State, and had managed to accumulate unheard-of fortunes. They were farmers-general, 'partisans', army contractors, tax collectors, the 'leeches of the people'. The King in person conducted through the fairy-lands of Marly a certain Samuel Bernard, who was worth sixty million; and indeed Bernard well deserved the honour. During the War of the Spanish Succession he had, with diabolical skill, contrived to make the enemies of France pay for the armies which were fighting them.[1]

The daughters of such personages had huge dowries, and the nobles did not scruple to grasp at them: the Duc de Gesvres married a Boisfranc, the Maréchal de Lorge a Frémont, a Crossé allied himself to a Béchameil, a Choiseul to a Crazat. Mme de Grignan wrote graciously on the marriage of her son: 'Of course one must sometimes manure one's estates.'

Money brilliantly usurped the rights of birth. 'Butchers have been seen to play with blue ribbons![2] cried the astounded curé of Versailles. All a butcher had to do was to amass some money, buy his son a position as an officer of the Crown and thus ennoble him.

Today it does not appear that this was the age of the noblemen whose privileges and precedences were so ardently defended by Saint-Simon. Rather it was the first golden age of the bourgeois, whom Molière delighted to portray from Harpagon to Monsieur Jourdain. Louis xiv had entrusted the government to this class and it had by now bought up the principal administrative, judicial, financial, municipal and purely honorary functions.

[1] Cf. Jacques Saint-Germain: *Samuel Bernard*.

[2] That is to say the dignitaries of the Order of the Saint-Esprit.

The Fêtes of Versailles

The Palace of Versailles.

Are de Triomphe du Carefour de la Fontaine sainct Gervais

Above. The temple of the Muses, represented on a triumphal arch erected in Paris for the great festival on 26 August 1660 to celebrate the peace with Spain and the marriage of Louis XIV and the Infanta.

Opposite top. The Sun King receives the obeisance of ambassadors from the Emperor of Siam.

Opposite bottom. The scene of joy in Paris at the birth of the Dauphin in 1674.

Opposite. Versailles and Paris emulated at the Viennese court of the Hapsburgs: Burnacini's design for the apotheosis of Leopold I in *Il Pomo d'Oro*, an opera given at the marriage festivities for the Emperor and Infanta Margarita of Spain in 1668.

Opposite bottom. Equestrian ballet at the Holy Roman Emperor's marriage festivities in Vienna.

Right. A fountain in the Gardens of Versailles.

Below. Water pageant at Versailles, part of the *Pleasures of the Enchanted Isle*, a three-day festivity given at Versailles in May 1664.

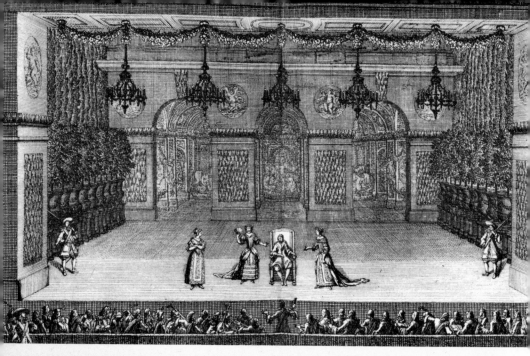

Top. Molière in *Le Malade Imaginaire*, acted before the king at Versailles in 1679.

Bottom. Lulli's tragic opera *Alceste* performed during the festivities of June 1679 in the Marble Court of the Palace.

Top. Frontispiece of Caspar von Lohenstein's *Cleopatra*, one of the allegorical political dramas popular at the German courts.

Bottom. The astonishing effects possible in the baroque theatre exemplified in a scene where Perseus descends from the heavens on horseback to rescue Andromeda.

Design for a '*Gloire*', and the machinery used
to produce it. From the theatre of San
Salvatore in Venice, 1675.

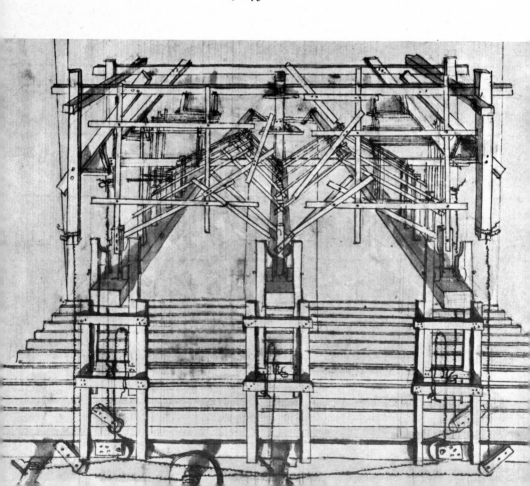

Pontchartrain said to the King: 'Every time Your Majesty creates an office, there is a fool to buy it.' But the bourgeois was not so foolish, for this road led to his advancement. If his parents had saved and he himself had saved, he had won a rare advantage in a country where cash was so scarce.

He was a parvenu, but he would have his *hôtel*, his *château*, his *objets d'art*, his livery, his magnificent clothes, like a gentleman. The moralists denounced his opulent tastes, compared his gilded apartments with the austere interiors of his ancestors, reproached him for replacing stinking candles at four sous a livre by tapers at twenty-two sous. Once upon a time Monsieur would have been content with a valet, Madame with a maid-servant. Now they employed as many as thirty domestics who, incidentally, did not cost much, for the impoverished country people flocked to such employment.

The bourgeoisie obtained yet another increase in prestige thanks to the privileged situation which was accorded to the intellectuals. In fact, if La Rochefoucauld, Bussy-Rabutin, Mme de La Fayette, and Mme de Sévigné were high-born (the writings of Retz and Saint-Simon were not to be known until the eighteenth century), nearly all the geniuses who made 'the Century of Louis xiv' were of bourgeois origin.

Never before had writers and artists found themselves so well understood, supported, stimulated and pensioned as they were during this reign (on the condition always that they did not meddle with politics). Lulli almost cut the figure of a favourite, for the King was intoxicated by music. A schism between official and non-conformist art would have been ridiculed. With the exception of La Fontaine, who was too friendly with Fouquet, and La Bruyère, who was lost among the Condés, the great writers gravitated round the throne. Molière had to contribute to the court entertainments, but this was worth while because it ensured the protection necessary to write the masterpieces which, without royal assent, would have brought him ruin. Boileau, satirical, flattering and well liked by Louis, was His Majesty's historiographer; likewise Racine. That may seem unworthy, today, of the author of *Phèdre*; at the time it was considered an honour. Bossuet exercised an all too strong influence on philosophy and religion. It was an age, unlike others, in which no genius was ever neglected or misunderstood.

It is true that the *Journal des Savants*, whose appearance in 1665 marked the birth of the literary press, had serious difficulties with Parliament over its 'mad and inept way of criticizing everyone'. But the impetus had been given, all the same, and the Dutch gazettes which were smuggled in kept the public informed of what was claimed to be secret. *Le Mercure Galant* satisfied the frivolous curiosity of people of fashion.

It was at this time that the Académie Française, placed under the protection of His Majesty and sitting at the Louvre, assumed the importance which it still keeps today. The salons were already preparing for elections, and Academic receptions conferred great prestige. Literary production was considerable; between 1660 and 1700 there appeared some six hundred novels and as many collections of poems.

The reign of the Sun King was a period of extremes. While the court displayed its splendour, while the cities became the most modern in the world, while creative genius flourished, the people lived in misery, epidemics and famines laid waste to the country, and pitiless fiscal laws stirred up revolts and carnage as in the time of Richelieu.

The peasants were not exactly as La Bruyère had painted them: 'wild animals . . . black and livid and scorched by the sun', who 'withdrew at night into dens where they lived on black bread and water and roots'. At least they were not all like that. About one-fifth of the land belonged to them, and, when he was not the victim of some calamity, the small rural proprietor led a life that was poor but bearable. The famous 'roots' of La Bruyère, which have sometimes caused misunderstanding, were vegetables, and people also lived on butter, milk, fruit, black bread, nuts and chestnuts. This was not enough, of course, for a labourer who toiled throughout the day. As for the unskilled workers, the farm labourers, their conditions were pitiful indeed, for they were hardly paid at all.

Colbert himself scarcely troubled about the common man, who bore, almost alone, the ever-increasing burden of taxation. The court never thought about him, and Vauban grew indignant about it in the *Dîme Royale*: 'It seems to me that people in France have never given enough thought to humble people, that they have had too little consideration; and so they are the most ruined and the most wretched people in the kingdom.' Louis XIV thought such ideas were seditious.

The problem of wheat was acute, because the impediments to its free circulation could mean a dearth in one province while the neighbouring province had a surplus. In certain circumstances there was also the obligation to lodge troops, not to mention the spasmodic ravages of war. Throughout the reign the crises grew worse until the disastrous year 1709.

Here is some evidence. From Saint-Simon: 'The nakedness and exhaustion [of the people] means that the fields are left uncultivated, the species of cattle die out, and nothing remains for the harsh tax-collector but the ruins of their dilapidated houses.' From Pesant de Boisguilbert: 'It is a fact that more than half France is lying fallow or badly cultivated . . . This is even more ruinous than abandoning the ground completely, because the product cannot repay the expenses of cultivation'. From Mme de Maintenon: 'There are now no market-days without sedition.' From Mme de Sévigné, during a stay in Brittany: 'I see only people who owe me money and weep.' From the Intendant of the Limousin in 1692: 'I have found more than 70,000 people, of every age and both sexes, who find themselves reduced to begging for their bread until March; in the meantime they are living on the remains of half-rotten chestnuts.' From the advocate Tourton de Sainte-Etienne: 'Not only is horse-flesh commonly eaten, but they have eaten all the dogs.' From Madame, Princesse Palatine, in 1709: 'If you go out, you are followed by a crowd of poor people crying out that they are hungry . . . The humble people are dying of cold like flies.'

But does this mean, as Georges Mongrédien sensibly enquires,[1] that the common people in the provinces did nothing but suffer for fifty years? It would be a mistake to believe so:

There are good years, and perhaps more good years than bad. Memoirs and descriptions abound in accounts of family or parish fêtes. . . . The peasant, who makes the earth productive, . . . is rarely at the end of his resources. He guards them jealously because it is important for the tax-collector not to see a display of excessive comfort . . . So he knows both difficult times and happier times, in turn. But the characteristic of country life, as compared with the regularity of to-day, is instability, and uncertainty of the morrow. This is explained by the economic régime.

The so-called classical order reached its apogee during the first twenty-five years of the personal reign of Louis XIV. The subject of the Sun King, the King whom the élite of the western world accepted as a model, liked the discipline and the authority which he imposed, he liked the indisputable dogmas: in a word, he welcomed constraint. After the tumults of the Renaissance and the Reform, he considered that the great problems had been solved, he was opposed to excessive and dangerous curiosity, adventure and experiment. Pascal declared that the whole misfortune of men came from the fact that they could not stay in peace in one room. 'The classical spirit . . . wanted to be stability itself . . . Politics, religion, society and art were submitted to interminable discussions, to endless criticism . . . People were afraid of space because it contained surprises and they wanted, if it was possible, to stop time.[2]

During the 1680s, the apparently indestructible order began to disintegrate under the barrage of the new critics.

If one ideal was sacrosant, it was the cult of Antiquity. From the King himself, whose statue was clad as a Roman Emperor, to the most provincial scribe, appeal was made to the Ancients. Then, quite suddenly this cult was denounced, a group of men proclaimed themselves *modern* and, using the word like a magic formula, they discredited all that belonged to the past. The quarrel of the Ancients and Moderns broke out, and novelty

---

[1] Georges Mongrédien: *La Vie Quotidienne sous Louis XIV.*
[2] Paul Hazard: *La Crise de la Conscience Européenne.*

became the new cult which Paul Valéry would one day define: 'Novelty, that most perishable of qualities, is still a quality of such eminence that its absence spoils all others for us and its presence replaces them.'

To the French, and to many others, Descartes preached the doctrine of reason. Pierre Bayle was not afraid to write: 'It is pure and simple illusion to pretend that an opinion which is passed down from century to century and from generation to generation cannot be entirely false'. People saw that they must reconsider the accepted ideas on history, nature, astrology and, in fact, on most things. Even Holy Scripture did not escape the critical spirit. Nothing was accepted on faith any more.

Bossuet thundered indignantly at the iniquities of the unbelievers: 'Their judgments, which they take for guides, offer nothing but conjectures and embarrassments to their minds; the absurdities into which they fall by denying religion become more than the truths whose loftiness astounds them, and, as they will not believe incomprehensible mysteries, they follow incomprehensible errors one after the other'. The illustrious prelate had a hard task. To tell the truth 'he was not the peaceful builder of a sumptuous cathedral, . . . he was much more like the workman who ran busily, hurriedly, to repair the breaches which grew more threatening with every day'. (Hazard)

The Church had been imperilled, the monarchy was likewise attacked, for it rested on divine right. Now, from Holland, from Germany, and, above all, from England, there sprang the conception of *natural right* which was substituted for the doctrine of 'the will of God'. In 1697, at the Treaty of Ryswick, and again, in 1713, at the Treaty of Utrecht, Louis XIV, the very incarnation of divine right, was to be forced to accept the fall of the Stuarts and thus to recognize *natural right*.

At this moment the whole classical system was about to collapse, and the individual, too, was to be transformed. The successor to the Courtier of Baltazar Gracián, was the *honnête homme*. The *honnête homme*, who hated excesses and showed exquisite politeness, who sought conciliation 'between ancient wisdom and Christian virtues, between the everyday and the sublime'. He was to keep his prestige until the end of the seventeenth century, and then become, in his turn, the victim of the general ferment. He was to yield to an entirely new character, one concerned with the future and not with the past, for his earthly happiness and not with his salvation, impatient to travel, to discover; a devotee of knowledge and a believer in progress. This character was to inaugurate the Revolution.

14 Spain

Philip IV had numerous children, but his sons did not survive. The political alliances sanctioned by the Treaty of the Pyrenees and by the French marriage of the Infanta Maria Theresa were decided on with the tacit assumption that he would die without a male heir. Then, four years after the Treaty, a new Infant, Don Carlos, was born. He was so frail that no importance was attached to him. But, to the general astonishment, the abortive, rickety child survived his father and became King Charles II. He was to reign for thirty-five years, balanced on the edge of the grave.

His entourage, who were anxious only to prolong his days, thought little about his education, so that he could barely read or write. Velasquez has recorded for us a terrifying portrait of his degeneracy; the extraordinarily long, narrow face with its disproportionate features; the body remained that of an invalid child.

The portrait of such a fiancé horrified the pretty, petulant Marie Louise of Orleans, niece of Louis XIV,[1] who had been betrothed to him to seal the Treaty of Nijmegen.

'People like you belong to the state,' the King said, in order to break her resistance. 'I could not do better for my daughter.'

'You can do better for your niece,' replied the unhappy girl, who loved her cousin, the Grand Dauphin.

She thought she was exchanging Paradise for the Inferno when she had left the pleasures of the court of the Sun King, and discovered the sombre Escurial, the tomb of so many young queens. Marie Louise inspired the wretched Charles with a violent passion. She was none the less the prisoner and the victim of the great noblemen in whose eyes a Frenchwoman was the incarnation of the Devil and they used the etiquette of the court to undermine her. Her French servants were accused one day of plotting the death of the King, and her nurse was tortured. She herself nearly died from a fall from a horse because it was forbidden to touch the

---

[1] She was the daughter of Philip of Orleans (Monsieur) and Henrietta Maria, sister of Charles II of England.

Queen. A bold man, who had the courage to go to the Queen's assistance, then escaped as fast as his horse would take him.

Charles reproached his wife for not giving him an heir, and as a last resort, agreed to submit to exorcisms which came nearer to magic than to religion. But it was no use. Marie Louise died at twenty-eight, probably poisoned at the instigation of the Austrian party.

She was succeeded by Maria Anna of Pfalz-Neuburg whom Victor Hugo was to make the heroine of *Ruy Blas*. Although she was wholly devoted to the cause of Austria, she, too, led the existence of a prisoner. 'She showed little piety,' wrote Villars, the French Ambassador, 'little modesty and restraint; one saw her all day at the palace windows (strictly forbidden to the Queens of Spain). She was making signs and sometimes speaking aloud to miserable Frenchmen, who seemed to be her lovers [i.e. her admirers] as much as the lovers of her waiting women.'

Beautiful, scheming, devoid of willpower, she abandoned herself entirely to her favourite, a Protestant: Gertrude Wolff von Gudenberg, Countess Berlepsch, nicknamed 'the partridge'. A voracious partridge she was too who 'took everything she could lay her hands on and sold the highest offices'. According to Louville, the French envoy, she transferred to her own account nearly all the capital of the kingdoms of Naples and Spain as well as the army funds! Not long before the King's death, she removed all her treasures to Germany.

This reign was marked by a regression towards the Middle Ages and by an extraordinary dearth of money. In the age of Molière and Newton, the King of Spain was living among visionary monks, exorcisers, dwarfs, nurses, duennas, buffoons, and black gentlemen adorned with monstrous spectacles – and all this enveloped in fumigating mists of 'supernatural virtue'.

The Inquisition, ever present, grew rampant. Here is the account which Villars has left of it:

There was a great ceremonial public account of the trial and condemnation of several people guilty of crimes against religion. They had been collected from all the inquisitions in Spain. A great theatre had been erected for the occasion in the Plaza Mayor in Madrid, and here, from seven in the morning until nine at night, one was busy seeing criminals and hearing them sentenced. Eighteen Jews, as many men as women, obstinate creatures, and two relapsers and a Mahometan, were condemned to the flames. Fifty other Jews or Jewesses, caught for the first time and repentant, were sentenced to several years' imprisonment and to wearing what is called Sambenito, which is a yellow jacket with a red St Andrew's cross front and back. Ten others, guilty of double marriages, witchcraft and other sorcery, appeared with great cardboard caps, a rope round the neck and a candle in the hand: the sentence for these is generally the whip, the galleys, or banishment.

The following night, those who had been condemned to the flames were burnt outside the city, on a piece of ground which had been built up for the purpose; and here, before they were executed, these wretches had to suffer a thousand tortures, even the monks who attended them burning them slowly with flambeaux to convert them. Several people, who had climbed up on the piece of ground, thrust at them with swords, and the crowd hurled stones at them. ... Those who were sentenced to be burnt were brought back to the theatre, each of them held by two Grandees of Spain. Monks who were utterly ignorant were vehemently haranguing these Jews without giving them any explanation of their heresies, while some of the criminals answered with as much learning as sang-froid, and others were gagged, for fear that they should speak. They appeared throughout, until they died, with a countenance which deserved a better cause, and some of them threw themselves into the fire.

These horrors, a climate of informing and police terror did not prevent either entertainments or love-affairs. In the noblemen's liaisons with the ladies of the court, there was an element of the grotesque. To quote the French Ambassador once again,

... it was not so much a pleasure as an illness. The liaison was highly imaginary: it consisted of presenting oneself in a square in front of the palace and there, in a carriage, talking by signs to a mistress who replied in the same fashion from a very high window ... Though the King had forbidden it, one saw the first gentlemen of the Court, married, old, and some of them grand-fathers, ruining their House by these passions and bringing down upon themselves everything unpleasant which the jealousy of their wives and domestic division could inflict.

This magnificent monarchy, the mistress of the greatest colonial empire in the world, lived from top to bottom in incredible destitution. The provinces were so exhausted

... that in some parts of Castile one was obliged to barter merchandise in order to live, because there was no more money to buy it ... Nothing was paid for in the King's household, and things reached such extremes that when most of the lesser domestics had given in their liveries and were to leave the service, it was very hard to find the means of making them stay ... The Household of the Queen-Mother, which had always been large, had been without pay for quite a long time, and all the servants had been obliged to live at their own expense, because the appropriate funds were lacking, and the treasurers were in no position to make advances on the rations which had to be paid for every day. ... In the meantime the Queen had been for more than six months without money, either for her amusements or for the many expenses which she had incurred on her journey ... She was finally settled with five hundred pistoles a month ... It was not much, after six months during which she had been secretly obliged to borrow money to give to her French women and to feed some horses which she had brought and was not allowed to ride ...

And so one saw, simultaneously, two very different things: an extraordinary dearth of money, an extreme expensiveness of food and merchandise. Both reached such a pitch that very many people in Madrid pawned and then sold their furniture to subsist; and this gave foreigners a new means of despoiling the Spaniards, who were forced by necessity to part with their silver plate and jewels and their most valuable possessions for much less than they were worth. (Villars)

The taxes, the number of functionaries busy collecting them, and the number of tribunals charged with prosecuting defrauders, grew all the time; and, by a strange phenomenon, these enormous levies of money hardly profited the state at all. Spain was living like a noblewoman, that is to say she did no work and she despised trade. And so she had neither manufacturers nor raw materials to sustain her. She had no ships, either. Foreigners provided them for her, and did not hesitate to confiscate two out of every three galleons laden with gold and silver from the East Indies. Nearly 7,000 Frenchmen immigrated in order to perform the tasks which the Spaniards disdained. They did not earn much, but they worked hard and accumulated their savings with which they returned to France. It was an army, which ebbed and flowed, continually draining the country of its substance.

Spain was becoming depopulated. In half a century Seville had seen the number of its inhabitants reduced by three-quarters, its cultivated soil by nineteen twentieths! On the other hand the cost of living continued to rise. Money was 'irregular' to an unbelievable degree. A great quantity of copper pieces in circulation were found to be counterfeit. When the Duke of Medina Coeli became prime minister, his first care was to devalue these 'tin reals'. But, as Villars wrote,

... the remedy was essential, but it was applied in a way which made it worse than the ailment. This first chance caused the gold and silver coins, reduced to half their previous value, to be taken from the kingdom in vast quantities, and strangers made considerable profits from them, especially the Portuguese, who gained nearly one-third ... The administrators and contractors of public money, who had only collected this kind of money in their coffers, found themselves insolvent, and private people were reduced to the same condition. And so the King and his subjects were deprived both of their incomes, and the whole kingdom found itself without money. Bankers lacked the funds and credit to satisfy bills of exchange ... Whole bodies of merchants had to be given letters of reprieve, first for four months and then for a further period. But they could not re-establish themselves all the same, for the money was still lacking, and therefore trade remained interrupted as well. Foreigners found fresh profit in this new Spanish affliction. They bought the forbidden 'tin' cheaply and sent it to Genoa, England and other places where they advantageously traded the metal which had a quite considerable silver alloy.

To foreign observers, the behaviour of individual people was no less astonishing than that of the State. Mme d'Aulnoy, who was staying in Spain, described it in her letters:

I knew a man of great family who was very badly off but still wanted fifteen thousand masses to be said for him when he died. His last wish was fulfilled, and this money was taken before the money he owed his poor creditors; for, however legitimate their debts, they could be given nothing until all the masses requested in the will had been said . . . if a great nobleman dies, and he has a hundred servants, his son keeps them on, though he will not reduce the number of those already in his house. If the mother happens to die, the women enter the service of her daughter or daughter-in-law in the same way, and this continues down to the fourth generation, for they are never dismissed. They are put into these neighbouring houses which I've mentioned to you, and they are paid their allowance . . .

People have a great number of slaves here, and they are bought and sold very dearly. They are Moors and Turks. Some of them are worth as much as four or five hundred écus. Once upon a time one had the rights of life and death over them. An employer could kill his slave as he could have killed a dog; but it was decided that this barbarity did not accord with the maxims of Christianity and the custom has now been forbidden. However, they still sometimes beat them until they break their bones, and they are not summonsed for it . . . As for the other servants, it would be dangerous to maltreat them; most of them claim to be as well born as the master whom they serve . . . They say that one must not insult them in their misfortune; that though they are reduced to being servants, they have not renounced their honour. Even the poor have their vanity, and when they ask for alms, they do so with an imperious and commanding air. If you refuse them, you have to do so politely, and say to them: 'I am sorry, cavalier, I have no money at all.'

Women's fashions caused Mme d'Aulnoy no less astonishment:

For the first time [she wrote], I dressed like a Spanish woman. I cannot imagine a more uncomfortable dress, your shoulders have to be so tightly bound that they hurt, you can't raise your arm, and you can hardly get it into a sleeve. I was put into an enormous bulky *guardingant* (because they must be worn in the Queen's presence). I didn't know what to do with this strange machine. You can't sit down . . . My hair was dressed *à la Melene*, that is to say it was all straggling over my neck and tied up at the end with a nonpareille . . . Finally I put on some *chapins*, they were more for breaking my neck than for walking . . . I was surprised when I arrived at the Princesse de Monteleon's to see several young women with great pairs of spectacles propped on their noses and attached to their ears; what astonished me even more, was that they did nothing which made these glasses necessary. They talked and still did not take them off. I got worried about it, and asked the Marquise de la Rosa, with whom I have become great friends, why they did so . . . She told me they did so for gravity's sake, that they did not need to wear them, they only did so to attract respect.

L

This respect did not earn them the prestige which was enjoyed by actresses, even though these were condemned by the Church:

It may be said [to quote Mme d'Aulnoy again] that actresses are adored at this Court, there isn't one of them who isn't the mistress of a very great nobleman, and for whom he has not engaged in several duels, and killed a number of people. I don't know what they say that's so pretty, but, to tell the truth, they are the most miserable carcasses in the world. They spend with wild extravagance, and people would rather let their whole household perish of hunger and thirst than let a wretched actress lack the most superfluous things . . .

The empire was exhausted, and Charles II, who feared the dismemberment of the twenty-three kingdoms, left them as a whole to the grandson of Louis XIV. He, too, had been brought up in ignorance and was a pious Christian. He greeted his extraordinary destiny 'with the gravity of a king of eighty', noted Mme de Maintenon. But he was in fact only seventeen and stood in fear of his grandfather.

'Be a good Spaniard,' said the King, 'it is now your first duty. But remember that you were born a Frenchman so preserve the union of the two nations.'

He strove for several weeks to give Philip 'instructions on the art of reigning'. Philip V left Versailles on 4 December 1700. After two centuries of war, how would the Spanish people receive a sovereign from the rival nation? How should a French prince behave in the presence of subjects of whom he knew nothing? Before he crossed the frontier a simple question of dress posed the problem:

Would the new King adopt the Spanish costume, sombre and entirely black? And, in particular, would he wear that sort of ruff, that golilla, which, he said, would be a torture to his neck? The costume was the national insignia. In coloured dress, with lace round his neck, the King would always appear like a French prince. Philip hesitated. People whispered that he should resist. The black costume, the carcanet at the neck, was Philip II's invention. Could the French dynasty not bring a costume of its own? Was he going to make his entrance in dead men's shoes? Louis XIV was consulted and made the wise, oracular pronouncement: one must not begin by shocking the Spaniards. Yes, Philip was to give up his neck to a golilla, and then, on occasion, he might relax, and appear again, in private, in a gayer, more comfortable French dress. Gradually his subjects would adopt it, too. Nothing abrupt. Nature proceeds by imperceptible steps to such metamorphoses. Changing the costume was touching the way of life, the character. Black expressed the religious gravity of the monarch, the golilla announced an almost hieratical majesty. A man with his neck caught in a golilla did not turn his head with every wind, he did not rush off madly to the hunt; he stayed in his palace, he went to church, he was careful. The French dress was that of a madcap.[1]

[1] Mme Saint René Taillandier: *La Princesse des Ursins*.

Philip v was disagreeably impressed when the French Ambassador advised him never to smell flowers or scents and not to open his letters himself, for fear of poison. But the Spaniards charmed him by their enthusiasm.

The King of Spain [wrote Saint-Simon] finally reached Madrid on 19 February 1701. He had had crowds and continual acclamations everywhere on his road, and in the cities there had been fêtes and bullfights, and a quantity of ladies and nobility from the surrounding countryside. On his arrival at Madrid, there was such a multitude that sixty people were found to be suffocated. Outside the city and in the streets an infinity of carriages lined his route, filled with much-adorned ladies; and the whole Court and the nobility filled the Buen Retiro, where he would dismount and stay. The junta and many of the Grandees received him at the door, and Cardinal Portocarrero wanted to throw himself at his feet to kiss his hand. The King would not allow it: he raised him and embraced him and treated him as his father; and finally came all the counsellors, everyone who was illustrious, a crowd of people of quality, an infinite nobility, and the whole Spanish household of the late King Charles II. The streets through which he passed had been decked with hangings and, in the Spanish fashion, they had been filled with tiers of seats filled with fine pictures and an infinity of silver, with magnificent triumphal arches at intervals. It would have been impossible to see a greater and more general demonstration of joy. The King was well made, in the flower of his early youth, fair-haired, like the late King Charles and like his grandmother Maria Theresa, grave, silent, circumspect, restrained, made to live among the Spaniards.

Once the festivities were over, the adolescent King felt the insurmountable wall of etiquette close round him, and he became a prey to tedium. He had to be rescued as soon as possible, and he was obliged to marry Maria Louisa of Savoy, an ardent young girl endowed with the grace of Italian princesses and with a fire, tenacity and courage which were unusual for her age. Her under-developed body inspired Philip with a lust which alarmed him. In order to satisfy his carnal fury, he never left his wife, day or night, and became her slave.

A sovereign of thirteen endowed with such power needed a guardian angel. Louis xiv and Mme de Maintenon gave her the Princess Orsini, who had changed her name to the Princesse des Ursins. She was *La Trémoille*, twice widowed, once by an exiled rebel and once by a Roman nobleman. Thirty years at the Papal Court had taught her diplomacy and intrigue and the art of seducing and managing the princes of this world.

Appointed *Camarera Mayor*, she conquered the heart of Maria Louisa, domineered the court, bent dignitaries to her will, and reduced the ministers to nonenities. The King nominally reigned as the absolute master, but the Queen governed the King, and Mme des Ursins governed the Queen.

This is how the *Camarera* described her ''employment'':

I have no rest at all and I don't even find time to talk to my secretary. There is no longer any question of resting after dinner, or of eating when I'm hungry. I am only too glad to snatch an inadequate meal and even then it is very rare for me not to be called the moment I sit at table ... To tell the truth, Mme de Maintenon would laugh heartily if she knew all the details of my situation. Do tell her that I'm the person who has the honour of taking the King of Spain's dressing-gown when he goes to bed, and giving it to him with his slippers when he rises; if that were all, I could bear it patiently, but every night, when the King goes into the Queen's room to go to bed, the Count of Benavento entrusts me with His Majesty's sword, with a chamber-pot and a lamp which I usually spill over my clothes. That is a little too comic for me. The King would never get up if I didn't go and draw his curtains, and it would be sacrilege if anyone but myself went into the Queen's room when they were in bed. The other day the lamp went out because I had spilt half the oil in it; I had no idea where the windows were, I hadn't seen them open because it was dark when we arrived at that particular place. I thought I was going to break my nose bumping against the wall and we spent a quarter of an hour, the King of Spain and I, knocking into each other as we looked for them. I am leading the life of a galley-slave, but I am well, Madame.

Thanks to the Princesse des Ursins, Louis XIV was able to impose his mark on the government of Spain, teach it something of the order and unity so important to him, and to revive the economy.[1] Thanks to Maria Louisa herself, who spoke of her 'heart of fire' and fell in love with her kingdom, Philip V became a purely Spanish king, adored by his subjects. Thanks to both women the young King, assailed by half Europe, twice obliged to abandon his capital to the Austrians, deserted for a moment by France herself, was able to overcome the trials, defeats, and the nameless miseries of a twelve years' war. He was able to found his dynasty on the love of the people even more solidly than he did on treaties.

Neither the misfortunes of this sombre period, nor the resistance of the Inquisition and the Jesuits prevented Spain from being open, now, to outside influences. Her own exhaustion had infected her intellectual élite, her art had become a mere foible of the court. And so the invasion of French taste met with little resistance, it was enough for the court to be French and for the national art to be French. Philip V felt nostalgia for Versailles. He summoned French architects and painters, and adorned his palaces with furniture made in Paris to the designs of Robert de Cotte, and he created a manufactory of tapestries. Mme des Ursins, who knew 'no more agreeable occupation than that of furnishing houses', inspired him to build. René Carlier, the pupil of Robert de Cotte, came and submitted

---

[1] The centralization of the kingdom was completed, the provinces lost their privileges, the government was reorganized on the model of the French Government.

plans to him: none was accepted unless it had received the guarantee of the great ancestor.

By 1714 a moribund Spain had returned to life. But the young Queen was to pay for a miracle which was largely her work. Maria Louisa of Savoy was victorious, but she died of her victory. The privations, the agonies, the sleepless nights in the icy rooms defeated her at last. Imposing doctors, clad in black, their swords at their sides, filed pompously past Her Majesty, and examined her from a distance, because etiquette forbade them to touch the Queen. Mme des Ursins consulted all the faculties of Europe, and the Hippocrates prescribed the waters of Bagnères. Unfortunately Spain was one of those jealous mistresses who preferred the death of the loved one to the danger of losing him: her *Savoyana* was not permitted to go, so Maria Louisa resigned herself, and died on the threshold of her twenty-seventh year. Until the last minute the pious Philip wanted to enjoy those delights which he could not know again for a long time, without sinning. He had to be torn from the deathbed.

According to the rites, her remains were laid in the crypt of the Escurial amidst the candles, reflected a hundred times in the black marble. Other Queens and Infantas had succumbed to grief and langour. The *Savoyana* alone had been consumed by heroism and love.

Philip v shut himself up in the palace of Medina Coeli with only Mme des Ursins for company. He wept for his wife and waited eagerly to replace her, for his health could no more be satisfied with his celibate life than his conscience would permit him a mistress. *La Camarera* anxiously perused the genealogies, and looked for a queen who might become a docile instrument in her hands.

The imperious governess had near her, at the time, the former secretary of the Duc de Vendôme: a compliant Italian, obliging and bubbling over with ideas. The Abbé Alberoni, the son of one of the Duke of Parma's gardeners, suggested his master's niece, Elizabeth Farnese. This princess belonged, in a certain degree, to the Austrian clan, for she was also the niece of the dowager Empress and of the widow of Charles II; but poverty, and the ravages of smallpox, predestined her for the part of pupil; Mme des Ursins accepted.

While Philip v burned with impatience, Elizabeth Farnese, symbolically married in Italy, prolonged her journey for several months, despite many messages, and caused much anxiety to the agents of the King of France. It was on 23 December 1714 in the little town of Jadraque, that she finally met Mme des Ursins. The two women shut themselves up together, and then the astonished crowd heard exclamations, an order, a clank of arms.

The gilded carriage, surrounded by guards like a criminal's cell, was already bearing off the old *Camarera*, in full court dress, towards the Pyrenees, in disgrace and exile.

A revolution had been accomplished. Philip v fell into the power of an impulsive, violent woman whose will was guided by the disquieting Alberoni. Not once in thirty years, did this indefatigable husband leave his wife. She was to exhaust him, until he fell into complete insanity. Even their commodes were next to each other in a single closet.

15 Italy

For two centuries Italy had served as a model for Western civilization. She in turn submitted to a foreign influence: the influence of French philosophy, French science, the French theatre, to the influence of classicism, 'the last triumph of order which the modern world would know'.[1] The élite adopted the character of the *honnête homme*, 'which contained, in equal proportions, the humanist of the Renaissance, the knight of the Middle Ages and the Christian of the Catholic Reform'. The doctrine of Gassendi was taught at Pisa, Padua, Naples and Rome. Descartes gradually conquered the peninsula. People admired Mabillon and his rivals.

This breath of fresh air was beneficial; for the creative faculties, awaking from a long sleep, once again revealed themselves. They were seen in the experimental sciences with Redi and Vallisnieri; in tragedy with Maffei; in history and criticism with Muratori and the great scholars; and in music with Corelli and Vivaldi.

In the meanwhile, the tireless Bernini was creating the prototype of the pontifical or royal portrait. He erected the gigantic statues of the Confession of St Peter and the tomb of Alexander VII, prepared the decoration of the St Angelo Bridge, and scattered fountains across the Eternal City. Each of his works revived the traditional mannerism; it was a baroque 'repertoire' to which generations of artists from every land would turn.

The Rome which he endowed with new finery had lost a little of its facility and its sometime scandalous picturesqueness. Its morals were certainly still very free: Queen Christina of Sweden, newly converted and installed in the Corsini Palace, kept gossips busy with her eccentricities, but the Holy See watched attentively to make sure that dogma and morality were respected.

Pope Alexander VII condemned those who 'dared to attack, in public or in private', the dogma of the Immaculate Conception, and he put a work on casuist morality by the Jesuit Father Pirot on the index.

[1] Casella: *Histoire des Papes.*

Innocent XI showed more severity and energy than his immediate predecessors. He re-established finances by proscribing extravagance and avoiding nepotism. He would even have fulminated in a bull against this abusive practice, if the Sacred College had not begged him to desist.

Struggling with an extraordinary outburst of unorthodox doctrines, Innocent XI fought probabilism, quietism and Jansenism. Gallicanism caused him serious anxiety. There was an open struggle between the Sovereign Pontiff and the Most Christian King, to whom the French bishops seemed ready to grant the omnipotence in the realm of the spirit that he already held on earth.

'If I listened to them,' Louis XIV used to say with a smile, 'I should be Mahomet.'

At the end of his reign he himself assured the victory of Ultramontanism to obtain the *Unigenitus* bull, which was designed to give the death blow to the Jansenists (1713). But the Church was already forced to confront serious dangers of another order. As a reaction against the aridity of classicism, there arose, 'a sentimental Christianity, breaking away from all authority, ready to swoon in a pantheistic or vaguely deistic mist'. Reason, on the other hand, ceased to be subject to faith. Analytic and critical, it now questioned everything, and claimed 'to treat with God as with an equal'. Individualism and scepticism were looming ahead, and they found supporters even among those whose vocation it was to fight them.

It was now that the Grand Duke of Tuscany's subjects discovered what absurd situations the dynastic principle could create – like any other principle when carried to extremes.

On the death of Ferdinand II (1670), the House of Medici was represented by his two sons, Cosimo and Francesco Maria. The younger one, according to custom, became a cardinal, and the elder one, his father's successor, made a splendid marriage: to Marguerite Louise of Orleans, niece of Louis XIII, first cousin of Louis XIV.

Cosimo III liked magnificence and exotic fashions, and spent recklessly. His young wife shared his taste for splendour, but that was their only point of agreement. The Grand Duke, who had been influenced by a bigoted mother, displayed an ostentatious devotion which made him a prey to hypocrites, upon whom he showered largesse. Both soldiers and functionaries were bereft of their pay in order that he could devote huge sums to pious ceremonies and to the conversion of infidels. Cold, withdrawn, devoid of grace, and subject to hypochondria, he inspired the French princess with genuine repulsion. She was accustomed to the gallantry and gaiety of the youthful court of the Sun King.

Their married life was disastrous, and in order to escape it, Cosimo travelled abroad, but every time he returned home, their animosity flared

Religion and Science

Children Instructed in the Catechism, detail from a painting by Magnasco.

Neüe Schwarm geister=Brut.

Above. Gerard Dou's portrait of Rembrandt's mother reading the Bible.

Opposite top. The Court Chapel in Dresden, where Heinrich Schütz, leading German composer of the seventeenth century, conducts the court choir.

Opposite bottom. Nonconformists of various persuasions – a Quaker, a Ranter, a Robins (whose wife is to give birth to the Messiah), and a Jew.

Top. A 'witches' sabbath'.

Bottom. Alchemy gave a lead to much of the advancement of science in the seventeenth century. Here an alchemist and his wife pray by their furnace that the mystical union of the sun and moon will take place in their 'vessel of Hermes'.

Louis XIV visiting the French Academy of Sciences, which he had founded in 1666.

Above. 'The Doctor versed in all the Sciences', engraving by Mitelli.

Below left. Valentine Greatraks, the Irish healer, 'famous for curing several Diseases and distempers by the stroak of his Hand only'.

Below right. The doctor's visit. Many developments in surgery and pharmacology in the seventeenth century greatly improved the lot of the patient.

David Teniers, *The Dentist*.

Vermeer, *The Geographer*. Advances in mapping, navigation and transport opened up the world, and broke down the boundaries of the old medieval European society.

up again. Three children were born, none the less, but so far from appeasing the Grand Duchess, they served only to intensify her grievances until, on the verge of madness, Cosimo relegated her to a villa from which she tried to escape. At last they decided on separation. Marguerite went back to France, where she led a miserable life first incarcerated in the Convent of Montmartre, and later in the Convent of Saint-Mandé.

Her two sons, Ferdinand and Giovan Gastone, became debauched in the extreme, but nevertheless Giovan Gastone received the inevitable red cap, while Ferdinand married a Bavarian princess, who was so virtuous and gentle that, faithful to his maternal heredity, he took a dislike to her. Since this unhappy union proved to be sterile, Giovan Gastone had to be restored to the laity in order to perpetuate the dynasty. They found him a wife who was as violent as his sister-in-law was gentle: Anna Maria of Saxe-Lauenburg, the widow of the Count of Neuburg, who only liked hunting and horses. She led a wild life in the depths of the forests of Bohemia, and, even when she was married, never wanted to leave them. Giovan Gastone used to visit her, but, after ten years, when these meetings failed to produce the hoped-for result, abandoned her.

Were the Medicis, then, to become extinct? Was Tuscany to become a vacant country? There remained one last resource, Cardinal Francesco Maria, the Grand Duke's brother. Cosimo III obliged him in his turn to leave the Church and the purple, and be married to the Princess Leonora di Gonzaga. Alas, when she discovered a husband in his fifties, obese, and dreadful, this charming young girl was horrified. She refused all contact with him, thus settling the fate of the dynasty and the state.

Cosimo III closed his account with all round bankruptcy. He had failed to assure his posterity, to relieve the poverty of the countryside, to make the Maremma healthy, or to bring the Greek Church nearer to the Roman Church as he had hoped when he welcomed the Greek families driven out of the Morea.

Giovan Gastone succeeded him, but, even in the course of his lifetime, the Great Powers disposed of Tuscany. One fine day Florence woke up to find that she was Austrian, in order that Poland should still belong to the Elector of Saxony and that Lorraine should be annexed to France.

On 11 August 1687, Venice received sensational news, when the *felucca* announced from the Lido the victories of Francesco Morosini who had just reconquered the Morea. The Senate bestowed unprecedented honours on the fortunate captain-general of the fleet, by erecting a bronze statue of him, surmounted by the standards captured from the Turks, in the very Hall of the Council of Ten. It was the last time that the intoxicated Venetians experienced the feeling of being a great nation, the mistress of an empire – even if this empire was in tatters.

However, they did not even manage to keep their monopolies. Although the Republic was very jealous of its industry, and gave privileges to its workmen, it forbade them to export or to trade with any foreign countries whatsoever. The emigration of a workman from Murano was equivalent to an attempt on the safety of the State. Colbert, who was resolved on the triumph of French industry, left nothing undone in order to attract the famous glass-makers. Many of them listened to their tempters, and did so despite the danger, for the tribunal of the Inquisition was daily informed of their actions in France, and they also ran the risk of assassination.

The glass-workers of Murano who had broken the ban were installed in the Faubourg Saint-Antoine. Louis XIV solemnly paid them a visit, promised a pension to their master, Antonio de Rivetta, and left a hundred and fifty doubloons as a gratuity to the workmen. 'My eyes are wet with tears,' wrote the Venetian Ambassador, 'to see how they have been brought here, through the unpunished wickedness of some of our citizens: these manufacturers which Providence, nature and industry had so specially allotted to us.'

The xenophobia of the Most Serene Republic of Venice did not prevent the ambassadors from being received with unparalleled magnificence. The Comte d'Avaux, the French Ambassador, won a victory worthy of his master's prestige: he had a procession of four gondolas each with four oarsmen, while his colleagues contented themselves with three. His successor, M. Amelot, increased the number still further. On 23 September 1682, in a jerkin completely embroidered in gold, he left his palace in his procession of gondolas, followed by the officers of his household and by forty gentlemen, including five Knights of the Order of Saint Michael.

The first and second of the Ambassador's five gondolas were all sculpted and gilt and enriched with hundreds of figures and bas-reliefs . . . The assembly of nobles and gentlemen, with and without masks, was very great, this being the only occasion on which it is not a capital offence for the nobles to enter an ambassador's house . . . Twelve violins could be heard in the portico at the top of the embassy, concerts in the private rooms, and fifes and trumpets at the second-floor windows . . . Downstairs all the populace were given wine to drink.[1]

The flotilla proceeded to the Piazzetta, where the Ambassador was conducted to the Staircase of the Giants. He mounted it, crossed the gallery, slowly climbed the gilded staircase, found the doors of the Anti-Collegio open, and entered the Council Chamber to find the Doge surrounded by the twenty-six principal members of the Government. The Ambassador made three bows, the ministers rose to their feet, the Ambassador made a speech to which the Doge replied. Thirty senators escorted him home.

[1] Manuscript in the Bibliothèque de Troyes.

It was the custom to decorate one of the entrances of the embassy and sometimes the portico with magnificent sideboards or dressers covered with handsome pieces of silver plate.

In order to avoid continual outbidding, which no longer corresponded to the state of French finances, the last envoy of Louis XIV, the Abbé de Pomponne, laid down the 'French ceremonial in Venice' in a detailed memorandum. And henceforth it was rigorously observed.

During the endless war against the Ottomans – unfortunately marked by the destruction of the Parthenon – the Republic still played a political and military rôle, but already the city of Venice was becoming a closed, mysterious and disturbing world which was ruled only by pleasure or by adventure. There was a striking contrast between the oppression and the freedom which existed side by side. The shadowy terror of informers hung over public life, the Inquisition controlled religious faith and intellectual inquiry. This inflexible discipline however, failed in all matters of government.

A curious custom – virtually a law – forbade any man of consequence to go out and be seen in public with his wife. This custom had given rise to a singular character, the *cicisbeo*. It was the *cicisbeo*, whom the husband accepted at marriage, who was entrusted with serving and entertaining the wife. He lived close beside her in the house, and he escorted her everywhere outside. The innocence of such intimacy was not questioned. And yet . . . conjugal morals were so lax that only the eldest child had the reputation of being legitimate. As for the others, all that was done was to save appearances. The Venetian Republic itself helped in this. If a husband was sent on some mission abroad and his wife became pregnant, he was recalled at once. Many of these complaisant husbands sought consolation with another kind of *cicisbeo ;* so much so that one day the Senate grew anxious about the future of the race and took measures to stimulate sexual proclivity. The public prostitutes were authorized to walk in certain streets with their breasts bare.

For a long time Venetian women had worn shoes with remarkably high soles, designed to protect their dresses from the mud in the alleyways and, in a practical way, to protect their virtue. How could they run to a secret rendezvous with these cumbersome pieces of equipment? The suppression of clogs, which were supplanted by flat-heeled shoes, caused a small revolution in morals as well as in dress.

As the respectable women grew emancipated, the courtesans saw their influence decline. The art of seduction ceased to be their monopoly. Literary, musical and entertaining, these disquieting beauties still, however, kept a clientèle, and among them were statesmen who revealed to them their secrets. Thus the courtesans were often the best source of information for foreign diplomats, who were forbidden close association with the patricians. The courtesans showed no respect for the sumptuary laws. They generally lived on the Grand Canal, where they flaunted themselves in provocative attire, and they were not afraid to parade in the Piazza San Marco when people came out of Mass, audaciously wearing white veils, like young brides.

Their less fortunate sisters, the prostitutes, were part of the décor of Venice. A traveller, Misson, noted: 'There are whole streets full of prostitutes, who give themselves to any passer-by ... They are dressed in red and yellow like tulips, their breasts are almost bare, their faces are heavily painted, and they always wear a bunch of flowers over the ear. You can see them by the dozen in the doorways and at the windows'.

Gambling was a serious occupation, often a profession. The decree enacted against its excesses was so harsh that it was ignored. The *ridotti*, *ritori*, *casini*, were real bandit dens, and functioned day and night. Marked cards and loaded dice surprised no one except the honest traveller. The state decided to reform this abuse and to control gambling by giving it legal status. Marco Dandolo opened an official establishment in his Palazzo San Moisè: the *Ridotto*. First came a huge ante-room, then two rooms devoted to the sale of sweetmeats and drinks (tea, coffee, chocolate); ten rooms were reserved for tables for *basset*, *faro* and *biribi*. Nearly a century later, someone thought of appeasing the plebeian fever, too, and *lotto* was instituted. The Republic did not fail to take its share of the squandered fortunes.

Patricians were expected to set the example of an irreproachable life. They succeeded without undue constraint, thanks to the carnival which allowed them take every liberty with impunity. The carnival was Latin; joyous, tumultuous, a brilliant form of hypocrisy which in England assumed the lugubrious look of respectability. Under the *tabarro* (black domino), the *bouta* (a veil which covered the head and shoulders), the tricorne and the bird-mask, desire and cupidity, chance and delusion culminated in the wildest frolics.

The carnival was held from the first Sunday in October until Christmas, then from Epiphany to Easter, and the *feria* added another fortnight. So for several months of the year Venice was populated with unrecognizable people and disguises. The characters of Italian comedy enjoyed themselves to their heart's content, Harlequin with his wooden sword, Mettacino in white with his plumed hat, Magnifico with his red jerkin and his black gown, Brighella with his huge pantaloons, Dr Graziano and Dr Balanzon who held burlesque consultations, and Signor Pantaloon,

the embodiment of the elderly Venetian merchant, always busily buying and selling in the Piazza San Marco, in turn father, husband, old bachelor or widower, rich or poor, miserly or prodigal, always full of himself and always ridiculous. As a rule he is plagued by two young ladies, Isabella and Smeraldina, who plot with their *soubrettes* to deceive him one way or another. In Venice and on the *terra firma* poor Pantaloon is always somebody's victim. (J. Gourbault)

The spirit of the age was not so much end-of-the-century as it was end-of-the-world. Optimism and forethought seemed out of date, and the mask of the Carnival of Venice concealed only cynical despair. It was the despair of a society whose arteries had hardened like those of an old man: a society in which further evolution was impossible.

16 Germany

The difference between 1600 and 1650, between before and after the Thirty Years' War, cannot be exaggerated. The German humanist as an ideal was replaced by the French *homme du gens*, local costumes by Paris fashions, theological quarrels by rival codes of etiquette. The history of the Holy Roman Empire changed into the histories of an association of sovereign states. The German people, reduced by one half had even changed ethnologically. Some regions like Austria, some towns like Hamburg were spared by the war, but Würtemberg, Berlin and Augsburg were reduced to one eighth, one fifteenth and one quarter respectively, of the former population. Nine hundred thousand people were killed in Saxony in two years. One hundred villages in Bavaria, three hundred in Hesse were destroyed. In Silesia and Brandenburg the number of deer exceeded the number of peasants. 'One can walk ten miles without seeing either man or beast'. It was the same with property and money: Wallenstein and Montecucoli had robbed the March of Brandenburg of 20,000,000 thalers. In Silesia both the middle classes and the peasantry had to contribute one half, officials and nobles two thirds of their income to the Imperial army. Estates with houses and farms were given away to obtain services.

Germany was parcelled out into 1,800 sovereign states, 300 of which belonged to the Reichstag in Regensburg. Austria had a tiny German core which was surrounded by foreign peoples; on one side, Prussia a province which did not belong to the German Empire. People considered themselves not as Germans but as Bavarians, Prussians or Hessians. A common language remained, however, together with a common criminal code and a common court of appeal in Wetzlar; and a common history. The nobility, the militant knights, the proud lords of the manor had changed into courtiers, servants of the 1,800 sovereigns. Gustav Freytag estimates that courtiers numbered five to six thousand, exclusive of domestics. The creation of new nobles, started by Ferdinand II, became a privilege of all sovereigns. Liselotte of the Palatinate mocked the new nobility, and the immortal figure of the *bourgeois gentilhomme*. The nobility had not only lost its independence but also its wealth. 'Power decreases but the titles increase', wrote the Duchess Sofia of Hanover in 1680. The race for titles produced the 'court tailor', the 'court watchmaker' the 'court chimney sweep'. Every successful man sought a title. The Fuggers became counts; the minor absolute princes were deified: 'If God were not God who could be God but Your most Serene Highness,' was written to an unimportant man like Ernst Ludwig of Hesse.

Compliments grew into an art, and there were no limits to the pomposity of address or to the humility of old families seeking a favour, let alone the minor official who demanded the same obeisance from his subordinates. 'Lord Chamberlains', 'Treasurers of the household', 'Equerries', 'Controllers of the Household', 'Really secret Councillors' graced many a puny court, and behind them the endless array of flunkeys and servants in the same hierarchical order. However, although absurd, it was preferable to the brutalities of war.

The German language had been corrupted by the hosts of foreign soldiers on German soil for many years. Literary people used French, sometimes Italian, university men, Latin, as of old, and the Austrian Court, Spanish. Christian Thomasius, an early figure of the enlightenment, was expelled from Leipzig university when he announced lectures in German. The Language of courts and of diplomacy became French, even where, as in Denmark a hundred years earlier, the reformation had introduced German.

Gryphius wrote a new version of the *miles gloriosus*, the boasting soldier of all times now characterized as a polyglot:

To make peace without me! Have I not shot the King of Sweden? What would it have been on the White Mountain without me? E che fama non m'acquistai, quando contesi col Gran Turca? Fi donc, go away because I get furious to death if I am bitter. Vinto dal ira calda e bollente e dallo sdegno arrabiato, I take St Stefan in Vienna by the spires and press them down, si forte in terra, that the whole world turns like a skittle.

In order to protect the German language, societies had been founded in the sixteenth century which only now flourished: 'The Palm Order', 'The order of the Swans of the river Elbe', 'The Shepherds from the Pegnitz'. Looking for an equivalent of the *honnête homme* they invented *deutsch gesinnter Tugendmut*. Among the 527 members of the Palm Order were the Great Elector, forty-nine dukes, nineteen princes, sixty counts and 125 other members of the aristocracy. Not all questions of property, restitution, expulsion were solved by the Peace of Westphalia. The Swedes and the Protestant Estates fought for restitution of Protestantism in Austria and Bohemia. The Emperor opposed them. Only in Lower

Austria and in Silesia did the Protestant nobles possess any rights. The Protestants from Inner and Upper Austria were forced to emigrate. Many secret Protestants remained in the Salzkammergut. In 1620 Ferdinand II had confiscated all the estates of the rebels in Bohemia, amongst them Hohberg, who instituted legal proceedings against this confiscation because he had fought with Wallenstein on the Emperor's side 1632–41. His estate was returned to him in 1650. His father-in-law who had been a leading Bohemian rebel, also had his estates returned to him. Hohberg took over the estates of his four stepdaughters, and this was typical of the absorption of the small estates by the large ones, which resulted in the disappearance of the small landed gentry in the course of the century. Likewise the situation of the Protestant Austrian nobility was deteriorating. The Catholic church, however, was striving to maintain its spiritual decisions, independantly of the state.

Meanwhile, there was a struggle for religious tolerance: Leibniz wanted to reconcile Lutherans, Calvinists and Catholics. Karl Ludwig of the Palatinate built a church in Mannheim for all creeds. Liselotte of the Palatinate wrote: 'Genuine Christians leave the quarrels to the clergy, superstitions to the mob and serve God in their hearts'. But the struggle was premature: Emperor Leopold I who reigned for fifty years, heard mass three times a day, Protestant Court pastors aspired to the position held by the confessors in catholic courts. 'I am not anxious to see the Pope,' wrote Duchess Sofia of Hanover from Rome in 1664, 'I have met too many Popes in Germany'. Christian Thomasius said: 'Lutherism has changed the wooden yoke of papistry into the iron one of Lutherism'.

It is an index of German energy that within ten years of the destruction of thousands of villages, the depopulation of the country and an atmosphere of utter demoralisation there began an era of splendid architecture. To demonstrate the rebirth of Catholicism, Jesuits employed the exuberance of Italian baroque with which they beautified the churches of Austria and Southern Germany, and ambitious princes, imitating the court of the Roi Soleil, built new palaces in their war ravaged lands. The architects were to start with mostly Italians: Carlone and Lurago in Prague, and Agostino Barelli, who built the Theatiner Church in Munich (1663) and the monasteries of Ebrach and Banz. But after about 1700 German architects had begun to flourish: in Vienna Fischer von Erlach designed the town-palace of Prince Eugene (1703), and Lucas von Hildebrand the Palais Belvedere (1693) and the Palais Kinsky (1709–13); in Dresden Pöppelmann designed the Zwinger (1711–22), and Nette built Ludwigsburg near Stuttgart in 1707. Paul Dury, one of the Huguenots who made their home at Cassel, built a French church in 1684, and also an Orangery for the sovereign. The two most important buildings in Berlin were erected at the end of the century: Nehring's Armoury in 1695 and Schlüter's Royal

Palace in 1698–1706. Thus, whilst literature and painting languished, architecture was unsurpassed. Likewise music, which found its supreme genius in J. S. Bach. His house at Eisenach shows wide stairs, high rooms and a feeling for space that was worthy of a palace.

It took longer to rebuild the towns. Twenty years after the war somebody found in Brandenburg 'half destroyed little places and the poor inhabitants strangely odd and ugly'. As late as 1681 the Great Elector was to prohibit pigs in Berlin, and since 1671 every peasant coming to Berlin to market was obliged to take with him a load of rubbish on his departure. Berlin had no street lighting until 1679, ten years after London, Paris and Amsterdam; but ten years before Vienna and seventeen years before Hanover. However, Germany was the first country to provide against fire: Bremen had fire fighting equipment by 1656, Nuremberg two years later. This was very important, as town houses were still half timbered and mostly covered with straw. Furniture was scarce everywhere but tapestries, known since the middle ages, became very popular. There were tapestry works in Berlin, Dresden, Munich, Vienna. The Bavarian Court had tapestries worth 8,000,000 thalers in 1687. Among the middle classes wainscoting was popular: Wallpapering was to come later.

Traditional and regional costumes were at last forsaken, and the new fashions were set by Paris and 'À la mode' became a form of abuse amongst contemporary satirists.

In 1626 Elector Maximilian of Bavaria introduced special dress regulations for all classes: peasants, lower middle class, artisans, clerks of the court, patricians, knights and nobles, doctors and licentiates, counts and baronets. Materials and trimmings were prescribed down to the smallest detail. The Duke of Gotha did the same for six classes of his subjects. Dresden forbade wigs in 1662, Brunswick ribbons, Leipzig trains in 1680. The regulations were never effective, although many people were punished for failure to comply. In 1661 in Nuremberg the printer Christoph Ender and his wife did not only wear too elegant dresses, they gave their dog a silver necklace and were fined as a result; but nothing could check the new fashions. 'The collars are changing with the moon,' complained Harsdörffer. In 1650 when the Electress of the Palatinate showed her many dresses to her sister-in-law, Sofia said: 'It is not any more à la mode to have many dresses, one has to change with the fashion.' New hair styles were equally challenged: Moscherosch, reactionary like most satirists wrote: 'These long hairs are veritable thieves, invented by Latins whose ears have been lopped in punishment for some crime.' In 1624 a nobleman stabbed the peasant Thomas Schlegel in Zittau because he dared wear his hair as long as if he were a gentleman. Nothing caused greater outrage than the wig. The clergy who had warned their flock of the fate of Absalom for years now began to follow this fashion after special permission had been granted.

M

Etiquette became more pronounced than ever. The Reichstag in Regensburg was entirely occupied by questions of protocol. The most important question in the court of Louis XIV was who was allowed to sit down in the presence of the Queen, who had the right to an armchair, who to a stool, who was allowed to drive up to the Louvre. Hundreds of German Princes followed suit. Moscherosch laughed about the new method of bowing: 'You snap from head to feet like a pocket knife.' But Moscherosch was equally disdainful of new eating habits: 'This stupidity of eating salad with a fork. À la mode!' A gentleman had to know how to carve; and a whole literature about carving was published in Germany. He should also be conversant with the art of folding napkins into turbans, crowns, etc.

Dancing also had become extremely formalized. The *Maître de Plaisir* selected one couple at a time, who alone occupied the whole floor. Tempos were reduced to walking pace; and distinction in dancing an aristocratic preserve. Thus Bolise warned a young bourgeois to avoid excellence in case he should offend the nobility.

Travelling was hazardous in the extreme, owing to the poor state of the roads and the danger of highwaymen. The journeys from Berlin to Stettin, from Heidelberg to Nuremberg and from Frankfurt to Paris, all took six days. The first really comfortable carriage was built in Berlin in 1660. It was called a Berline, and was in use for 200 years. The inns were uncomfortable; a bed was provided for each traveller, but several to a room. In Wismar there was an inn 'with so many little rooms that almost each person can have a private room', wrote Pastor Hartmann. Hainhofer found the best inn of Germany in Jüterbog.

To avoid the tedium and coercion of etiquette a kind of masquerade existed in Vienna called *Wirtschaft*. Emperor and Empress dressed up as publican and wife, the ladies and gentlemen of the court as waiters and maids. Occasionally this served to solve problems of protocol. In 1698 Emperor Leopold and Czar Peter the Great could arrange to meet only at a 'Tavern', and they played their respective parts as innkeeper and peasant excellently.

At the Vienna Court gambling was also very popular, with *Piquet* and *tarochino* introduced by the Italians, and the Spanish *l'hombre*. 'Anybody rich and of old descent and not afraid of playing for high stakes can find much pleasure in Vienna and will not be barred from any society', wrote Herr Mathias von Wolzogen about Vienna at the end of the century:

A great crowd living near one another above and below makes acquaintance easy. There are no vagrant knights, romantic heros, poets and so-called 'Precieuses' in Vienna. The splendour is more rich than artistic, everything causing trouble and requiring thought is abhorrent. More is spent on dogs, horses, and dresses than on books or works of art. The streets, overcrowded with men, horses and carriages, are dangerous for the pedestrian. The coachmen and the carriers of sedan-chairs call continuously 'Look up'! 'Look up'! But when avoiding the one, one bumps into the other. Any visitor to the court or to the upper classes, must have a carriage. One sees here people from everywhere, Hungarians, Poles, Hussars, Heydukes, Muscovites, Persians, Turks, Spaniards, Italians, and it is certain that one cannot see anywhere else more different costumes although one must admit that in London and in Amsterdam even more foreign people are gathering because of the port.

The preparation for the wedding in Vienna of Emperor Leopold and Infanta Margarita of Spain took nine months. The Austrian aristocracy, the families of Lobkowitz, Dietrichstein, Colloredo, Starhemberg, Waldstein, and the Emperor himself took part in the processions of dryads, fauns, nymphs, shepherds, knights, Indians, furies, horse quadrilles, fireworks, serenades. In the horse ballet for the betrothal celebrations each horse was carrying a caparison worth 100 florins and ostrich feathers worth 100 ducats. The manager was ennobled and received 20,000 florins from the emperor and a yearly pension of 1,000 florins.

The first theatres were built during the Thirty Years War, as at Ulm in 1641, but after the war the building of theatres began in earnest. Dresden's theatre of 1664 could seat 2,000 people. Everybody was soon stagestruck, princes, school boys and girls and nuns. The documentary was popular. Gryphius staged *His murdered Majesty Carolus Stuardus*, August Adolf von Haugwitz dramatized the murder of Wallenstein. Very soon followed the opera houses. The Viennese court spent 15,000 florins on each new opera . . . The staging of Medea in Munich cost 70,000 florins. The Elector of Saxony spent 8,000 thalers annually on his orchestra. However the most important opera house was not at a court but at Hamburg, opened in 1687. Sixty-three different operas were performed in the first eighteen years, and the composer Reinhard Keiser composed 107 operas for this house.

17 Low Countries

'The people here live like citizens of the world,' wrote Temple,[1] 'bound to each other by the ties of civility and peace, under the impartial protection of moderate laws.' And Saint-Evremond said: 'It is a country where the laws protect us from the whims of men, a country where, in order to be sure of everything, we only need to be sure of ourselves.' Hospitality had no limits in this land of refuge. Spinoza, excluded from the synagogue, polished optical glasses. Bayle, professor of philosophy and history at Rotterdam, compiled his celebrated dictionary. The French Protestants, escaping from the dragonnades, formed a little Huguenot France in the Netherlands. They opened schools whose reputation lost many Dutch establishments their pupils, they taught fencing, dancing, hairdressing and culinary art.

Foreigners like Parival never tired of 'admiring the happiness of the Dutch States and of envying their condition'. Individuals certainly had a greater margin of choice and more scope for initiative here than anywhere else, but their 'freedom' had to comply with a narrow conformism, a strict morality, and with the axiom that success guarantees virtue. Unshakeable ideas about religion, work, economy and propriety undermined any real audacity. And the government was not democratic in the sense in which we understand the word.

Although slavery did not exist in the United Provinces – if a negro had the luck to set foot there, he regained his freedom – the liberal and pious Republic did not hesitate to traffic in slaves. Ruyter, organizing an expedition against the Gold Coast, did so with the sole purpose of procuring this living merchandise. In Angola every year the Dutch bought about 15,000 slaves at thirty florins a head. They re-sold them in America at between 300 and 500 florins.

This traffic did not in the least disturb those intractable consciences, which apparently worked according to a unique mechanism. Originality

[1] Sir William Temple, the English Ambassador.

was unknown; everyone alike among the Batavians execrated idleness and ostentatious luxury. 'Never,' noted Temple, 'had a people negotiated so much and consumed so little. 'The Dutch are always buying in order to re-sell at once. They dominate the spice market, but they eat their own fish and vegetables. They sell the best products of their textile industry in France, and buy the coarsest cloth in England for their own use.' The Comte de Guiche, who paid a visit to the illustrious Ruyter on his flagship, found the great man busy sweeping out his cabin and feeding his hens with grain. And yet Ruyter, like his colleague Tromp, was a popular hero who earned massive profits from his victories. He was said to get from 6,000 to 50,000 florins in prize money. Religion and frugality went hand-in-hand with him. Psalms were sung on board his ship, prayers were said before every battle, besides which the Admiralty favoured every expression of religious feeling, assimilated to a national ideology.

The Dutch, although great travellers, never settled abroad. Nothing pleased them except their homes, which had become the central theme of contemporary painting. There was the vestibule, the centre of family life, often large and lit by windows looking on to the street. Round it and beneath it a complicated system of little staircases, steps and doors joined the ground floor and the basement rooms (the cellars and the dependencies of the kitchen). In the typical Dutch house, no room was on the same level as another. One always had to go up or down. The house was built round the two rooms which had once been enough in themselves: the 'front room' and the 'back room'. In the seventeenth century town, only the poorest dwellings still kept to this simplicity. These two original rooms remained, divided by a wooden partition, which was sometimes glazed in, or by a passage. The passage opened on to several little intermediary rooms; a few stairs, a wooden archway divided it in the middle: through an open door one saw a clair-obscure room in which a young woman's dress made a splash of colour, one glimpsed the spring-time reflections of a garden. The subject more than once attracted a Jan Steen, a Vermeer, a Pieter de Hoogh, a Metsu ... Leading from this passage, or directly from the hall, was a spiral staircase which led to an entresol room – 'the suspended room' – and thence to the upper storey. These rooms were again divided. Sometimes a dividing wall rested on the axis of a window, so that each of the two contiguous rooms had half of it. Another, narrower, staircase, little more than a ladder, went up to the loft and attic, under their framework of enormous black beams and joists.

Three pieces comprised the basic units of furniture: the table, the chair and the cupboard. They were to be found in all the rooms, and were the pride of the housewife and the object of the carpenter's principal decorative efforts. In 1600 the table was still a thick rectangular platform resting on bulbous legs, sometimes covered with a serge tablecloth, or damask in a wealthy home. Later, various types introduced from abroad became popular: Italian-style tables with two flaps supported by vertical ledges, folding tables, three-legged pedestal tables designed to be placed against the wall, and various other English and French styles. Chairs kept more of their traditional Dutch styles, with their leg-rails, high backs and low leather-covered seats on which one or even two thick cushions were placed. The habit gradually spread of covering the chairs with moquette or velvet attached by copper nails. At the same time various designs were carved in the chair-backs and the whole framework became lighter.

The classic furniture in good Dutch society was the cupboard. Modest townfolk and peasants had old-fashioned medieval chests set flat on the floor, which opened with a lid and were painted in green and red and decorated with rudimentary drawings. But the cupboard was an expensive article at that time, the basic luxury of the household, symbolising success, social ambition, wealth and comfort. During the course of the century the original square, deep, massive, clumsy cupboard carved in plain wood also became lighter and began to resemble the French type of 'cabinet', inlaid with decorative panels of mother-of-pearl or ivory. From 1670 onwards wealthy householders flanked their cupboards with real cabinets, valuable chests fitted with drawers and standing on long legs. A well-furnished house included at least two cupboards. First there was the sacrosanct linen-cupboard, perfumed with sweet woodruff, entirely under the control of the mistress of the house. The linen-cupboard in the home of the wealthy Vrouw Blijenborgh of Dordrecht, for example, contained the following treasures: sheets from the East Indies, from Haarlem, Flanders, Amsterdam, Alkmaar, Friesland and Emden, arranged according to their origin; bonnets, handkerchiefs and neckerchiefs dating back to her grandmother's childhood; twenty-four dozen shirts, forty dozen tablecloths and napkins set aside for her children's dowries. As another example, an Amsterdam bookseller of modest fortune managed to squeeze into his cupboard sixty sheets, thirty table-cloths and more than 300 table-napkins. Some fashionable people replaced the linen-cupboard by an Indian chest veneered with copper or silver, or by a chest carved in Holland which they covered with blue cloth.

The second indispensable cupboard was the china-cupboard, given the place of honour in the main reception-room, displaying on its shelves plates, pots, dishes painted with designs and sometimes musical instruments. Dressers were also in use, with pyramidal rows of shelves and many people, even in the country, possessed also a cupboard with glazed doors in which they displayed precious objects. Here the mistress of the house often kept the presents she had received at her baptism and her marriage souvenirs.

From the 'back room' or from the end of the corridor a few steps led down to the yard surrounded by a fence, painted green or red-brown.

Some artisans made their yard into an extension of their workshop and tradesmen might use it as a store-yard. But most citizens, even in modest circumstances, arranged their yard as a garden, however small it might be (and sometimes it measured only a few square yards). At least a grass lawn would be grown, a flower-bed and a few patches of moss. If the space available was sufficient, an elder tree or laburnum would be trained against the wall and two or three fruit-trees would be planted. The higher the family stood in the social scale the larger became the space devoted to the garden, although this never assumed really large proportions – land was scarce and valuable in the city. For this reason people of independent means began, during the second half of the century, to buy a second garden just outside the town limits, where they took the whole family on Sundays and holidays during the summer months.

The typical arrangement of a Dutch garden consisted of four square lawns separated by crossing pathways. There were flower-beds in the lawns and trees all around them and, in the centre crossing, a wooden (or, later, stone) pavilion with a domed roof; or, instead of a pavilion, an arbour under which the family ate meals and, when it became fashionable, took tea. The entire garden was neat, trim, geometric and Lilliputian – a doll's garden.

Much to the disgust of a few arbiters of morals, the entire nation nourished a passion for flowers. These were very little used in the interior decoration of houses and were left to provide a mass of colour in the garden. They were arranged in separate beds according to species: roses here, irises there, lilies elsewhere; hyacinths farther down the garden and wild roses along the back; yellows on one side and reds on the other. Flowers were planted without the slightest creative imagination but in a way which reflected the methodical spirit of their growers. At least, the scents of the flowers were allowed to intermingle! And, in the tiny gardens in the centre of large towns, their scent was also mingled with the odours rising from the canals and, on hot days, stifled by them.[1]

Since the beginning of the reign of Louis XIII, French fashion had raised the tulip to the rank of the queen of flowers. Dutch horticulturists who had produced more than a hundred species provided tulips for the whole of Europe. In 1637 the wild speculations in bulbs had caused bankruptcies without number. Now the cultivation and the sale of the *Admiral Van Enckuysen*, the *General Van Eyck*, the *Marvels* and *Paragons* were rationally continued.

To tell the truth, cool reason never lost its natural influence, even in matters of love.

The evidence of most foreigners agrees on this point. The men in the Netherlands were mostly big, strong and robust, plump, well-built, with white skins and high colouring. But no sexual passions animated them; business affairs seemed more important to them than love-affairs, and for their diversion alcohol was preferred to women as being simpler. For their part, the women refused to allow themselves any signs of flirtatiousness, partly because of a very strong attachment to their independence but also because the men's coldness very soon cured them of any inclination to indulge in amorous wiles. They gained thereby an extraordinary freedom of action with regard to the opposite sex, and were outspoken on erotic matters to a degree which astonished the French of the time. In Paris, about 1660, there was a pleasantly allusive saying: 'To make love like a Dutchwoman'. René Le Pays, visiting the Netherlands during this period, remarked ironically that the

---

[1] Paul Zumthor: *Daily Life in Rembrandt's Holland*

Dutchwomen did from stupidity what the girls in Paris did through licentious-ness: 'At the climax of pleasure they start eating an apple, or break nuts with their teeth.' Apart from such pleasantries, there was a more subtle analysis by Saint-Evremond in his statement that, once they had reached adulthood, Dutch men and women tended to become generally cold and aloof, presumably as a result of marriage and maturity, whereas young bachelors were radically different. (Zumthor)

From 1650 the corrupting influence of France had begun to make itself felt. Twenty years later, the cafés and the smoking-rooms had multiplied, and the evening at home, which had so long been sacred, became an exception. The bourgeois went home as late as possible, his wife and daughter went out independently. 'Serious people grew anxious . . . The old bourgeois austerity, the pious conservatism, everything which made the strength of the Netherlands people was disappearing or degenerating. The family was no longer really the family, nor was the home the home'.

Of course this picture is exaggerated, but it cannot be denied that in 1670 the Dutch bourgeois dreamed above all of peace and well-being. The Dutch had lost their American colonies, but they had defeated the English, they had sent their fleet into the port of London itself, and forced Louis XIV to break off his conquests (Treaty of Aix-la-Chapelle). Sure of their power, they had abolished the functions of Stadtholder, and dispensed with the officers who were faithful to the House of Orange; they had refused direct taxation and military credits, and let the fortifications fall into ruin.

Suddenly they saw a formidable danger loom up before them, the Anglo-French Alliance which would crush them. The war in which they had long refused to believe was not only caused by the rancour of Louis XIV, his hatred of republicans and Protestants. The French economy was linked to the Dutch economy, and Colbert wanted to free it of this mort-gage. His mercantile policy consisted in giving a formidable impulse to French expansion and in refusing imports from abroad. But French capitalism saw itself powerless before the banks of Amsterdam and Rotterdam, just as its merchant fleet of 500 vessels was powerless before the 15,000 Dutch ships. These audacious merchants had therefore to be brought to heel.

Impelled by public fear and indignation, the bourgeois Republic, led by the brothers John and Cornelius de Witt, then turned to William, the young heir of the Princes of Orange, and made him captain-general and admiral-general. And so began the career of that strange personage who, from treachery to treachery, from defeat to defeat, would become the triumphant rival of the Sun King, the 'bastard Themistocles of European resistances'.[1] As a child, William did not like laughing, or playing, or

[1] Michelet

264

The Life of the People

Adriaen van Ostade, *Peasants Playing Backgammon.*

Traditional celebration of May Day in an Austrian village.

The Portuguese bull-fight, in the Terreiro do Paço in Lisbon.

Above. Travelling players
in Holland at the end of the
seventeenth century. The
performances had gained
somewhat in sophistication
since the days of Brueghel.

Illustration of a hold, from
a manual on wrestling.

Top. Devastation of the Dutch country in 1673, when the dykes were broken down to prevent the advance of the French.

Bottom. Mass execution in Moscow of rebellious *stryeltsi* in 1698 under Peter the Great. Illustration from an eye-witness account,

Opposite. Street-urchins in Seville, painted by Murillo.

MARZO.

GIVGNO.

OTTOBRE.

The young man, the whore and the beldam in a London brothel.

Opposite and below. The Harlot's Progress by Mitelli: March, June, October and December.

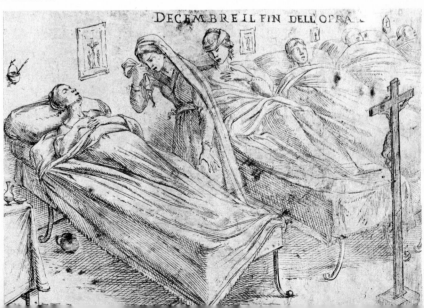

DECEMBRE IL FIN DELL'OPRA

The Coffee-house Mob: a print of 1710 celebrating the new places of entertainment, notable for the novelties of coffee (introduced via Vienna after the defeat of the Turks in 1686), and newspapers. The first English daily paper, the *Daily Courant*, appeared in 1702.

learning. Only theological discussion and the study of languages seemed to excite his mind, of which Saint-Evremond nonetheless recognized the exceptional quality. At twenty, William was already what he would always remain: taciturn, underhand, fiercely egostical, hostile to luxury, firm, tenacious, impossible to discourage, secretly burning with two passions to the exclusion of all others: the passion for power and the passion for fighting.

If he was guilty of allowing the de Witts to be horribly massacred, he can claim the glory of the first resistance to Louis xiv's armies, and the glory of the flood which was Holland's answer to the invasion. It was extraordinary that Louis xiv and Charles ii of England, renewing their treaty, agreed that he should be put at the head of the State. They demanded the man who was going to break the hegemony of the one, and ruin the dynasty of the other.

The Dutch had opened the dams, and cut through the dykes. For two years they remained submerged. It was an enormous sacrifice. It was not, as in other lands, the meadows that they flooded, it was the richest houses in the world, the greenhouses, the exotic gardens, the treasures of the museum of the world. The war soon became European and, though Louis xiv emerged victorious, Holland, by a paradox, lost nothing.

But William was bitter. He was constantly defeated in battle – and this in spite of a real act of treachery: he attacked the French army on the day that peace was signed. He also felt himself inferior to the other monarchs of the Coalition. If he was to become the head of the great anti-French league of which he dreamed, he had to have a crown. His first step towards his goal was to pull off a *coup* which stupefied Europe. English opinion had forced Charles ii to break the alliance with France. William went to England and simply asked for the hand of Princess Mary, the daughter of the Duke of York, the niece of the King and the possible heiress to the British throne. Charles ii tried to resist, but he was borne away by the current – unless, that is, he was frankly deceived. He told the French Ambassador: 'This will destroy the cabals . . . This alliance will end my subjects' suspicion that my liaison with France is founded on a change of religion'.

Eleven years later, William dethroned his father-in-law, James ii, and, with his wife, he reigned over England. Surrounded by immense prestige, he figured henceforward as the Protestant champion of freedom. In fact he killed the freedom of Holland by submitting the country to a veritable dictatorship and committing it to endless wars. The War of the League of Augsburg lasted eight years, the War of the Spanish Succession lasted eleven. William died just as it began, the new massacre he had prepared with furious zeal, but his successor, the Grand Pensioner Heinsills, showed an equal determination in pursuing his own policies. In the process, Holland was ruined, and lost its rank among the nations. The debt rose to 250,000,000 florins for an annual income of 13,000,000.

This absorption of capital, and the competition from England which closed all commercial outlets, brought the decline of the navy, commerce and fishing. The United Provinces maintained themselves by banking and foreign loans. From a nation of manufacturers, ship-builders, merchants and traders, they became a nation of stockholders and speculators. This inferior form of activity followed a military effort which had exceeded the material and moral strength of the country; resolution collapsed, and the creative force disappeared, and, with it, disappeared idealism.

The bourgeois wanted to enjoy themselves. They built themselves houses full of tapestries, hangings figured with gold, high chimneypieces with marble columns, expensive pictures, gold and silver plate. Public spirit was in complete decline, no-one cared any more about the general interest. Nepotism and corruption triumphed among these bourgeois, who monopolized the public offices. The tax-farmers gave gratuities to the magistrates. It was not long before an historian would laugh at the sailors in the war of independence, who had blown themselves up rather than strike their flag. The taste for literature and the arts gave way to the taste for useful knowledge, law, and experimental sciences. Religious feeling weakened and rational deists abounded. Artistic sensibility grew less, and the great palaces of the Kaisergracht and the Heerengracht were Louis xiv in style; painters repeated Italian lessons like automata. The people, degraded by growing poverty, were driven to insolence and to beggary. (Roland Mousnier)

18 England

Charles II was welcomed back with widespread rejoicing, for many people felt that a restored monarchy would end the various difficulties and deadlocks which had accumulated in the last years of the Commonwealth. But although their hopes were largely frustrated, there was nothing like a return to the earlier Stuart period. At first Charles kept round him the men who had served his father or aided his return, but these were soon replaced by unscrupulous politicians who knew how to amuse the king and win over what Evelyn called the court's 'buffons and ladies of pleasure'. Later Danby tried to build a more honest administration; but Charles himself remained thoroughly cynical and taken up with his women, though clever enough not to push things to extremes. He brought back from exile a definitely French taste in fashions and modes of living, with new standards of comfort and display. Huge periwigs came in, with gaily-feathered broad brimmed hats, falling bands of rich lace enveloping the shoulders, short cloaks slung across the shoulder, long straight doublets swelling out from the waist, wide puffed-out petticoat-breeches decorated with knee-ribbons and with lace-ruffles underneath. Country-folk continued with the more sober styles that had been coming up with the 1640s. The Sacheverell couple at Morley in 1662 are examples of the plainer gentry. The man has a simple white cap with white border, a large collar, cloak and doublet, also simple in style; his wife wears a long black veil and a small black hood tied under the chin.

Evelyn was astonished at the costly furnishings of the Countess of Arlington's new dressing-room at Goring House: two fine mirrors, 'silver jars and vases, cabinets, and other so rich furniture as I have seldom seen; to this excess of superfluity were we now arrived, and that not only at Court, but almost universally, even to wanton profusion'. At court the Duchess of Portsmouth had her apartment at the end of the Long Gallery. Evelyn describes it:

Following His Majesty through the gallery I went with the few who attended him, into the Duchess of Portsmouth's dressing-room, within her bed-chamber, where she was in her morning loose-garment, her maid combing, newly out of her bed, His Majesty and the gallants standing about her; but that which engaged my curiosity was the rich and splendid furniture of this woman's apartment, now twice or thrice pulled down and rebuilt to satisfy her prodigal and expensive pleasures, while Her Majesty does not exceed some gentlemen's wives in furniture and accommodation. Here I saw the new fabric of French tapestry; for design, tenderness of work, and incomparable imitation of the best paintings, beyond anything I had ever beheld. Some pieces had Versailles, St Germains, and other palaces of the French King, with huntings, figures, and landscapes, exotic fowls, and all to the life, rarely done. Then for Japanese cabinets, screens, chimney furniture, sconces, branches, brasiers, etc., all of massive silver, and out of number; besides some of His Majesty's best paintings.

When her sister was widowed, several ships were needed to take her belongings back to France; among them were a cabinet table in old Chinese lacquer and a Chinese incense-burner. Such burners were often used, or scented powder was scattered round the dressing-room. The court-ladies studied an elegant negligence. Glossy ringlets escaped from a simple bandeau of pearls or were graced with a single rose; they fell in careless charm on to bared shoulders. Bosoms did not have a transparent lawn to cover them. The arm, bare to the elbow, rested on the loose satin petti-coat, with satin heaping up its train in the background.

Pepys gives us many glimpses of the fashionable clothes and adornments:

[March 1662, La Belle Pierce brings his wife] a pair of perukes of hair, as is the fashion for ladies to wear, which are pretty, and of my wife's own hair.

[With his wife at the New Exchange] We saw some new-fashioned petticoats of Sarsnet, with a black, broad lace, printed round the bottom and before, very handsome.

[The Queen in] a white waistcoat and a crimson short petticoat, and her hair dressed a la negligence mighty pretty.

[30 Oct. 1663] £3 worse than I was last month; but it has chiefly risen from my laying out in clothes for myself and my wife viz. for her about £12, and for myself about £55, or thereabouts, having made myself a velvet cloak, two new cloth skirts, black, plain both; with a new shag gown trimmed with gold buttons and twist; with a new hat and silk tops for my legs; two periwigs, one whereof cost me £3 and the other 40s. I have worn neither yet, but I will begin next month, God willing.

[1666] The King hath yesterday in council decreed his resolution of setting a fashion for clothes, which he will never alter.

[15 Oct.] This day the King begun to put on his vest, and I did see several persons of the House of Lords and Commons too, great courtiers, who are in it; being a long cassock close to the body, of long cloth, and pinked with white silk under it, and a coat over it, and legs ruffled with white ribbons like a pigeon's leg, and upon the whole I wish the King will keep it, for it is a very fine and handsome garment.

Three days later Evelyn saw the King who 'had put himself into the Eastern fashion of vest', resolving 'to leave the French mode which hitherto obtained to our great expence and reproach'.

The spirit of the court has been preserved in the witty *Life of de Grammont* by Hamilton, with its tales of the main amours. He calls the court:

the Seat and Fountain of *Sports*, *Pleasures*, *Enjoyments*, and all the *Polite* and *Magnificent* Entertainments, which are generally inspir'd by the Inclinations of a *tender*, *amorous*, and *indulgent* Prince. The *Beauties* studied to *charm*, the *Men* to *please*: And all, in short, improv'd their Talents the best they could. Some distinguish'd themselves by *Dancing*, others by *Shew* and *Magnificence*; some by their *Wit*; many by their *Amours*, but very few by their constancy.

But, compared to the courts of Elizabeth, James I, Charles I, the whole edifice sounds hollow and trivial.

The foreign mistresses were unpopular, as we see from the tale of the London mob threatening Nell Gwynn in her coach, taking her for the Duchess of Portsmouth – till she put her head out and said, 'Pray, good people, be civil, I am the Protestant whore'. Later in 1688 the apprentices wrecked brothels in Moorfields, remarking that they did 'ill in contenting themselves with pulling down the little brothels and did not go to pull down the big one in Whitehall'. Eight rioters were hanged, and a pretended Remonstrance was drawn up in the names of the whores and addressed as a petition to the King's mistresses.

To illustrate the change in manners, in the idiom of lovemaking, which had come about, it is amusing to compare, say, a letter from Kenelm Digby, probably to Venetia:

If you will be happy in this world, or if you will not weare out to no purpose a dull and uncomfortable life; you must have yr. hart fixt upon something; and you must suffer yr. loue (wch. is as naturall and necessary in mankinde, as thinking or breathing) to settle somewhere. Which being so; consider how the measure of him who may best deserue that divine blessing from you; is not to be taken by any admired excellencies of witt, nor any endowments of fortune nor gracefulnesses of person (in all which, I acknowledge I shall fall short) but by his intrinsecall richnesse in the same coyne, and by his profusiue straining himselfe to purchase yours with his while stocke. By the eternall God, in this ballance (which, is the onely true one, to weigh returnes of friendship in) j am heauier then all yr. world of louers and seruants besides that are or euer haue bin; were they all together putt into the scale agt. me.

And compare it with a letter of 1661 from the Earl of Chesterfield to Barbara Villiers, Duchess of Cleveland, who became one of Charles II's mistresses:

Madam After so many years service, fidelity and respect, to be banished for the first offence is very hard, espetially after my asking so many pardons, if heaven with you should be as rigorous as you are with mee, I doubt never would see it, but in your Glasse; therefore use mee as you doe your Domesticks, that is, blame mee for the first fault, and if I do not mend, turn away your very humble servant.

Both letters use a religious idiom in the service of love; but whereas it is seriously and deeply pondered in the first, in the second it appears only to turn a witty phrase.

In May 1654 Evelyn noted, 'I now observed how women began to paint themselves, formerly a most ignominious thing and used only by prostitutes'. He seems to be remarking a swing away from the comparative plainness of dress and lack of cosmetics in the war-years and the first years of the Commonwealth. (On 7 June 1650 Parliament had ordered 'an Act against the Vice of Painting and wearing Black Patches and immodest Dresses to Women to read on Friday morning next', but we hear nothing more of it.) However the strong dislike felt by Pepys for painted faces suggests that the practice, at least in obvious forms, was not yet widespread. In 1667 his cousin Mrs Pierce, a surgeon's wife, took to paint: 'still very pretty, but paints red on her face, which makes me hate her'. He was also upset when he saw Nell Gwynn and Mrs Knipp painting themselves in the tyring-house at the king's theatre (where a big mirror had been bought for nine pounds in 1660): 'and yet what a show they make on the stage by candlelight'. Margaret Huggins, who played Lady Wisfort in Congreve's *Way of the World*, used the lines to scold her dresser: 'The Red, sweetheart, Complexion, darling. Paint, fool! Paint, Paint'! Near the end of the century the moral issue of paint or no-paint reached the climax of its debate, which took up many columns of *The Ladies' Dictionary* of 1694. An affirmative answer was finally reached by the publication of *Several Letters between Two Ladies*, said to be a posthumous work by Jeremy Taylor, which ended the old type of attack based on Biblical precedent and reaching far back into medieval times.

Patches persisted. Lady Castlemaine declared they could be worn on all occasions but those of mourning. Even the Duchess of Newcastle, who retired from the fashionable world to write plays and lay-sermons for women, had 'many black patches, because of pimples about her mouth'. Pepys allowed his wife to use them after learning that Lord Sandwich approved of them. One night at the theatre he observed Lady Castlemaine call an attendant 'for a little patch off her face, and put it into her own mouth and wetted it, and so clapped it upon her own by the side of her mouth. I suppose she felt a pimple rising there'. Under Anne patches were used as party-favours: Whig ladies had them on the right side of the face; Tories on the left; ladies who wanted a coalition or who ignored politics, put them on both cheeks. The Duchess of Marlborough, who defied the Queen by wearing patches in a period of court-mourning, assiduously patched her face in the electioneering months of 1710.

All Europe was raided for hair; and Scotland sent its quota before the act of union. 'Forty guineas a year for a periwig, but ten to a poor chaplain'. They grew larger and larger. Lord Foppington in *The Relapse* wears periwigs to his knees and declares they should be to a man as a mask to a woman, 'nothing should be seen but his eyes'. Some women grew their hair long, to have a wig made of their own hair; the phrase of a woman seen 'in her own hair' appeared. Dyes were common. Mr Thynne, mad to marry a redhead, chose Lady Jersey's daughter, and the shock of finding how much henna did for her hair seems to have killed him off after a few months' marriage. Women headressers appeared, accepted finally by the Company of Barber Surgeons. The sophisticated styles involved much hard work. Betty Verney, unable to afford a maid, complained, 'I am confident going to plough would not make me more sick than reaching up my arms does when I set my hair.' The ringlets of the court-ladies were called heartbreakers as opposed to the men's lovelocks; and were often set on wires to stand out from the head. When Mrs Pepys was attracted to the new style 'because it is the fashion', Pepys was horrified and made a scene.

James II did his best to reform the Court. He did not give up his mistress Catherine Sedley, but kept her in a house in St James's Square, not at Whitehall. The French ambassador wrote that his aim was 'to observe every formality and to preserve exactly all the externals'. It was found necessary to issue express instructions that a courtier was not to be drunk in the Queen's presence. The Queen, Mary of Modena, was forced to use rouge, though she daily repented of it to her Italian confessor. But James had nothing new to contribute to the political scene and lacked his brother's cynical tact. A popular uprising under the Duke of Monmouth was ruthlessly supressed; an alliance of the landed magnates and the city-merchants were then safely able to depose James without any fear of irruptions from below. Court-life lost its importance. Burnet tells us:

> The King, a very few days after he was set on the throne, went out to Hampton Court, and from that palace came into town only on council days: so that the face of a court and the rendezvous, usual in the public rooms, was now quite broken. This gave an early and general disgust. The gaiety and diversions of a court disappeared.

A cold and formal man of business, William preferred the closet to the public rooms, where he stood unsmiling and detached, and Hampton Court to Whitehall, which, as if to mark the end of an epoch, was burnt down in 1698 – except for Jones's noble Banqueting House. William refused to pretend that the laying on of his hands could cure scrofula, and he infuriated the clergy by keeping his hat on in Church: a Dutch custom which reminded them of the Quakers. When his wife died of smallpox, he became even less approachable. The Duchess of Marlborough records his rudeness at table to Princess Anne early in his reign:

There happened to be just before her a plate of green peas, the first that had been seen that year. The king, without offering the Princess the least share of them, drew the plate before him and devoured them all. Whether he offered any to the Queen I cannot say, but he might have done that safely enough, for he knew she durst not touch one. The Princess Anne confessed, when she came home, that she had so much mind for the peas that she was afraid to look at them, and yet could hardly keep her eyes off them. She was at the time near childbed.

Anne was not averse from cardplaying and tippling; she was practically crippled with dropsy and gout, often appearing covered with bandages 'in extreme pain and agony, everything about her in much the same disorder as about the meanest of her subjects'. She bore six children and had about twelve miscarriages. (She seems certainly to have been the victim of James II's venereal disease.) Yet she liked to drive in her *chaise roulante*, with two gentlemen holding the reins and walking either side of the horse's head, and even hunted in the same chaise, which, Swift says, 'she drives herself and drives furiously like Jehu, and is a mighty hunter like Nimrod'. One day he insists, she drove forty miles, after a stag. He attended a levee at Hampton Court. 'We made our bows, and stood, about twenty of us, round the room, while the Queen looked at us with her fan in her mouth, and once in a minute said about three words to some that were nearest to her; and then she was told dinner was ready, and went out.' Burnet sums up, 'She had lain down the splendour of the court too much, and eats privately; so that except on Sundays, and a few hours twice or thrice a week at night in her drawing room, she appears so little that her court, as it were, is abandoned'. Yet she was the last monarch to preside at all regularly over cabinet meetings. In the next reign the Prime Minister has definitely arrived in the person of Walpole.

With William there was a lessening of the elaborateness of costumes. Nobles and gentry wore low-crowned hats edged with gold and adorned with feathers; coats with lace and embroidery, the sleeves ending in huge cuffs; neckcloths with Brussels lace. Claret-colour was liked. Men took their periwigs off in public, set them on their knees, and combed them. Snuff had come in. Misson in his *Travels*, 1697, says curtly of the gallants: 'Creatures, compounded of a periwig, and a coat laden with powder, as white as a miller's face, a face smeared with snuff, and a few affected airs'.

The Factious Citizen, 1685, describes a fop changing into a citizen's costume:

Off with your clothes, your sword, wig, hat, put yourself nimbly into a black suit of grogram below the knees, a broad skirted doublet, a girdle about the middle, and a short black coat squirted down before with black taffety; a broad brimmed hat, with a great twisted hat-band, with a rose at the end of it. Your hair is slink enough and of the precise cut without your periwig.

The wives wore 'green aprons and grogram gowns or petticoats, with little wings upon their foreheads, a straight hood and a narrow dimunitive colverteen pinner, that makes them look so saint-like'. Ladies used a new hair-style. Ringlets were given up. The hair was drawn back from the forehead and combed over a cushion; the back hair was arranged above this in a wreath of curls and brought sloping down each side of the face; some women supported the hair on rows of lace, one row over another in a succession of plaits, from which long streamers hung over the shoulders. Much fine hair was needed for these effects, and so a further step was taken in the use of artficial hair. In 1711 Addison says that ten years earlier women's hair had shot up and made them taller than men; indeed men looked like grasshoppers. But now women had shrunk. He knew some who had been seven feet high and now had dwindled to some inches of five. Fashions were still slow in reaching the country. Near the end of Anne's reign the *Spectator* says a Cornish congregation had been astonished when the squire's wife, after wintering in London, came down the aisle in a little head-dress. The lawyer telling this tale had ridden the western assize-circuit and had always noticed how old fashioned even the girls looked the further they lived from London. The intrusion of a new middle-class censorship, different from the furious attack of certain Puritan sections in the past, is to be read in such warnings as that of Isaac Bicker-staff against the shoes and slippers in a big shop near the St James's end of Pall Mall, 'which create irregular thoughts and desires in the youth of the realm'.

Soap was cheaper. Soapmakers were among the first tradesmen to advertise in the journals now circulating; by the end of the century some sixty-three factories were making twenty-five million pounds a year. Baths, however, were still not much used. The Duchess of York in the St James's Palace had a splendid bathing-closet. The curtains were of Indian silk, but they enclosed only a couple of wooden tubs. Pepys, making alterations in his house, never dreamed of a bathroom. With all his care for minute details, he only mentions his wife having a bath once. 'My wife busy in going with her woman to the hothouse to bathe herself, after her long being within doors in the dirt, so that she now pretends to a resolution of being hereafter very clean. How long it will hold I can guess'. On the Continent bathing establishments had long been popular. In the Commonwealth Chamberlain, who had been Charles I's physician, tried to introduce baths of the German and Scandanavian kind; both Parliament and the College of Physicians opposed him, considering that the result would be debauched morals. One or two hothouses were set up, but that was all.

The great lords still lived sumptuously. At Badminton, under Charles II, the Duke of Beaufort had above £2,000 a year, 'which he managed by stewards, bailiffs and servants', says Roger North. He bred all his horses, and had 200 persons in his household, with 'nine original tables covered every day' in the house. Except for soap, candles and ale (made on the premises), 'all the provisions of the family came from foreign parts as merchandise'. Suitors for his favours were lodged at an inn at a nominal charge.

There was no time of the day without diversion. Breakfast in her [the Duchess's] gallery that opened into the gardens, and parks with their several kinds of deer, to be visited: and if required mounting horses of the duke's were brought for all the company.

Old elements of display are present, but the self-sufficient manor-house was coming to an end. Gentlemen went into the large vaults to drink wine; and the Duke 'always had some new project of building, walling, or planting, which he would show and ask his friends for advice about'. Building in the grand manner continued, sometimes so slowly that a nobleman had little time to inhabit his mansion. The Duke of Devonshire took eighteen years in rebuilding Chatsworth and died the year it was done; the Duke of Marlborough died before completing Blenheim.

Gardens were still formal. Charles II had admired the French systems. Rose, his gardener at Hampton Court, was an expert at show-pieces, such as dwarf yew trees; under William the maze was introduced. However, Evelyn at Deptford had fine walks and hedges, especially holly, and a small pretty greenhouse. 'He has four large round philarias, smooth clipped, raised on a single stalk from the ground, a fashion much used. Part of his garden is very woody and shady for walking; but his garden not being walled, has little of the best fruits'. Thus into the formal garden intrudes the Natural, which looks towards the Romantic. (We may compare Marvell's garden-poems.)

Though many new suggestions for bettering agriculture were being made, the gentry were backward. 'Our gentry are grown ignorant,' noted Pepys, 'in everything of good husbandry.' They were content with protective corn-laws and the absence or landtaxes. Samuel Butler stressed the strong regionalism. The squire 'is a clown of rank and degree; his homely education has rendered him a native only of his own soil and a foreigner in all other places, the custom of being the best man in his own territories has made him the worst everywhere else'. The real wages of labourers and husbandmen either stood still or fell. King estimated that the yearly income of a family of 'cottagers and paupers' (some 400,000 in 1688) was £6 10s. per head. Poor rates kept rising, and by the end of the century a fifth of the nation survived by occasional alms, mostly parish-relief. The House of Correction became less a workhouse and more a gaol. Irons and fetters were provided and by 1680 the inmates are called prisoners.

Richmond, Jan. 1675–6: for diverse years last past there hath been great increase of idle vagrant persons there . . . it is therefore Ordered that from and after February 6th next, there shall be a Ho. of Corrn. at Richmond . . .

Richmond, Jan. 1677: To pay 26s to Mich. Harrison gent. for reimbursing him for fetters for Ho. of Correction.

Middleham, March 1680: £3 10s. 0d. unto Peter Hood Gov. of the House of Correction at Richmond for buying of irons to secure his prisoners and amende a sink and the doors, bolts and irons of the gaol.

The Act of Settlement under Charles II empowered parishes to send back to his native parish any man trying to settle down in their area, so that he might not at some future date become chargeable on the rates. In Cambridgeshire the statutory wages rarely met the needs of a large family. In 1670 Levellers were rioting in Worcestershire, and indictments for riot and trespass were common at quarter sessions. There were also corn-riots, troubles among London silkweavers, and revolts of apprentices every now and then. In 1671 the game laws were strengthened. The act forbade all freeholders of under £100 (this is, most of the class) from killing game even on their own land. Sir Roger de Coverley (intended to be a good-natured man) remarks that the yeomen 'who is just within the Game Act' would be a good neighbour 'if he did not destroy so many partridges' (on his own land). Shooting now superseded hawking, and gentlemen often stalked pheasants and shot them roosting on boughs. The catching of birds by ground-nets or limed twigs was common. Decoys lured wild ducks, and manors had decoy-ponds. Heather and bracken with grouse and blackcock could be burnt only at certain times; a whipping was the likely fate of a disobedient shepherd. Addison's Tory squire said that the new Game Law was the only good law since the Restoration. The breaking-open of deer parks in the Civil War and the scarcity of stags had led to the fox-hunt. (Foxes had previously been dug out or killed by peasants as vermin.) The idea of a gentleman hunting in his own parkland gave way to that of the hunt across open country. Hares were still much hunted.

Censorship was now carried out, not by royal prerogative, but by act of parliament, the Licensing Act of 1663; revived under James but going out with William. From 1694 a man was free at last to publish what he liked, liable only to a charge of libel or sedition before a jury: Milton's longed-for Liberty of Unlicensed Printing. Meanwhile, however, the Licensing Act had reduced the number of master-printers to twenty; and apart from the University Presses they were all in London. When William occupied Exeter after his landing at Torbay, he could not find a single printer in the west for his manifesto. Except for the few years under Charles II when the censorship was in abeyance, there were practically no newspapers apart from the slight official Gazette. So handwritten newsletters were sent out from London, enabling the Whig and Tory parties to develop and close their ranks; the former favouring toleration, the latter wishing to crush dissent. Various other sorts of newsletters (literary, commercial, general) were also sent out, with a host of scribblers at work in London. (Though the terms Whigs and Tories now appear, we must not for a long time yet, think of organised parties in the modern sense. The Crown could exert much influence, buying up Members of Parliament or relying on a loyal rally.) When censorship ended, a number of Courants, Intelligences, Gazettes, Posts, appeared; and in 1702 the first daily, consisting solely of news. In 1704 Defoe began his weekly *Review*, a forerunner of *The Tatler*, 1709, and *The Spectator*, 1711. The government, disturbed by the press's influence, introduce a stamp tax as a curb in 1712. *The Spectator* was promptly killed off.

In 1662 the Common Prayer Book was enforced by law, and many severe penalties and prohibitions were imposed on dissenters. The Fifth Monarchists, who looked for the completion of the revolution by the advent of Christ, had risen in the previous year. After their failure the dissenters became quietist; they turned their backs on politics and struggled simply for freedom of conscience. The story of Bunyan illustrates their sufferings and their steadfast endurance. From 1689 they were permitted to meet under license though excluded from public affairs. There were, however, mob-riots against them and chapel-sackings during Sacheverell's impeachment under Anne. The ethic of thrift and hard-work was to bear fruit in the next century when the Quakers emerged as bankers and iron-founders.

The roads were so bad that often doctors could not get to patients and remedies were prescribed by letter. Even a conscientious surveyor could call out workers for only six days a year to repair roads, and he had no funds to pay them. An Act of 1633 had allowed turnpikes to be set up, so as to pay for keeping the roads in order; but the money was seldom if ever used for that purpose. Riders often fell from horses; coaches were turned over, sunk in quicksands, lost in floodwaters. They carried tools for repairs. The increase in industrialisation, slight as it yet was, had deforested many areas; thus the ironworks round Birmingham and the Black Country put an end to the Forest of Arden. The workers in the mines were being crushed by worsening conditions, as the pits went deeper, with falls of earth and explosions caused by firedamp. Women and children were taken underground as bearers; and in Scotland the miners were reduced to a state of serfdom.

Stage-coaches had come up about the mid-century. In 1663 there was one every month to Edinburgh, with the journey taking twelve days; by

1697 the coach from York to London took six days. Those on the boot were liable to road-sickness. In London the hackneys were such a nuisance as to be called 'hell-coaches'. Noblemen had coaches with six to twelve horses, with which they showed off in Hyde Park. Pepys was proud when he rose to a coach and noted that 'the people did mightily look upon it'. A pamphleteer of 1675 denounced coaches at length for causing all sorts of economic ills, bringing about the decline of the horse and of a large number of trades connected with riding as well as ruining inns. Regular posts had come in under Charles I, but not until William were there cross-posts between various towns without touching London. (The government had benefited from all letters going through London as it was then easier to open them and watch out for conspiracies.)

Dissenters continued to open charity-schools, with some pious Anglicans following suit. In 1712 there were a 120 in the London area. After 1660 the grammar-schools were in some disrepute as nurseries of rebellion; and schoolmasters refusing to conform to the new Book of Common Prayer were liable to be ejected. Thinkers with the more practical view-point fostered by Puritanism, like Petty, James Harrington, Locke, wanted to break down the domination of Latin and abstract Logic. John Wallis, who became an important geometer, learned at Felsted Latin, Greek and a little Hebrew, with Logic; he had to teach himself arithmetic and the other branches of mathematics as well as music and French; at Oxford he was back again on Latin, Greek and Logic. Private schools were sometimes more advanced than the grammar schools.

The administrative services still had many of the old weaknesses and corruptions. But we see in Pepys, son of a City tailor, how a new sort of conscience was in process of birth. He stayed at his post all through the Plague and ended by doing excellent work at the Admiralty. The diary of Henry Teonge, chaplain on three ships in 1675–9, however, illustrates the laxities of naval life. Received by a lieutenant with 'bottles of claret', he set sail on 3 June 1675.

Many of our seamen's wives follow their husbands, and sing *Loath to Depart*, in punch and brandy; so that our ship was that night well furnished, but ill man'd; few of them being well able to keepe watch, had there beene occasion. Thence we passed to the Boy on the Redsands, thinking to go the nearest way over the Flatts; but fearing we should be calmed, wee tack about and goe the other way. And heare we begin our warlike acchievements; for, seeing a merchant-man neare us withoute taking the least notice of a man of warr, we gave him a shott, make him loare his top-gallant, (*id est* putt off his hat to us), and our gunner presently goes on board of him, makes him pay 6s. 6d. for his contempt; abreing him 2d. becuse it was the first shott.

13 June : This day preached my first sermon on ship-board; where I could not stand without holding by boath the pillars in the steerahe; and the Captaines chayre and others were ready to tild downe sometimes backwards, sometimes forwards. All the women and olde seamen sick this day; I was only giddy.

20 June: And now may you see our mournefull ladys singing *lacrimae* or *Loath to depart*; while our trumpets sound, *Mayss where are your harts*, etc. Our noble Capt. (though much bent on the preparation for his voyage) yet might you see his hart full of trouble to part from his lady, and his sonn and heire; whoe so younge, yet with his mayde to lead him by his dading sleeves, would he goe from gunn to gunn and put his finger to the britch of the gunn and cry Booe; while his mother, like a woman of greate discretion, seems no whit troubled, that her husband might be the lesse so. But our lieutenant's wife was like a weeping Rachell, or mournful Niobe; also was the boatswain's wife; indeede all of them like turtle-doves or young pigeons, true emblem of mourning. Only our master's wife, of more masculine spirit, or rather a virago, lays no such grief to her hart; only like one that hath eaten mustard her eyes were a little redd.

24 June: Midsummer Day, as wee are calmed still over against the Ile of Wyte, and within kenn of Portland, though 30 leagues from us. This day two seamen that had stolen a peice or two of beife were thus shamed; they had their hands tyd behind them, and themselves tyd to the maine mast, each of them a piece of raw beife bobbing before them like the knott of a crevatt; and the rest of the seamen cam one by one, and rubd them over the mouth with the raw beife; and in this posture they stood two houers.

By 1700 London had some 674,000 persons, more than a tenth of the whole population of England and Wales. The abundance of money for investment led to the establishment of the Bank of England in 1693, the subscription of £1,200,000 being completed in ten days, although for some time pamphleteers attacked it and there was only partial confidence. The colonial and commercial gains made in the wars under Anne brought in yet more money, and English shipping gained a virtual monopoly of the slave trade, which provided the main basis of the great expansion of ports like Bristol in the following century. Division of labour was increasing, and Defoe was soon to paint a picture of widening activity in trade and industry.

Leystalls or rubbish-dumps, established in 1670 at regular sites, were a great nuisance with their odure, decaying vegetables and other food. Those near the river were shovelled in occasionally on an ebb tide. An odd work, *The Floating Island* of 1673, describes a fantasy-journey to the various sanctuaries in the town. In the Savoy was Alsatia, open to debtors but not to felons and traitors, where bailiffs at times forced their way in by pretending to have a warrant for the latter offenders, but at the cry 'Arrest! arrest!' everyone flew to arms and drove the invaders out, perhaps with loss of their ears. In Milford Lane was another refuge for debtors, originally occupied and defended by hard-up officers and now turned into a 'most absolute Hance [Hanse] and free Town of itself, without dependency'. Baldwin's Gardens was a perilous passage 'by reason of the straggling Troops of the Enemy, who lie Purdue in every ale-house thereabouts. The safest way of Sally is that through the Walks, from whence the Red Lyon in Garies-Inn Lane receives them with good quartering, and passes them through the back way into the Main Land.' The precinct of St John of Jerusalem had lost its privileges; and in Blackfriars only some of the oldest trades kept them, in a few houses belonging to the Friars; Great St Bartholomew's was in decay:

Upon whose platform a whole Army of Borrowers and Book-men might have been mustred and drawn out at length, or into what form or figure it had pleased them to cast themselves. What works, yea what variety of Art and Workmanship was within it; What an excellent Half-Moon was there cast up without it, for defence to the Eastward; What excellent Sconces, in the fashion of Tobacco-shops and Ale houses in all parts of it. But alas these are demolisht, for the most part, the old Soldiers discharg'd, and all delivered up into the hand of the Enemy upon composition.

North of Blackfriars was Ludgate Prison, with its Hell's Gate which all the rogues and beggars of the sanctuaries sought to avoid. The lairs had their own customs and laws. Among the Ram Alley folk:

In case of Linnen, it hath been adjudged, that if three good fellows and constant Companions have but one shirt between them, and that these three (seeing none of their other shifts will do them any good) jointly consent this shirt shall be sold, it shall be lawful for them to expose it to sale, vended and condemned for the common good of three, and that forthwith the money be spent in the cherishing that blood that retired from the extream parts, being chil'd with the fright of parting with so dear and near a friend.

Under Charles II there were the Scowerers, and under Anne the Mohawks (as well as Whipping Tom who caught and flogged women), who indulged in various violences. But there is not much authentication of their deeds; behind the Mohawks there seem to be rumours of Jacobite conspiracies. Genuine dangers were those of the naval pressgang and the agents who 'crimped' men for ships.

In 1665-6 came the disasters of the Plague and the Fire. For the Plague we have Pepys' diary and Defoe's narrative. Defoe was only four years old at the time, at his father's shop in Cripplegate; but he must have heard many stories of it as he grew up, and his details are remarkably precise.

When any one bought a joint of meat, he would not take it out of the butcher's hand, but took it off the hooks himself; on the other hand the butcher would not touch the money, but put it in a pot full of vinegar which he kept for that purpose. The buyer carried always small money to make up any odd sum, so that he might take no change.

Pepys preserves the day-to-day impact:

16 Aug. Lord! how sad a sight it is to see the streets empty of people and very few upon the 'Change. Jealous of every door that one sees shut up, lest it should be the plague; and about us two shops in three, if not more, generally shut up.

28 Aug. To Mr Colvill the goldsmith's, having not been for some days in the streets; but now how few people I see, and these looking like people that have taken leave of the world.

He gives too a powerful account of the Fire:

We staid till, it being darkish, we saw the fire as only one entire arch of fire from this to the other side the bridge, and in a bow up the hill for an arch of above a mile long; it made me weep to see it. The churches, houses, and all on fire, and flaming at once: and a horrid noise the flames made, and the cracking of houses at their ruine . . .

It was pretty to see how hard the women did work in the cannells sweeping of water: but then they would scold for drink, and be drunk as devils. I saw good butts of sugar broke open in the street, and people go and take handsfull out, and put it in to beer and drink it. And now all being pretty well, I took boat . . .

The fact that the plague did not recur was no doubt in part due to the rebuilding of London with much more brick and stone; but the filthier areas, the slum Liberties, had not been burned. No doubt the extermination about this time of the medieval black rat by the brown rat, which was much less a carrier of plague-fleas, had its effect. The Fire raged for five days and destroyed almost all the City between Tower and Temple, the central residential and commercial region, with eighty-nine churches and streets of old lathe-and-plaster houses. However the merchants were so well supplied with funds that the rebuilding took only four or five years, and was done 'most stately in brick' (Reresby). The old Gothic cathedral was burned; the new St Paul's was a communal effort, to which a tax on coal entering the port was dedicated. Vast quarries were opened at Portland, and roads and piers built for the carriage of the stone.

Since the Restoration the custom of putting the whole dinner on the table at once had changed to that of presenting dishes one after another in some sort of order. There was much dining together, and merchants seem to have stopped work after the midday-meal. For a big dinner a man had the food brought from the cookshops in a regular procession through the streets, with the aproned and white-capped server in front. Fiddlers and trumpeters went round the cookshops to find where they might be hired. The most fashionable tavern for long was Locket's at Charing Cross. 'With evening wheels we'll drive about the Park, Finish at Locket's and reel home i' the dark'. Here is a grandiose menu from Pepys (4 April 1665):

A Fricasse of rabbits and chickens, a leg of mutton boiled, three carps on a dish, a great dish of a side of lamb, a dish of roasted pigeons, a dish of four lobsters, three tarts, a lamprey pie (a most rare pie), a dish of anchovies, good wine of several sorts, and all things mighty noble and to my great content.

Odd items were goose-pie, buttered shrimps, oyster-stuffed mutton, pigeons stuffed with green gooseberries, grapes boiled in butter and served with sips of bread and sugar, turkey stuffed with clove. Supper was at five or six, informal like breakfast: cold meat with a salad, a tankard of ale, a pipe of tobacco. Small ale was consumed everywhere in preference to the possibly contaminated water. Chamberlayne gives some idea of the abundance of drinks:

Since the late Rebellion, England hath abounded in variety of Drinks (as it did lately in variety of Religions) above any nation in Europe. Besides all sorts of the best wines from Spain, France, Italy, Germany, there are sold in London above twenty sorts of other Drinks, as Brandy, Coffee, Chocolate, Tee, Aromatick, Mum, Sider, Perry, Mede, Metheglin, Beer, Ale, many sorts of Ales, very different, as Cock, Stepony, Stitch-back, Hull, North-Devon, Sambridge, Betony, Scurvy-grass, Sage-Ale, Colledge-Ale, etc., a piece of wantonness whereof none of our Ancestors were ever guilty.

Even such a heavy drink as metheglin was considered a morning draught. Apoplexies were not uncommon. In December 1681 Luttrell notes, 'The countess of Suffolk was seized with an apoplexy the 12th, and died the same day. The Lady Betty Felton, her daughter, was seized also with a fitt of the same the next day, and died of it'.

Taverns were now not the only meeting places. The first coffee-house was opened in 1652 in St Michael's Alley, Cornhill, by Pasqua Rosa of Ragusa (though Evelyn mentions seeing coffee drunk at Oxford in 1637). Rosa's handbill claimed extravagant virtues for coffee: it helped digestion, quickened the spirits, checked rheums or consumption, dropsy, gout and scurvy, the spleen and hypochondriac winds. Coffee-houses soon multiplied, as good places for political and other discussions. The government in alarm tried in 1675 to suppress them, but failed. Some houses provided music, songs, even tumblings; others, a show of curiosities (probably brought from the East by sailors). Pepys tell us:

(3 Feb. 1664) In Covent Garden tonight going to fetch home my wife, I stopped at the great coffee-house there, where I never was before: where Dryden the poet, I knew at Cambridge, and all the wits of the town, and Harris the player, and Mr Hoole of our College. And, had I had time then, or could at other times, it will be good coming thither, for there, I perceive, is very witty and pleasant discourse.

A pamphlet of 1675 attacks coffee-houses, but also advocates the stopping of any more new buildings in London, the obligatory residence of the gentry on their estates for so many months of the year, the suppression of all or most stage-coaches and caravans, the reduction of craftsmen's wages, and the setting up of Courts of Conscience in every main town.

By 1713 Defoe was deploring the shops that sold newfangled luxuries and the fact that coffee, tea, chocolate, 'are now become capital branches of the nature's commerce'.

Chocolate-houses were also places of resort, more elegant with mirrors and decorations. But many folk were still afraid of a cup of chocolate without a dram to fortify the stomach. 'Bring in,' says the gallant, 'two dishes of chocolate and a glass of cinnamon water.' Tea had been introduced near the end of the Commonwealth, also accompanied by claims for its beneficial effects, but city-ladies, inviting friends to drink it, finished off with cordials to offset any bad consequences. Millament's lover in *the Way of the World* allows her to be 'Sole Empress of her Tea-table', if she promises to banish from the table 'orange brandy, aniseed, cinnamon, citron and Barbadoes water, together with ratafia and the most noble spirit of clary'.

Shops had been mainly warehouses piled with staple manufactures, such as the cloths and kersies of the draper, or small structures like stalls. Goldsmiths alone seem to have made much of their display, and even they did not set out their most valuable wares. Shops in the modern sense were now coming in. Defoe regarded with distrust the gaily-decorated shop with glass windows – plate-glass supplanting the old lattice windows with diamonds or circles of leaded glass. He was particularly angry at a pastry-cook's shop; the walls of the front and back shop were lined with galley-tiles, and in both sections there were large pier looking-glasses, well-lighted, each with a larger branch candlestick or chandelier as well as great glass lanterns (three large and eight small) and twenty-five sconces against the walls. The painting of the ceiling, the gilding of the lanterns and the carved-work had cost some fifty-five pounds; and altogether with china and 'other things to make a shew' the cost was more than 300 pounds. Such an outlay, he thinks, 'will hardly be believed in ages to come'.

There were also many open-air places of resort and promenade; Hyde Park; St James's Park; Mulberry Park (where now is Buckingham Palace) with arbours for supper parties and with dark paths in the Wilderness, till 1675 – here were 'gentlemen and ladies that made love together, till twelve o'clock at night'; New Spring Gardens at Vauxhall where Pepys observed the gallants to take hold of every woman there; heard the nightingale, the fiddles, the harp and the Jew's trump; partook of cheesecake, syllabubs and wine, and listened to the young men, 'Lord, their mad talk did make my heart ake' Lawyers and their ladies had Gray's Inn Gardens; the folk of Holborn and Fleet Street, Lamb's Conduit Fields. The galleries of the Royal Exchange and the Piazza of Covent Garden were used by gallants and others. Spas were increasingly popular: Bath, Buxton and Harrogate, with the rustic cottages round Tunbridge Wells for courtiers and rich Londoners.

The Restoration in England

Nell Gwynn, celebrated mistress of Charles II, painted for him by Lely.

The burning of St Paul's in the Great Fire of London of 1666.

Scenes of the Great Plague of 1665.

Samuel Pepys,
unrivalled chronicler of
English social life under
the Restoration.

Pepys's diary, open at 6 September 1666, where he is describing hour by hour the course of the Great Fire of London.

Self-portrait of Sir Peter Lely with his family in an 'Idyll'. Lely's paintings
recorded the great beauties of Charles's court.

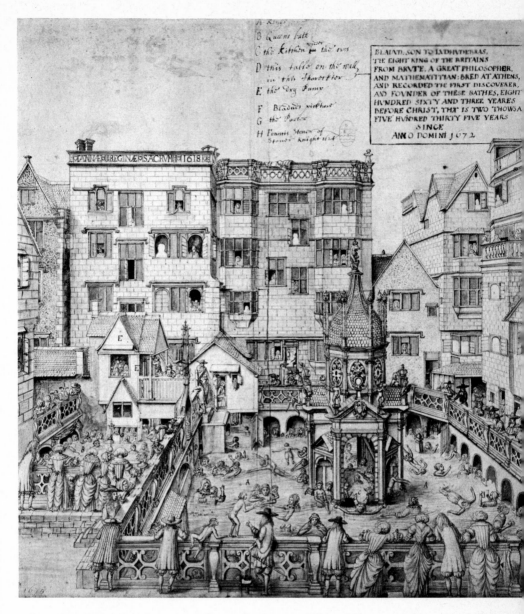

Above. The 'King's and Queen's Bath' at Bath, already a fashionable resort under the restored monarchy.

Opposite. Four of the famous beauties of Charles II's court: Hortense Mancini, one of Cardinal Mazarin's *Mazarinettes*, who came to London and became a favourite of the king's; Elizabeth Hamilton, wife of the Comte de Grammont; the 'wicked Countess' of Shrewsbury, said to have held the horse of the Duke of Buckingham, disguised as his page, while he fought and killed her husband; and Nell Gwynn.

Detail from *The Tichborne Dole*, Van Tilborgh's painting which illustrates a lively country ceremony enacted in 1670.

An attempt of the court under Charles II to carry out a frolic in the country is amusing for its failure to fulfil the pastoral idyll:

There being a Faire neare Audley End, the Queen, the Dutchess of Richmond, and the Dutchess of Buckingham, had a frolick to deguise themselves like country lasses, in red petticotes, wastcotes, &c., and so goe to the Faire. Sir Bernard Gascoign, on a cart-jade, rode before the Queen, another stranger before the Dutchesse of Buckingham, and Mr Roper before Richmond. They had all so overdone it in their deguise, and look'd so much more like Antiques than Country volk, that as soone as they came to the Faire the people began to goe after them.

But the Queen going to a booth to buy a paire of yellow stockins for her swete hart, and Sir Bernard asking for a paire of gloves, sticht with blew, for his swete hart, they were soon, by their gebrish, found to be strangers, which drew a bigger flock about them. One amongst them had seen the Queen at dinner, knew her, and was proud of his knowledge: this soon brought all the Faire into a crowd to stare at the Queen. Being thus discovered, they, as soon as they could, got on their horses; but as many of the Faire as had horses got up with their wives, children, swete-harts, or neighbours behind them, to get as much gape as they could, till they brought them to the Court gate. Thus, by ill conduct, was a merrie frolick turned into a pennance. (N. Henshaw)

Horse-racing at Newmarket was patronised by Charles II, who rebuilt the place. He improved the breed of the horses by introducing Arab and Barb blood. Wrestling, singlestick, boxing, swordfighting, hurling, and football were common sports. A French traveller in 1672 describes a fencing match:

We went to see the Bergiardin, which is a great amphitheatre, where combats are fought between all sorts of animals, and sometimes men, as we once saw. Commonly, when any fencing masters are desirous of shewing their courage and their great skill, they issue mutual challenges, and before they engage, parade the town with drums and trumpets sounding, to inform the public there is a challenge between two brave masters of the science of defence, and that the battle will be fought on such a day.

We went to see this combat, which was performed on a stage in the middle of this amphitheatre, where, on the flourishes of trumpets and the beat of drums, the combatants entered, stripped to their shirts. On a signal from the drum, they drew their swords, and immediately began the fight, skirmishing a long time without any wounds. They were both skilful and courageous. The tallest had the advantage over the least: for, according to the English fashion of fencing, they endeavoured rather to cut than push in the French manner . . .

The tall one struck his antagonist on the wrist, which he almost cut off; but this did not prevent him from continuing the fight, after he had been dressed, and taken a glass of wine or two to give him courage, when he took ample vengeance for his wound: for a little afterwards, making a feint at the ham, the tall man, stooping to parry it, laid his whole head open, when the little one gave him a stroke, which took off a slice of his head, and almost all of his ear. For my part I think there is an inhumanity, a barbarity and cruelty, in permitting men to kill each other for diversion.

The smaller man was finally defeated by another blow on his wrist. Next day there was to be a battle of bears and dogs. On 27 May 1667 Evelyn had watched in the same pit a butcher and a waterman fight. The latter dropped his sword and the butcher cut him over the wrist. 'In a minute the whole stage was full of watermen to revenge the foul play, and the butchers to defend their fellow, though most blamed him; and there they all fell to it knocking down and cutting many of each side. It was pleasant to see, but that I stood in the pit, and feared that in the tumult I might get some hurt.' When a cultivated man like Evelyn found such a sight pleasant, we can imagine the emotions of the rougher sort.

From the diary of Roger Lowe, a Lancashire apprentice: September 1663, 'I went to a bowling alley and lost 12d., at which I was sore grieved'. He also watched a cockfight and hunted with hares; but the provinces seem less barbarous than London. Betting was a widespread passion. On 21 December 1663 Evelyn was at a cockfight in a new pit in Shoe Lane; he noted a Member of Parliament who had been Deputy-Governor of the Tower and a 'strange variety of people' down 'to the poorest prentices, bakers, brewers, butchers, draymen, and what not; and all these fellows one with another cursing and betting'.

The Restoration had brought in a theatre of a new kind, with women acting the female parts, and with proscenium arch and complicated scenery aiming at a realistic effect. Things were much more refined, but the stage had now lost its old popular roots and the audience had narrowed; by the end of the century the new middle-class was genteelly exerting its influence. Pepys was delighted at the refinements:

The stage is now by his pains a thousand times better and more glorious than heretofore. Now, wax-candles, and many of them; then, not above 3 lbs. of tallow; now, all things civil, no rudeness anywhere; then, as in a bear-garden; then, two or three fiddlers; now, nine or ten of the best; then, nothing but rushes up on the ground, and everything else mean; and now, all otherwise . . .

He was pleased to be presented to Nell Gwynn and to kiss her, 'and a mighty pretty soul she is'; he saw her in Florimell, 'a comicall part done by Nell that I can never hope to see the like done again by man or woman'.

There was still much amateur activity in music. Pepys loved to sing songs and play on the lute, violin, viol, and flageolet; he even tried his hand at composition. He let his wife learn singing and dancing, and stimulated her interest till she at least learned the flageolet. Visiting Audley House in 1660 and 1667 he drank in the cellars: the first time playing the flageolet 'there being an excellent echo'; the second time, singing with his wife 'to my great content'. In 1683 sailing to Tangiers, one of the anticipated pleasures of the voyage was that 'of concerts (much above the ordinary) of voices, flutes, and violins'. The country-dance still had much vitality.

The professional literary man was arriving; Dryden was the outstanding example. He still depended upon patrons, but was beginning to detach himself and to find a definite (middle class) audience. Sciences of all kinds, including statistics, were supplanting the abstract logic of medieval preoccupation. The great scientific impetus gathering force in the later Puritan developments begot the Royal Society; and though the Society soon lost much of its experimental energies (by 1680), in almost all the contemporary scientific fields men were making important contributions. Hooke, Newton, Locke represent their decisive advance. The conflict between religion and science, latent ever since Copernicus, Bruno and Galileo, was coming into the open. Men like Locke tried to rationalise Christianity; and unashamed free-thinkers like Toland stated their views. The visions that had still been utopian in Bacon were coming down to earth. In comparison with the attitudes of 1560, those under Anne were highly secularised, basing their claims on reason and not on authority.

These remarks sum up the most important developments. The manners and the outlook of the medieval period in its later phases were transformed into those of a society standing on the threshold of the modern world. In the process there had been many strains and stresses, and more lay ahead. These were the pangs of a world changing from the medieval forms in which men were still close to nature, relating their lives to seasonal changes, making whole things with their hands and only very partially drawn into the network of money, and moving easily from work to festival relaxations – into the world of the clock, strict discipline and controls, with the money forces taking ever more control, begetting new rationalities, but also bringing about a division of labour and centralized administrations. Such a process involved great gains, and great losses. Despite the many distracting new pressures, there were also gains in humanity; a more humane approach to children was beginning; and marriage took on something of a new warmth and dignity.

Index